access to history

The People's Republic of China 1949–76 SECOND EDITION

Michael Lynch

HODDER
EDUCATION
PART OF HACHETTE LIVRE UK

Study guides revised and updated, 2008, by Angela Leonard (Edexcel) and
Sally Waller (AQA).

Hodder Headline's policy is to use papers that are natural, renewable and
recyclable products and made from wood grown in sustainable forests.
The logging and manufacturing processes are expected to conform to the
environmental regulations of the country of origin.

Orders: please contact Bookpoint Ltd, 130 Milton Park, Abingdon, Oxon
OX14 4SB. Telephone: (44) 01235 827720. Fax: (44) 01235 400454. Lines are
open 9.00–5.00, Monday to Saturday, with a 24-hour message answering service.
Visit our website at www.hoddereducation.co.uk

Michael Lynch 2008
First published in 2008 by
Hodder Education, part of Hachette UK
338 Euston Road
London NW1 3BH

Impression number   6
Year   2012 2011 2010

Cover photo by Camera Press, London
Typeset in Baskerville by Gray Publishing, Tunbridge Wells
Printed in Great Britain by the MPG Books Group, Bodmin

A catalogue record for this title is available from the British Library

ISBN: 978 0340 929 278

Contents

Dedication

Keith Randell (1943–2002)

The *Access to History* series was conceived and developed by Keith, who created a series to 'cater for students as they are, not as we might wish them to be'. He leaves a living legacy of a series that for over 20 years has provided a trusted, stimulating and well-loved accompaniment to post-16 study. Our aim with these new editions is to continue to offer students the best possible support for their studies.

Note on spellings

There are two main styles of transliterating Chinese names into English, the older Wade–Giles system and the more recent *Pinyin* form. In this book it is *Pinyin* that is normally used. To avoid confusion, the Wide–Giles or alternative form is added in brackets after the first appearance of the name. There is also a glossary of names at the end of the book (page 181) giving a list of names in both forms.

1

Introduction: China Under Mao 1949–76

POINTS TO CONSIDER

On 1 October 1949 Mao Zedong, Chairman of the Chinese Communist Party, stood on a balcony of the old imperial palace in Beijing to proclaim the formal establishment of the People's Republic of China. His pronouncement marked the final victory of the Chinese Communists over their enemies after two decades of civil war. How Mao went on to reshape China and the impact this had on the world at large are the main themes of this book. To lay the ground for this analysis the first chapter covers the following areas:

- China before 1949
- Mao's career before 1949
- The reshaping of China under Mao 1949–76
- Mao's China and the historians

Key dates

1840s	Europe began to impose itself on China
1911	Collapse of the ruling Qing dynasty
1925	Chiang Kaishek became leader of GMD
1937	Japanese occupation of China
1945	Japan defeated at the end of the Second World War
1945–9	Civil war between Communists and Nationalists
1949	Communist takeover of mainland China
	PRC established under Mao Zedong
1950–3	Korean War
1951	'Anti-movements' launched
1952	Political parties other than CCP banned
1952–6	China's first Five-Year Plan
1957	Hundred Flowers campaign launched
1958–62	The Great Leap Forward
1966–76	The Great Proletarian Cultural Revolution
1976	Death of Mao Zedong

1 | China Before 1949

Imperial China

At the start of the twentieth century, China was one of the oldest cultures and nations in the world. By tradition, Chinese society and politics were deeply conservative. China's principal shaping influence had been **Confucianism**, a philosophy that required the Chinese people to accept without complaint their place in an unchanging social order. Over two and a half millennia of development, this had produced a **hierarchical structure** in which the first duty of the citizen was to obey lawful authority, expressed in its highest political form in the rule of the emperor.

China's conservative character was also reflected in its attitude towards the outside world. Until the nineteenth century

Key question
What was the character of imperial China?

Confucianism
A pattern of thought based on the teachings of Confucius (551–479 BC), who emphasised the need for harmony in human relations.

Hierarchical structure
A pattern of government in which each class or group owes obedience to the authority above it.

Key terms

Map of China 1900–49, showing its main provinces, the treaty ports and the Jiangxi and Yanan Soviets.

Key terms

Unequal treaties
Agreements forced on China in the nineteenth century, which obliged it to surrender territory and accept trade on Western terms.

Republic
A form of government in which there is no monarch and power is exercised by elected representatives.

Key question
What fundamental changes did China experience between 1911 and 1949?

Key terms

Warlords
Powerful local generals in China who exploited the weakness of the central government to set themselves up as rulers in their own areas.

Nationalists
A Chinese revolutionary party created in the early twentieth century and based on the 'Three People's Principles': socialism, democracy and national regeneration.

Chinese Communist Party
Formed in 1921 and committed to a Marxist revolution in China.

China had essentially been a closed society. For over 2000 years it had deliberately avoided contact with other nations wherever possible. Largely isolated from foreign influences, it had developed a deep sense of its own superiority over all other cultures. However, this self-belief was suddenly and profoundly shaken in the 1840s when a number of Western industrial nations, principally Britain and France, used their greater military strength and more advanced technology to impose themselves on China. The Chinese were forced to open their ports to foreign commerce and to enter into a series of '**unequal treaties**'. By 1900 over 50 of China's key ports and towns were in foreign possession.

Chinese bitterness at such humiliation created mounting dissatisfaction with the imperial government. The Qing (Manchu) dynasty's inability to protect China encouraged the growth of a revolutionary movement. The remarkable feature of this movement was its desire to achieve 'a revolution against the world to join the world', to end China's subjection to the West by adopting progressive Western political and economic ways.

China from revolution to revolution 1911–49

In 1911 China underwent the first of its modern revolutions when the Qing government collapsed. Although a **republic** was set up in place of the imperial system, it was unclear where the real power in China now lay. For the next 40 years, rival **warlords** and factions struggled to assert authority. Two main revolutionary parties were in contention: the **Nationalists** or Guomindang (GMD) led after 1925 by Chiang Kaishek (Jiang Jieshi), and the **Chinese Communist Party** (CCP), whose leader from the later 1920s was Mao Zedong. Although the GMD was the nominal government of China from the early 1930s, it was never able to crush its Communist rivals.

Moreover, such power as the Nationalists had was seriously compromised after 1937 by their apparently half-hearted response to the military occupation of many of the richest and most densely populated parts of the Chinese mainland by China's neighbour and traditional enemy, Japan. In contrast to Chiang Kaishek's lack of fight, Mao Zedong led the CCP from its bases in Jiangxi (Kiangsi) and Yanan (Yenan) in a spirited resistance to the Japanese occupation.

By the time the Japanese had been defeated in 1945, Mao's Communists had become a more powerful force in China than the Nationalists. This was proved beyond doubt 4 years later when Chiang and the GMD forces were forced to take refuge on the island of Formosa (Taiwan) after suffering a series of shattering military defeats at the hands of Mao's armies. Mao and the CCP were now in a position to establish Communist rule over the whole of mainland China.

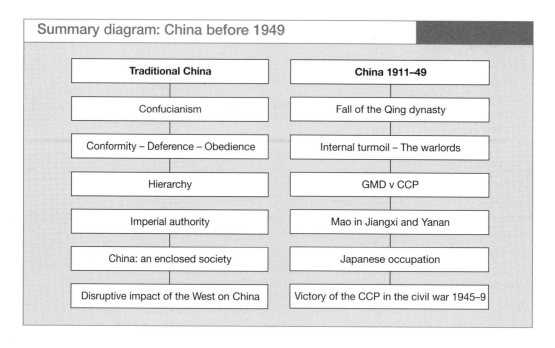

Summary diagram: China before 1949

Traditional China	China 1911–49
Confucianism	Fall of the Qing dynasty
Conformity – Deference – Obedience	Internal turmoil – The warlords
Hierarchy	GMD v CCP
Imperial authority	Mao in Jiangxi and Yanan
China: an enclosed society	Japanese occupation
Disruptive impact of the West on China	Victory of the CCP in the civil war 1945–9

2 | Mao's Career Before 1949

'A clean sheet of paper has no blotches, and so the newest and most beautiful pictures can be painted on it.' This was Mao Zedong's poetic description of the opportunity that lay before the new China in 1949. But behind the fine words was a fierce resolution. The picture that Mao intended to paint would allow no space for brushwork other than his own. He intended to create China in his own image. He would continue to use the methods that had brought him to power in 1949. Mao had been shaped by the brutal world in which he grew up.

The lessons that Mao learned as a young man in China were violent ones. All his experiences as a young revolutionary convinced him that unless he was prepared to use unyielding methods he could achieve little. He despised his countrymen who were not willing to use extremism in pursuing their goals for China. In the end, as he saw it, it was force which made things happen. Mao believed in the **dialectic** as the explanation of life. That was why he had become a **Marxist** and a founder member of the CCP in 1921. He held that all change, all progress, resulted from suppression of the weaker by the stronger. It was a belief that characterised his behaviour in all the major episodes of his career.

Mao's early years

Mao was born into a relatively well-to-do landed family in Hunan province. He was what might be termed a 'natural rebel'. Doted on by his mother, he fell out with his father and refused to show him the respect traditionally expected of a Chinese son. As a

Key question
What were the main influences that shaped Mao as a revolutionary?

Key terms

Dialectic
The Marxist notion that historical development occurs through a progressive series of conflicts between social classes.

Marxist
A believer in the theories of the German revolutionary Karl Marx (1818–83), who used the notion of the dialectic to explain history as a continuous conflict between the 'haves' and the 'have-nots', the exploiters and the exploited.

Profile: Mao Zedong (up to 1949)

1893	Born in Hunan province
1901–6	Attended primary school
1912	Joined anti-Qing army in Hunan
1912–18	Trained as a teacher
1918	Joined the Hunan independence movement
1919	Worked as a librarian at Beijing University
	Helped to organise strikes in Hunan
1921	Became a founder member of the Chinese Communist Party (CCP)
1923	Joined Guomindang (GMD)
1924–7	Involved in planning CCP–GMD alliance against the warlords
1927–34	Created the Jiangxi Soviet
1930	Suppressed a mutiny in the Red Army at Futian
1934–5	Led the Long March to Yanan
1935–45	Created the Yanan Soviet
1942	Crushed opposition within the CCP
1945–9	Led the CCP to victory over Chiang Kaishek and the Nationalists
1949	Declared the creation of the People's Republic of China

teenager, Mao played a small role as a volunteer soldier in Changsha in the Chinese revolution of 1911, which saw the collapse and abdication of the Qing. He then moved to Beijing where he furthered his education and in 1919 took up a post as librarian in Beijing University. It was there that he was introduced to Marxist ideas and developed the conviction that if China was to be truly regenerated it would have to undergo a profound social and political revolution.

Mao as a Chinese revolutionary 1911–27

Mao's belief was strengthened by his awareness that the 1911 revolution had brought China little benefit. Although a republican government had replaced the imperial system, it exercised only nominal power. Throughout China local warlords and factions struggled to assert authority. Mao recorded the savagery that became commonplace:

> During my student days in Hunan, the city was overrun by the forces of rival war lords – not once but half a dozen times. Twice the school was occupied by troops and all the school funds confiscated. The brutal punishments inflicted on the peasants included such things as gouging out eyes, ripping out tongues, disembowelling and decapitation, slashing with knives and grinding with sand, burning with kerosene and branding with red-hot irons.

The barbarity Mao witnessed greatly affected him, but it was not the cruelty that moved him so much as his realisation that it was the strongest and most ruthless who always won. He concluded that the only way to gain power was through violence. This helps to explain why throughout his career he was so ready to use brutal means in crushing political opponents. One of his most revealing sayings was, 'all power grows out of the barrel of a gun'. Another was, 'a revolution is not a tea-party; it is an act of violence, by which one class overthrows another'. He was impressed by the extreme methods used by the **Bolsheviks** in the Russian revolution that began in 1917.

Mao at Jiangxi 1927–34

In 1924 China's two major revolutionary parties, the Nationalists and the Communists, had formed a united front against the warlords, but the GMD–CCP unity was more apparent than real. The GMD's main aim under Chiang was to destroy the Communists. In 1927 it launched a systematic extermination campaign against them. Mao survived by taking his CCP forces to the mountains of Jiangxi province, where he organised guerrilla resistance against the Nationalists.

During the next 7 years Mao helped to establish the Jiangxi **Soviet**, dedicated to achieving a peasant revolution. While there, he showed himself unwilling to accept dictation from the **Comintern**. He frequently rejected the orders from Moscow that instructed the CCP to base its activities in the towns rather than the countryside.

It was also during the Jiangxi period (1927–34) that Mao revealed the calculated ferocity that marked his whole career. In the notorious 'Futian incident' in 1930 he had no qualms in torturing and executing some 4000 **Red Army** troops whom he regarded as rebels.

> [T]hey were brought out to be tortured, women as well as men … They were tortured to make them speak and they were tortured on Mao's orders. There is a document in the party archives which Mao approved which says, 'do not kill the important leaders too quickly, but squeeze out of them the maximum information; then from the clues they give you can go on to unearth others'.

The Long March 1934–5

Although the GMD became the official government of China in the early 1930s, it was weakened by the Japanese military occupation, beginning in 1931, of many parts of the Chinese mainland. Chiang Kaishek was seen to be more intent on crushing his Communist enemies within China than resisting the Japanese invader. In 1934 Chiang encircled the CCP's base in Jiangxi with a view to destroying it altogether. Again Mao survived, this time by joining and eventually leading the besieged Communists in their escape north to Yanan in Shaanxi province.

The journey to Yanan, which took over a year to complete, was later elevated by CCP propaganda into one of the great epics of Communist folklore: the Long March. It was never as glorious as the propagandists made out; of the 100,000 who fled from Jiangxi, scarcely 20,000 survived to reach their destination. Nevertheless, the march was certainly an important stage in the development of Chinese Communism. It was during the March that a critical strategy meeting took place at Zunyi. Mao outmanoeuvred his opponents in the CCP and imposed on the party his idea that to be successful the revolution in China must be based on the peasants in the countryside, not on the workers in the towns.

The Yanan years 1935–45

During the Yanan period Mao, by a combination of political and military skill and brutal suppression, succeeded in imposing his personal authority on the CCP. At the same time he fought off attempts by the Comintern to dominate the party. In the early 1940s he launched a series of **'rectification of conduct' campaigns** to consolidate his hold. It was also while he was at Yanan that Mao wrote his major political works setting out his revolutionary ideas.

Victory over the GMD 1945–9

With the surrender of Japan at the end of the Second World War in 1945, Mao turned on the GMD in a renewal of the civil war that had lasted intermittently since the late 1920s. A fierce 4-year struggle for supremacy ended with the complete victory of the Communists. Chiang and the GMD were driven from the Chinese mainland to their one remaining stronghold, the offshore island of Taiwan. In October 1949 Mao triumphantly declared that a new Communist society had come into being – the People's Republic of China (PRC).

Mao's policy in the countryside 1945–9

One of the most remarkable features of the civil war period was the brutal treatment of the peasants by Mao's Communists in the areas they controlled. Between 1945 and 1949, the CCP, continuing the policies that they had followed during the Jiangxi and Yanan periods, committed fearful atrocities against the peasants in order to force them to join the struggle against Chiang Kaishek's Nationalists.

It is interesting that Mao sent his son, **Anying**, to take part in the suppression of the peasantry. Mao thought his son needed toughening up. What Anying then experienced came close to unhinging him mentally.

One incident illustrates the type of horror he witnessed. In one set of villages which the Red Army had seized, the locals were rounded up and made to attend an anti-landlord rally. It was the middle of winter with temperatures well below zero. For five days the villagers were not allowed to leave the unsheltered area they had been herded into. They were forced to chant Maoist slogans and denounce the landlords who were publicly paraded before them. Some people froze to death standing up. The climax came on the fifth day when the condemned landlords were kicked and punched to death as the crowds shouted 'Kill, Kill, Kill'.

Anying recorded in his diary that the barbarity was worse than anything he had seen or heard of while studying Soviet Communism in **Stalin's USSR**. His attempt to come to terms with what he now saw in China caused him agonies of doubt. He was 'so full of pain' that he wept. What particularly disturbed him was the realisation that the party cadres carrying out the land policies were among the worst types of people in China. Anying described them as 'thugs' and 'the dregs of society'.

The reason why the savage policies of the CCP did not lose it the support of the peasants as a whole was that the record of the Nationalists was little better. Both Communists and Nationalists treated the Chinese peasants with deep contempt. The great difference was that while this might be understandable in the GMD since it was the party of the exploiting propertied classes, it defied sense for the CCP, a party that had come into being to liberate the people of China, to engage in their savage oppression.

It was their embarrassment over this that led many members of the CCP to protest against the appalling things being done in their name in the countryside. Mao, as he invariably did when his policies became excessive, simply blamed the mistakes on the failings of others. He declared himself guiltless and told **Liu Shaoqi** to shoulder the blame. Liu did as he was told, confessing to the party that he had let things slide until corrected by Mao.

Liu Shaoqi (1898–1968)
A gifted party organiser who was to become President of the PRC in 1959.

Key figure

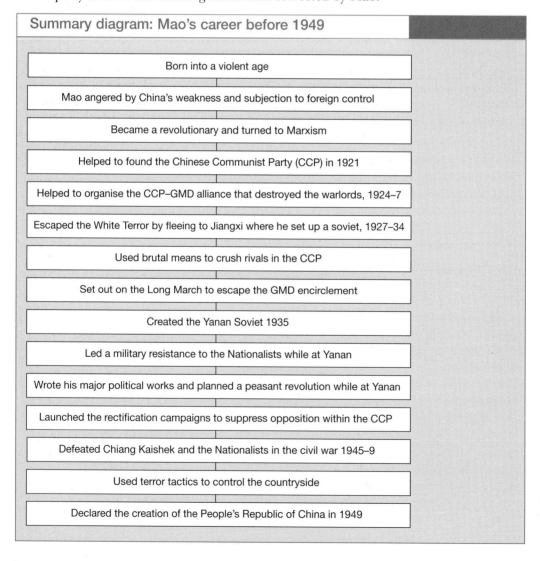

Summary diagram: Mao's career before 1949

Born into a violent age

Mao angered by China's weakness and subjection to foreign control

Became a revolutionary and turned to Marxism

Helped to found the Chinese Communist Party (CCP) in 1921

Helped to organise the CCP–GMD alliance that destroyed the warlords, 1924–7

Escaped the White Terror by fleeing to Jiangxi where he set up a soviet, 1927–34

Used brutal means to crush rivals in the CCP

Set out on the Long March to escape the GMD encirclement

Created the Yanan Soviet 1935

Led a military resistance to the Nationalists while at Yanan

Wrote his major political works and planned a peasant revolution while at Yanan

Launched the rectification campaigns to suppress opposition within the CCP

Defeated Chiang Kaishek and the Nationalists in the civil war 1945–9

Used terror tactics to control the countryside

Declared the creation of the People's Republic of China in 1949

Key question
What basic changes occurred in China under Mao's leadership?

Key dates

PRC established under Mao Zedong: 1949

'Anti-movements' launched: 1951

Korean War: 1950–3

3 | The Reshaping of China under Mao 1949–76

The consolidation of Communist authority 1949–57

During the Jiangxi and Yanan periods of the 1930s and 1940s, Mao Zedong had remorselessly enforced his authority on the CCP. His dominance became even greater with the creation of the People's Republic of China in 1949. Between then and his death in 1976, he was revered by the mass of the Chinese people as a living god. But the adulation that was lavished on him could not hide the huge problems he faced as leader of the new China. Mao's most demanding task was to bring stability to a nation that had been riven by decades of turmoil. His approach was a simple one; he would tolerate no opposition to the CCP. All other parties were outlawed and the total obedience of the nation to the new government was demanded.

Removal of officials

Initially, the officials and public figures who had previously served the GMD Nationalist government but had not fled to Taiwan were asked by the Communist authorities to stay in their posts. They were promised that if they pledged themselves to the new China they would suffer no retaliation for their past behaviour. For a short period this undertaking was honoured, but, once the officials had served their purpose by providing the young PRC with the necessary continuity of administration, they were turned on and persecuted as **class enemies**.

Key term

Class enemies
Those reactionaries who refused to accept the new China that the Communist government was creating.

The 'anti-movements'

The concept of class enemies was basic to the social and political strategies of the Communists in government. Invoking the traditional Chinese duty of respecting authority, Mao and the CCP leaders began public campaigns against anyone in public life who opposed official policy. From 1950 onwards an atmosphere of fear and uncertainty was systematically created by a series of 'anti-movements', launched against those whom the CCP regarded as socially or politically suspect. The Chinese people were encouraged to expose all who had co-operated with the former GMD government. China became a nation of informers. It was enough for individuals to be charged by their neighbours with having belonged to the privileged classes for them to be publicly denounced and to have their property seized. Their pleas of loyalty to Mao's new China were ignored.

The vengeful atmosphere was intensified by China's being drawn into the Korean War of 1950–3 (see page 28). This struggle placed great demands on the young PRC and made those who were less than whole-hearted in supporting it open to the charge that they were imperilling the nation's existence. Some of the worst excesses occurred in the countryside where millions of landlords were brutally dispossessed of their lands, which were then redistributed among the peasants.

A landlord being tried in 1953 by a people's court, one of many set up to deliver summary justice in the countryside. What clues does the picture offer regarding the way in which trials in the people's courts were conducted?

Purges of party members

Purges were also carried out within the CCP. Members who did not slavishly follow the **party line** were liable to be condemned as 'rightists' who were opposed to the progress of the PRC. Purges were alternated with periods when party members were encouraged to criticise current policies. This apparent liberalising was invariably followed by the imposition of even tougher restrictions on freedom of expression. A striking example occurred in 1957 when Mao, using the slogan 'Let a hundred flowers bloom; let a hundred schools of thought contend', called on members to air their grievances. Those who were rash enough to do so were then attacked as 'rightists'. Such purges were to become a recurrent feature of Chinese politics down to Mao's death in 1976.

Party line
Official CCP policy.

Key term

The Great Leap Forward 1958–62

In economic matters Mao's basic aim was to industrialise China. He hoped that within a short period the new China would be able to match the Soviet Union and the capitalist West in industrial output. To achieve this, he copied the Stalinist model of a series of 5-year plans. These involved prodigious physical efforts by the Chinese workers, but, since Mao deliberately chose to place his faith in mass labour rather than in advanced technology, the plans were only partially successful.

Key question
What economic changes were introduced under the Great Leap Forward?

Key date

The Great Leap Forward: 1958–62

The Second Five-Year Plan 1958–62

The limitations of Mao's approach were particularly evident during the second Five-Year Plan (1958–62). Intended to be the Great Leap Forward, the plan fell far short of its production targets. The true figures of the failure were hidden from the people, but what the authorities could not conceal was the widespread famine that accompanied the plan. The collapse of the food supply system was directly attributable to two factors, collectivisation and '**Lysenkoism**':

Key term

Lysenkoism
The agricultural theories of Trofim Lysenko.

- The land that had been given to the peasants after its seizure from the landlords had to be forfeited in a mass collectivisation programme which ended private ownership and obliged the peasants to live and work in communes.
- The dislocation this caused was made worse by Mao's decision to introduce into China the fraudulent crop-production theories of the quack Soviet scientist, Trofim Lysenko.

This combination of social disruption and false science produced a catastrophic famine throughout China. Deaths were numbered in millions. Characteristically, Mao declined to acknowledge responsibility for the famine, but in the early 1960s he withdrew into the political background, leaving two prominent party figures, Deng Xiaoping (Teng Hsiao-ping) and Liu Shaoqi (Liu Shao-chi), to tackle the problem of food shortages. Their attempts to repair the economic damage led them to reverse some of Mao's earlier policies. One major adjustment was the abandonment of collectivisation. Mao was upset by this move since he judged it to be an undermining of the socialist principles on which China's 1949 revolution rested. In a series of dramatic gestures, which included his swimming in the Yangzi (Yangste) River in 1966, the ageing chairman reappeared in public and reasserted his dominance in Chinese politics.

What inspired him to return was the fear that had always moved him, and which increased as he grew older, that the revolution he had led might not survive his death. He determined, therefore, to impose a political and social structure on China that would permanently define its character as a nation. This was the intention behind his introduction in 1966 of the great Cultural Revolution, an extraordinary movement that plunged China into a decade of deliberately engineered turmoil.

The Cultural Revolution 1966–76

Mao's aim in unleashing the Cultural Revolution was to oblige the party to acknowledge all its current errors and in so doing purge itself of all possible rivals to his authority. His chosen instrument for achieving this was the youth of China. In 1966 he called on the young to set themselves up in judgement over their elders. He urged them to form a mass movement to destroy everything from China's past that threatened its present revolution.

The Red Guards

The young people responded with an idealistic enthusiasm that soon deteriorated into a brutal fanaticism. Squads of teenagers, known as **Red Guards**, rampaged through China's cities and towns. No part of China's antique culture was sacred. Buildings – whether universities, libraries, museums or temples – which, in the eyes of the Red Guards stood as memorials to Chinese decadence, were smashed or burned.

Jiang Qing

The violence was part of a wholesale attack on China's traditional culture. All forms of artistic expression were subjected to crippling censorship. They had to pass the test of '**socialist integrity**' imposed by Mao's wife, Jiang Qing (Chiang Ching), who was entrusted with the responsibility for re-creating Chinese culture. In the event she achieved the reverse. Her demand that all forms of creativity must conform absolutely to her judgement of what constituted genuine socialist culture meant that nothing of lasting significance was produced or presented. China became an artistic wilderness.

The Cultural Revolution was an act of madness but there was method in it. The Red Guards were a highly visible and terrifying feature of the movement, but they were essentially a front. Mao was using the apparent anarchy to enforce his will on the CCP and the nation. It was a means of fulfilling his concept of '**continuing revolution**', the belief that unless the Communist Party was regularly purified it would cease to be a revolutionary force and China would cease to be truly socialist.

Mao's death and the end of the Cultural Revolution

For 10 years after 1966 the Cultural Revolution caused massive disruption within China and harmed its relations with the outside world. By the early 1970s, there were signs that even Mao himself considered the social and political extremism had gone too far. Although he never formally abandoned the Cultural Revolution, he allowed it to run down. By the time of his death in 1976 the movement had lost much of its violent fanaticism.

Key question
What were Mao's motives in deliberately creating disruption?

Key dates

The Great Proletarian Cultural Revolution: 1966–76

Death of Mao Zedong: 1976

Key terms

Red Guards
The revolutionary students whose name derived from their practice of wearing red arm bands, supplied to them by Maoist officials. Red was the traditional colour of the Communist movement.

Socialist integrity
The notion that a true work of art in Communist China must portray the triumph of the workers and peasants over their class enemies.

Continuing revolution
Mao's notion that revolution was not a single event but a continuous process.

The link between the PRC and imperial China

An important point to stress is that the PRC rather than being a break from China's past was in all major respects a continuation of it. The major question facing the PRC at the time of its creation was how could it establish the stability and permanence that all the preceding regimes since the fall of the Qing in 1911 had failed to achieve. The short answer was by a successful return to absolutism (see Figure 1.1).

The political character of China after 1949 has been much analysed and discussed. It is possible to argue that the PRC was no different in essentials from the traditional Chinese political system. Despite its title, the People's Republic, the PRC allowed no involvement in government by the vast majority of the people. The rule of the CCP was as uncompromising and self-perpetuating as that of the emperors. Maoist China was not, therefore, a new China except in certain outward appearances. The change in 1949 was one of form rather than of substance. Despite its revolutionary claims, China remained a politically reactionary society. All authority came from the top and the people's duty was to obey.

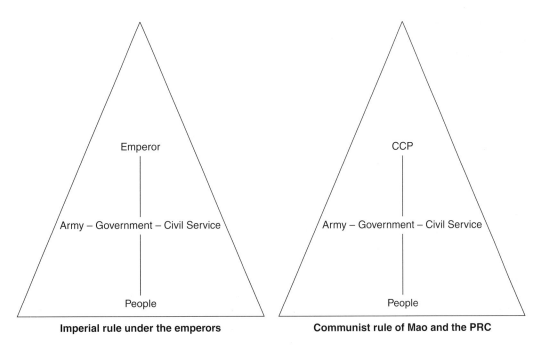

Emperor

Army – Government – Civil Service

People

Imperial rule under the emperors

CCP

Army – Government – Civil Service

People

Communist rule of Mao and the PRC

Figure 1.1 The unchanging nature of Chinese government.

Summary diagram: Reshaping of China under Mao 1949–76	

```
          ┌─────────────────────┐
          │    Consolidation    │
          └─────────────────────┘
                     │
          ┌─────────────────────┐
          │   Collectivisation  │
          └─────────────────────┘
                     │
          ┌─────────────────────┐
          │  Great Leap Forward │
          └─────────────────────┘
                     │
          ┌─────────────────────┐
          │  Cultural Revolution│
          └─────────────────────┘
                     │
┌──────────────────────────────────────────────────────┐
│ Continuity between Imperial China and Communist China │
└──────────────────────────────────────────────────────┘
```

4 | Mao's China and the Historians

The writing of history in China

China has always had chroniclers of its history, but it has no tradition of historical writing as the term is understood in the West, where the pursuit of evidence and its impartial interpretation are the ideal. China's ruling authorities have always required that writers and commentators when describing the past do so in such a way that reflects well on the present. Indeed, to Chinese governments the purpose of history is to justify the present.

Key question
What problems confront historians studying Mao's China?

Control of the media under Mao

After the creation of the People's Republic of China in 1949, the Communist authorities continued the practice of controlling all official publications. The news media in the PRC have always been heavily centralised. The state controls practically all of the output of the Chinese press. This means that the media are effectively the mouthpiece of the Beijing government, whose policies are invariably greeted with universal approval from China's newspapers and journals. The line established by **Xinhua** (Hsinhua) is toed both by the mass circulation dailies and by the internationally published Chinese newspapers and journals.

During the half-century of the PRC's existence from 1949 nothing was printed in these papers or in any other official publication that was critical of the CCP's record or its policies in government. Before 1976, everything that was published praised Mao Zedong without reservation and condemned China's internal and foreign enemies.

Xinhua
The PRC's government-controlled news agency.

Key term

Key question
How did official attitudes towards Mao change after his death?

Key term

De-Stalinisation
A campaign begun in the USSR 3 years after Stalin's death to reveal the truth about his development of a 'cult of personality', a reference to his having put his own reputation and interests above the needs of the Communist Party during his rule between 1929 and 1953.

Key figure

Deng Xiaoping (1904–97) The dominant force in Chinese politics from 1978 to 1997, Deng reversed many of Mao's policies.

Mao's changing reputation

With the death of Mao in 1976 his reputation began to decline and a number of adjustments to the official record were made. But these were very limited. There was no equivalent to the **de-Stalinisation** that occurred in the USSR in the wake of Stalin's death in 1953. The ensuing power-struggle between the hardline Maoists and the more progressive Communists, who believed that changes were necessary for party and national survival, resulted in the defeat of the die-hards. But this did not leave the victors entirely free to reject Maoism. If the members of the CCP had admitted that serious mistakes had been made by the party under Mao's direction it would have undermined their own standing.

So the CCP adopted a form of compromise. Mao could not be rejected entirely by his successors; after all, they had risen to prominence under him and had carried out the Cultural Revolution on his orders. But **Deng Xiaoping** in introducing his own revolution was eager that China should deliberately overlook those aspects of its recent past that it could not undo. He let it be known that the Cultural Revolution was now to be regarded as a closed topic. In 1984, the PRC government formally instructed China's book publishers not to produce any more works on the Cultural Revolution.

Forgetting the Cultural Revolution

The result has been that the Cultural Revolution, the great centrepiece of Chinese history since 1949, is now largely ignored in China. Politicians deliberately avoid referring to it and students are seldom taught about it. Middle-aged men and women who were once Red Guards will sometimes own up to the fact, but they will wearily, though politely, explain that it is a topic that no longer interests them.

Controlling the past

In 2006 China's education ministry announced that the history textbooks used in Chinese schools would not dwell on the 'negative' aspects of the country's past; instead they would be concerned with 'producing innovative thinking and preparing students for a global discourse'. This was a coded way of saying that China's pupils would not be taught any history that reflected badly on the record of the ruling Communist Party. When a celebrated historian, Yuan Weishi, protested against this in a powerfully written article in which he argued that China must face up to the dark incidents in its past, such as the Cultural Revolution, the newspaper which had published his piece was forced by the authorities to apologise and print a denunciation of Yuan.

The influence of the Cold War on Western attitudes towards Mao's China

The PRC's reluctance to face its past has meant that Chinese academics who are desperate for information about their country's history tend to rely on foreign **sinologists** for enlightenment. This obviously throws a great responsibility on non-Chinese historians. Here a particular difficulty applies. Keen though Western historians have been to convey the truth about China, they have understandably tended to interpret Chinese history very much from the standpoint of the West. The history of the PRC under Mao Zedong coincided with the **Cold War**. For much of that time China was looked on as the ally of the USSR and therefore as a threat to Western interests.

The American attitude in this respect is particularly instructive. The Communist victory in China in 1949 forced the USA, which had invested considerable time, energy and money in east Asia before 1949, to reassess Chinese history. A large number of universities in the USA established departments of Chinese studies in the 1950s. Their concern was to explain what they regarded as a Cold War calamity, the 'loss' of China to Mao's Communists and the forming of a Communist alliance between the PRC and the Soviet Union.

Key question
How did the Cold War influence interpretations of Mao's China?

Key terms

Sinologists
Experts on China.

Cold War
The period of tension (1945–91) between the Communist Eastern bloc, led by the USSR, and the Western democratic nations, led by the USA.

Western historians and Mao's China

Whatever the political motives behind it, the US initiative had a very valuable outcome. It produced some outstanding scholarship that made a major contribution to Western understanding of China. Particularly distinguished American sinologists were Stuart Schram, the first major Western biographer of Mao Zedong, Orville Schell, who produced invaluable collections and translations of Chinese documents, and John King Fairbank, whose published studies of China placed the PRC in the wider context of Chinese historical development. British historians have also contributed significantly to the study of China. Prominent among them are Roderick MacFarquhar, a leading authority on the Cultural Revolution, and Jonathan Spence, whose many studies of China's transition from an antique culture to a modern state have become required reading world-wide.

Key question
What special contributions have Western scholars brought to the study of modern China?

Balance and bias

The outstanding attribute of these historians is their objectivity. They treat the Chinese record in a balanced form, presenting both the creditable and the discreditable aspects of the PRC's history. Their approach has provided a valuable corrective to the one-sided accounts that had been produced earlier by writers who had allowed their political bias to influence their work. For example, at the height of the Cold War, many US-based studies had been distorted by their distaste for Communism, whether in its Russian or Chinese form.

There had been equal distortions at the opposite end of the political spectrum. Left-wing radicals, most notably in France and the USA, had glorified Mao Zedong as a great liberator whose progressive brand of Communism had superseded the decaying Soviet variety. It took a generation before such Western liberals were prepared to accept the truth about the horrors of the Great Leap Forward and the Cultural Revolution. Even now, in the early twenty-first century, there are Western writers who take a sympathetic view of Mao. One such is the American scholar Lee Feigon, who does not deny that the Great Leap Forward and the Cultural Revolution caused 'horrific damage', but argues that, nevertheless, without these movements the modern Chinese economy could not have developed in the powerful way that it has.

Co-operation among international historians in the study of China

An interesting fact is that Russia is a major holder of sources on Mao's China. Sadly, in the Cold War atmosphere that prevailed up to the 1990s the Soviet experts on China were not permitted to co-operate with their Western counterparts by allowing them to study the documents. It was not until after the break-up of the USSR in the early 1990s that Western scholars were granted access to the former Soviet archives. By the late 1990s co-operation between Western and Russian historians had begun to throw light on many previously hidden aspects of both the domestic and international history of the PRC.

Jung Chang's biography of Mao

In 2005 a book appeared which claimed to tell the 'unknown story' of Mao. It did not quite do that since many of the 'discoveries' in the book had already been presented in a less dramatic way by other scholars. Nonetheless, the biography of Mao by Jung Chang and Jon Halliday quickly caught the imagination of students of China in the West, largely because the writer was already popular with readers for her *Wild Swans*, a book which sold 10 million copies throughout the world and provided a fascinating account of her family's bitter experiences during the Cultural Revolution. As might be expected, Jung Chang paints a very dark picture of Mao, portraying him as a driven monster responsible for the deaths of 70 million of his people.

Given her sufferings under Mao, Jung's approach is understandable, but it is arguable that her book is too strongly critical of its subject. The insights of someone who lived through the grim times she describes are obviously highly valuable, but there is a danger that she may be too close to it all to give a balanced appraisal. It may be one of those cases in which the player does not see the game as well as the spectator. This is why it is important to pay attention to other biographies of Mao, such as those by Philip Short and Jonathan Spence, which are written from a more detached, dispassionate angle.

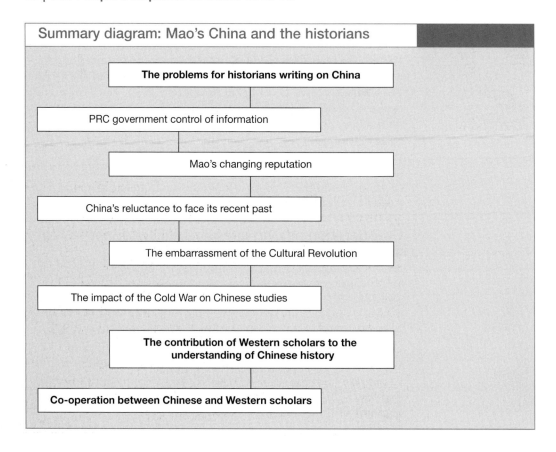

Summary diagram: Mao's China and the historians

The problems for historians writing on China

PRC government control of information

Mao's changing reputation

China's reluctance to face its recent past

The embarrassment of the Cultural Revolution

The impact of the Cold War on Chinese studies

The contribution of Western scholars to the understanding of Chinese history

Co-operation between Chinese and Western scholars

Some key books on Mao's China:
Jung Chang and Jon Halliday, *Mao: The Unknown Story* (Jonathan Cape, 2005).
Jung Chang, *Wild Swans* (HarperCollins, 1991).
Delia Davin, *Mao Zedong* (Sutton, 1997).
Lee Feigon, *Mao: A Reinterpretation* (Ivan R. Dee, 2002).
John King Fairbank, *China: A New History* (Belknap Press, 1992).
Michael Lynch, *Mao* (Routledge, 2004).
Roderick MacFarquhar, *Mao's Last Revolution* (Belknap Press, 2006).
Stuart Schram, *Mao Tse-Tung* (Penguin, 1966).
Frank Schurmann and Orville Schell, *Communist China* (Penguin, 1976).
Philip Short, *Mao: A Life* (Hodder & Stoughton, 1999).
Jonathan Spence, *Mao* (Weidenfeld & Nicolson, 1999).
Jonathan Spence, *The Search for Modern China* (W.W. Norton, 1990).
Ross Terrill, *Mao: A Biography* (Stanford UP, 2000).

The Early Years of the PRC 1949–57

Key question
How did Mao impose himself on the people of China?

Key term

Public utilities
Gas, electricity and the transport system.

1 | The Consolidation of Communist Power 1949–57

On taking power, Mao did not immediately rush to reform China. His initial moves were cautious. It is true that the property of those Nationalists who had fled with Chiang Kaishek to Taiwan was seized and the banks and the **public utilities** were taken under state control. All foreign assets, except for those of the USSR, were also taken over. But the new regime was prepared to offer compensation to those former owners and share holders who declared their willingness to work in the new China. Mao announced that the PRC was ready to use the resources of 'the national capitalists' to begin the reconstruction of China under Communism.

Mao was also aware that, although the Chinese **middle classes** were a relatively small part of a population overwhelmingly made up of peasants, their importance was greater than their numbers. It was they who provided the officials, the civil servants and the industrial managers. Those who had been unwilling or unable to flee with the defeated GMD were invited to stay in their positions and become loyal servants of the new government. Most accepted the offer and to these were added a significant number of **expatriate Chinese** who returned in a spirit of idealism, eager to serve the new regime.

The structure of the PRC

For administrative purposes, the country was divided into six regions, each governed by a bureau of four major officials:

- chairman
- party secretary
- military commander
- political commissar.

Since the last two posts were filled by officers of the **People's Liberation Army** (PLA) this effectively left China under military control, a situation which Mao Zedong considered offered the best means of stabilising China and guaranteeing the continued rule of the CCP. The overarching governmental power resided in the Central People's Government Council. This was composed of 56 leading party members, the majority of whom were veterans of the Yanan years. Six of these served as vice-chairmen under Mao who, as Chairman of the Council, was the unchallengeable figure in government.

The imposition of military control

A clear sign of how ruthless the new government intended to be was evident in the way it enforced its control over the outlying areas of China. In a series of **reunification campaigns** three separate PLA armies were dispatched west and south:

- one army was sent into Tibet (Xizang) in October 1950
- a second went into Xinjiang (Sinkiang)
- a third went into the southern province of Guangdong (Kwantung).

Tibet

The PRC's justification for invading Tibet was that the region had historically always belonged to China. The claim was an assertion, not a statement of fact. The Tibetans were markedly different in race, culture and religion to the Chinese and had always regarded themselves as a separate people. This was evident from the spirited resistance the PLA met with when it invaded; a hastily

National capitalists Those who had run China before 1949.

Middle classes Broadly made up professionally qualified people, such as lawyers, administrators and financiers.

Expatriate Chinese Chinese nationals living abroad.

People's Liberation Army The new name for the Red Army, which Mao had built into a formidable force in the 1930s and 1940s and which had carried him to power in 1949. The PLA's loyalty to Mao was his greatest single asset as leader of the PRC.

How was Communist authority imposed over mainland China?

Tibet invaded by PLA: 1950

Reunification campaigns The Chinese government's euphemism for forcibly bringing the invaded provinces into line in the 1950s.

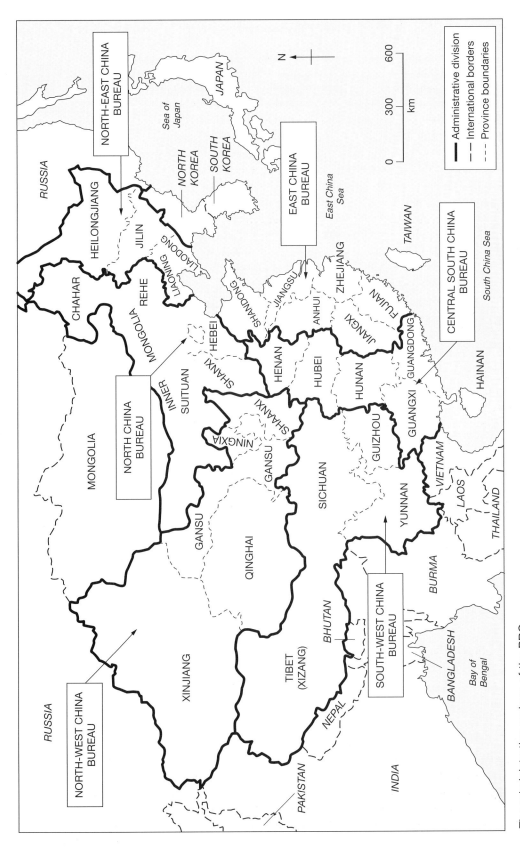

The administrative regions of the PRC.

assembled force of 60,000 Tibetans fought determinedly to preserve their land and culture.

However, the struggle was hopeless. Without a trained army and possessing only outdated weapons, the Tibetans had no chance of matching the occupying PLA. Within 6 months open resistance had been suppressed. The PLA then imposed a regime of terror aimed at wiping out all traces of separate Tibetan identity (see page 64).

Xinjiang and Guangdong

Similar PLA harshness was shown in Xinjiang. This distant western province, which bordered Soviet-controlled Outer Mongolia, had a large Muslim population. The CCP feared that it would either declare its independence from China or fall into Soviet hands. By 1951, within a year of their arrival, PLA detachments had imposed Communist authority over the region. At the same time, the Guangdong province in southern China, the traditional GMD base, was brought under PLA control.

Political control

The 'anti-movements'

Having tightened its military grip over China, Mao's government turned its attention to extending its political control. In 1951, in keeping with the Chinese love for classifying programmes under cardinal numbers, Mao announced the beginning of 'the three anti-movement', the targets being:

- waste
- corruption
- inefficiency.

This was expanded in 1952 into 'the five anti-movement', which was intended to stimulate the economy by attacking:

- industrial sabotage
- tax evasion
- bribery
- fraud
- theft of government property.

The main aim of the anti-movements was to destroy the remnants of what Mao defined as 'the bureaucratic capitalist class'. It was clear that 3 years after the Communist takeover Mao felt able to turn openly against the classes which he had been obliged to tolerate earlier in order to maintain continuity of administration. In 1952, Mao justified his tough line in a widely broadcast public statement:

> Our present task is to strengthen the people's state apparatus – meaning principally the people's army, the people's police and the people's courts – thereby safeguarding national defence and protecting the people's interests. We definitely have no benevolent policies towards the reactionaries or the counter-revolutionary activities of the reactionary classes. Our benevolent policy does not

Key question
What methods did Mao's government use to extend its political control?

Key date

'Anti-movements' launched: 1951

apply to such deeds or such persons, who are outside the ranks of the people; it applies only to the people.

Terror tactics

On the pretext of defending the people from their enemies, it was not long before Mao and the CCP began to resort to terror as a basic method of control. It soon became clear that China was to be turned into a one-party state. At the time of the Communist success in 1949 there had been over ten separate political parties in China. These included the Left GMD and the Democratic League, splinter parties that had broken away from Chiang Kaishek's Nationalists. By 1952 they had disappeared, destroyed in a set of repressive moves which denied the right of any party to exist other than the Chinese Communist Party.

The political purges were accompanied by a series of mass campaigns aimed at extending the CCP's authority over the people of China. A concerted attack was launched against 'counter-revolutionaries and imperialists', catch-all terms that were used to condemn anyone who showed signs of disapproving of the Communist regime.

Mass killings

Particular CCP severity was evident in the early 1950s in Shanghai and Guangzhou (Canton), cities which had been notorious for their underworld gangs and **triads** in the years of Nationalist rule. Having used the local knowledge of the former gangsters to consolidate its hold on the city, the CCP turned on them in a violent bloodletting. Of the 130,000 'bandits and criminals' rounded up by the authorities in Guangzhou over half were executed. A similar process led to a death toll of 28,000 in Shanghai.

Enforcing conformity

To maintain its control, the CCP turned China into a nation of informers. Local party officials created a system in which:

- neighbours spied on neighbours
- workers snooped on their mates
- children reported on their parents
- each street or tenement block had officially appointed 'watchers' who kept the local CCP informed on anyone or anything suspicious
- community associations, which were set with the declared aim of providing mutual help, became a major means of exerting control and conformity.

Such developments had the effect of forcibly politicising the nation. Individuals or families who declined to become involved were immediately labelled as class enemies. Indeed, 'labelling' became the chief means of enforcing conformity. Those Chinese who had a middle-class or non-revolutionary background knew that this would be enough to condemn them. To prove the

Key date
Political parties other than the CCP banned: 1952

Key term
Triads
Chinese secret societies, usually of a criminal kind, involved in drugs, gambling and prostitution.

Key question
What methods were used to impose conformity?

sincerity of their acceptance of the new proletarian China, they became especially eager to denounce others as 'bourgeois elements' and 'imperialist lackeys'. In the People's Republic there was to be no toleration of independent thinking, let alone dissent.

As part of the CCP's coercion of China, youth organisations were either closed down or taken over by party **cadres**. Religion was selected for special attack (see page 108); China had begun to take its first steps towards becoming a society of informers in which conformity was maintained by exploiting the traditional fear Chinese people had of being publicly exposed as political or social deviants.

The attack on China's middle class

Mao's aim in pressing these policies on the people was nothing less than the destruction of a whole class – China's **bourgeoisie**. Having used this class to help see the PRC through its teething troubles, he had no compunction in then turning on it in order to obliterate it. He regarded it as an essential step in the creation of China as a fully Marxist state in which only one class would exist – the **proletariat**.

Mao's view of the necessity of violence

Mao insisted that proletarian revolution could be achieved only through the use of violence. He had always contended that no class ever gives up power willingly; power has to be dragged from it by force. And even then, the dispossessed class will attempt to fight back; that is why there are always reactionaries.

The task was, therefore, to show no mercy in obliterating the bourgeoisie and all the other reactionary forces that were still to be found corrupting the new China. Mao spelled this out with great clarity when addressing a gathering of the party leaders in 1955:

> On this matter we are quite heartless. On this matter, Marxism is indeed cruel and has little mercy, for it is determined to exterminate imperialism, feudalism, capitalism and small production to boot. Some of our comrades are too kind, they are not tough enough, in other words, they are not [truly] Marxist. Our aim is to exterminate capitalism, obliterate it from the face of the earth and make it a thing of the past.

Registration as a political weapon

A notable method by which the party imposed its will was the system which required individuals to register themselves. There were three main types of registration:

- *danwei* – a permit without which an individual could not hold a job
- *hukou* – a certificate which entitled a family to obtain accommodation
- *dangan* – a dossier held by local party officials containing the personal details and record of every individual.

Key question
Why was Mao so determined to destroy the middle class?

Key terms

Cadres
Dedicated Communist Party workers whose special task was to spy and report on fellow CCP members and the public.

Bourgeoisie
The Marxist label for the middle-class capitalists who exploited the workers.

Proletariat
The Marxist term for the revolutionary workers.

Key question
How did the registration system enable the government to enforce control?

Of the three, the *dangan* was the most intrusive. A veritable army of party clerks spent their working hours collecting and collating material on everyone in the population. Hundreds of millions of records were kept. The *dangans* became the chief means by which the authorities maintained political and social control over the Chinese people. A person's right to employment, housing or a pension, or indeed to his freedom, depended on the contents of his dossier.

The Gao Gang and Rao Rashi affair 1954

Key question
What did the case of Gao Gang and Rao Rashi indicate about the nature of the terror?

The repression imposed on the nation at this stage has to be understood in relation to two developments that dominated the early years of the PRC: the Korean War (1950–3) and Mao's first Five-Year Plan (1952–6). The Korean struggle (see pages 28–33) placed huge additional burdens on the young Communist Republic and was used to justify the extension of state control.

The same applied to the industrialisation programme on which China embarked (see page 46). Mao claimed that many officials were only half-hearted in their efforts to promote it. He identified two major culprits, **Gao Gang** (Kao Kang) and **Rao Rashi** (Jao Shu-shi). Mao asserted in 1954 that these two leading party officials, rather than working to advance China's industrialisation, had misused their authority to establish 'independent kingdoms'.

Mao's charges resulted in the Central Council's dismissing both men from their positions. Gao Gang committed suicide, an act described by Deng Xiaoping, who had been highly active in hounding him, as 'the ultimate treason'.

Mao's distrust of his colleagues

Key figures

Gao Gang
(1902–54) The CCP leader in Manchuria.

Rao Rashi
(1900–75) The CCP leader in Shandong.

The high party status and reputation that Gao and Rao had enjoyed made their sudden fall all the more remarkable. It was clear evidence of the increasing centralisation of power in the party and government and of Mao's refusal to tolerate potential rivals.

Key terms

Power struggles
From the time of his helping to found the CCP in the 1920s through to his triumph in 1949, Mao had fought a series of fierce battles to assert his authority over the party.

Paranoia
A persecution complex, the feeling a disturbed person has that everybody is plotting against them.

Mao never forgot the lessons learned in the CCP **power struggles** in Jiangxi and Yanan. Notwithstanding the apparent harmony that the CCP leaders publicly displayed, tensions and rivalries were never far below the surface. The godlike status that Mao achieved among the Chinese people between 1949 and his death in 1976 did not make him more trustful of his colleagues. Indeed, his suspicions increased to the point of **paranoia**.

A characteristic of Mao that many biographers have stressed is that the more powerful he grew the more detached he became from his political and governmental associates. Such was the awe in which he was held that his colleagues did not find it easy to converse or to exchange ideas with him and it is doubtful that they ever gave him their honest opinions. While it is true that Mao made a point in the 1950s of '**going to the people**', his travels within China were largely stage-managed affairs. His claim that such journeys brought him into touch with the real feelings of the people is unconvincing; those peasants and workers who were selected for the privilege of speaking to him were coached into telling him only what he wanted to hear.

Terror on the land

Despite his admission that things had gone too far during the civil war period of 1945–9 (see page 8), the land policies that Mao adopted after coming to power in 1949 followed the same violent line. The property of the landlords was confiscated and redistributed among their former tenants. Some landlords were allowed to keep a portion of their land provided they became peasants, but the great majority were put on public trial and denounced as enemies of the people.

The evidence that later came to light revealed that as many as a million landlords were killed during the PRC's land reforms of the early 1950s. Scenes similar to those witnessed by Mao Anying earlier were repeated across China (see page 7). The Communist government argued, of course, that the stern measures were directed not against the peasants, but against the landlords and **kulaks** who had previously abused them. Moreover, the peasants had now been given the land as theirs, and it was certainly true that in the early 1950s many peasants rejoiced that the new regime seemed to have their interests at heart after all.

However, the joy was to be short lived. Within 2 years of the peasants' being granted the land, it was taken back from them. This was the prelude to a massive upheaval in rural China – the collectivisation of the peasantry.

The character of Communist Party rule in the PRC

It should be noted that despite the coercive society that Mao's China was in practice, in theory it was one of the freest in the world. The Communist Party claimed that all power rested with the people and that the party officials and the government acted as servants of the nation. Figure 2.1 shows a model of how the government supposedly operated. It was the workers and peasants who exercised authority through the various connected and overlapping bodies.

The Chinese Communists made much of the claim that elections for party officials and administrators were held in the villages, localities and regions and that the members of the National People's Congress, which was the body formally responsible for deciding national policy, were themselves elected as the people's choice. What was not emphasised was that only one party could stand for election, all others being outlawed, and that even those who stood as independents had to acknowledge publicly that the CCP had an absolute right to rule. An additional factor was that party officials oversaw all the elections, which meant that there was little chance of anyone critical of Mao or the government ever being successful.

Key question
What policies did the new government adopt towards the peasants and landlords?

Key terms

Going to the people
Used to describe Mao's practice of periodically travelling through parts of China, supposedly to listen to what the people had to say.

Kulaks
A word borrowed from Stalin's USSR to describe the rich peasants who exploited their poorer neighbours. As in the USSR, the existence of a kulak class was a deliberately created myth.

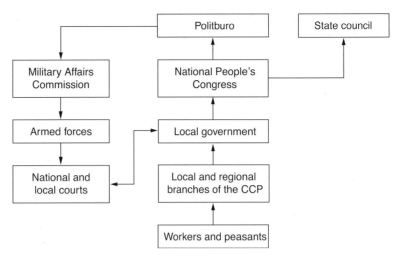

Figure 2.1 The pattern of Chinese Communist Party rule.

The Politburo

Key question
What was the role of the Politburo?

Key term

Politburo
An inner core of some 20 leading members of the Communist Party.

The reality in the PRC was that the Communist Party, not the people, ruled. Moreover, the party in this context did not mean all the members of the CCP. In effect, government was carried by the **Politburo**. The National People's Congress simply rubber-stamped the decisions made by the Politburo; its job was to applaud the party's leaders when they made their appearances on the platform. There was never a genuine case of the Congress's challenging, let alone reversing, party policy on any issue that mattered.

Mao's authority over the Politburo

The Politburo, in turn, was under the authority of Mao Zedong. This did not mean that he initiated every detail of policy; sometimes he chose not to attend Politburo meetings. Nevertheless, nothing could be done of which he disapproved. He was the ultimate authority. What adds to the oddity of Mao's position is that his power did not rest on any formal position that he held. It is true that he was Chairman of the party, but the title did not confer power on him; rather it was a recognition of the power that he already wielded. That was why he was able on occasion to withdraw from the political frontline, as at the time of the famine in the early 1960s (see page 73), and then later return with his power undiminished.

Democratic centralism

Key question
How did democratic centralism operate under Mao?

Western observers were sometimes puzzled by the Chinese situation in which a party, dedicated to the notion of the rule of the masses, allowed itself to be controlled by one man, Mao Zedong. Part of the answer lies in the concept of democratic centralism. This idea had first been formulated by **Lenin** in Russia. The argument, which Mao took up and applied to his own interpretation of revolution in China, was that true democracy in a Communist party lay in the obedience of the members to the authority and instructions of the leaders. The justification for this was that while, as representatives of the workers, all Communists were genuine revolutionaries, only the leaders were sufficiently educated in the science of revolution to understand what needed to be done.

In practice, democratic centralism meant the Chinese Communists' doing what Mao told them to do. One of the ironies of this was that in spite of the power he wielded, Mao became increasingly paranoid. The more authority he gained, the more he feared that opposition to him was growing. It is a feature of his personality that explains why he was so ready to launch anti-campaigns and purges against those he suspected irrationally of plotting to overthrow him.

Key figure

Lenin
(1870–1924) The great interpreter of Marx and the man who had led the Russian Communists to power in the 1917 revolution.

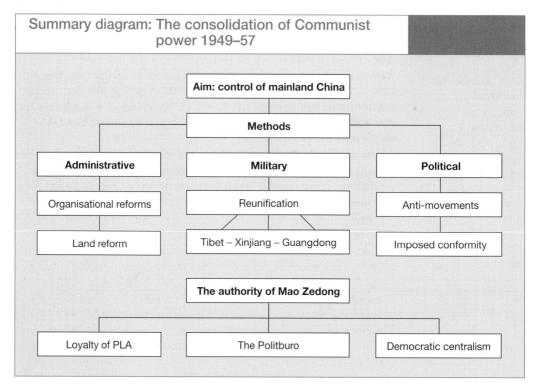

Summary diagram: The consolidation of Communist power 1949–57

2 | China and the Korean War 1950–3

The invasion of South Korea

Between 1910 and 1945 the Korean peninsula had been occupied by Japan. With the defeat of Japan at the end of the Second World War in 1945, Korea was partitioned along the 38th parallel; the USA took responsibility for protecting the area to the south of that line, with the Soviet Union playing an equivalent role in the region to the north. In 1950 the North Koreans crossed the parallel with the aim of imposing their Communist control over the whole peninsula.

Key question
How did the PRC, so soon after its formation, come to be involved in war?

Korean War: 1950–3

Key date

Key terms

US State Department
The US body responsible for foreign policy, equivalent to the British Foreign Office.

'Loss' of China
Refers to the USA's dismay at mainland China's becoming Communist in 1949.

UN Security Council
The permanent five-member body (originally made up of the USSR, the USA, Britain, France and Nationalist China) responsible for settling international disputes.

Veto
Each single member of the UN Security Council has the right to block the collective decisions of the other members.

There have been various attempts to explain this move. It was once believed that the whole affair had been initiated by Mao in collusion with Stalin. This was how the **US State Department** interpreted it at the time. Their sensitivity over the **'loss' of China** to the CCP in 1949 led the Americans to assume that the Communist invasion of South Korea was the first joint venture of the new Communist bloc formed by Red China and the USSR.

However, it is now known that although Mao eventually backed North Korea he did not initiate the invasion. Korea seems hardly to have been discussed at the meetings between Stalin and Mao in Moscow in 1950 (see page 138). China's current military plans were exclusively concerned with Taiwan, Xinjiang, Guangdong and Tibet. Indeed, the PRC had recently made the decision to cut back on military expenditure and redirect its resources into the rectification campaigns within China.

Stalin's role

What commentators now suggest is that Stalin had colluded with Kim Il Sung, the North Korean leader, in organising the venture and that he called on China to give support only after the fighting had started. Stalin was playing Cold War politics. Having been convinced by Kim that North Korea was capable of sustaining a major war effort against the Americans, Stalin anticipated that the USA would be sucked into a conflict in Asia which it could not win.

The great advantage as Stalin saw it was that war in Korea entailed no risk to the USSR since Soviet forces would not be directly involved. This gave particular significance to the USSR's decision not to attend the vital meeting of the **UN Security Council** in June 1950 which voted to send a UN army to Korea.

Cold War analysts used to believe that the USSR had miscalculated at this critical juncture by walking out of the Security Council in protest at the Western powers' recognition of Taiwan rather than the PRC as the true China. It was judged that the walkout left the remaining Security Council members free to vote for the sending of a UN army to Korea, knowing that the USSR could not use its **veto** to block the resolution. However, Andre Gromyko, the Soviet foreign minister, later admitted that the Soviet Union's decision to boycott the Security Council was a deliberate move by Stalin to entice the USA into the Korean conflict.

Mao's lack of awareness of Stalin's true intentions has led historian Jonathan Spence, one of the foremost Western authorities on China, to describe the PRC's involvement in the Korean War as 'a study in ambiguity'. The ambiguity arose from Mao's not fully understanding the situation; he remained in the dark regarding Stalin's motives. Stalin calculated that if the North Koreans could take the South and thus bring the whole of Korea under Communist control, the benefits to the USSR would be considerable. The USA would have been humiliated and the Soviet Union would have acquired a very powerful position in the Far East at very little cost to itself.

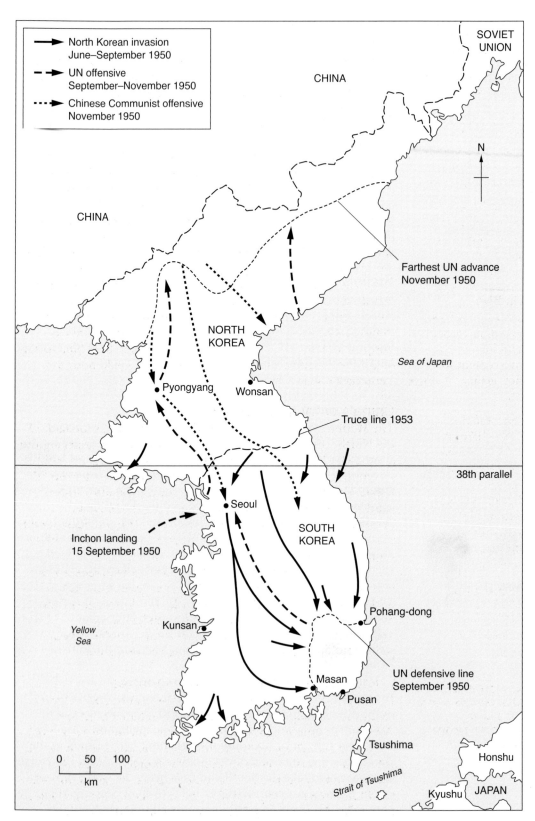

Map of the Korean War 1950–3.

Key question
What were Mao's reasons for committing China to the Korean War?

Key terms

Fait accompli
Something done in such a way that it cannot be changed.

Conscript army
Troops who have been compulsorily called up.

Key figures

Lin Biao
(1907–71) Mao's second in command until his involvement in a plot against Mao in 1971.

Zhou Enlai
(1898–1976) A veteran of the Jiangxi and Yanan years, who, as Mao's Foreign Secretary, became an outstanding international statesman.

Peng Dehuai
(1898–1974) The PRC's minister of defence and a PLA veteran.

Key question
What was the cost to China of its involvement in the war?

Mao's reaction

Since he had not been party to the plan devised by Stalin and Kim Il Sung, Mao was at first hesitant to commit China formally to the Korean struggle. But once he realised the affair was a *fait accompli* he felt obliged to enter. Korea was too close geographically for China to remain detached, and at this early stage in its development the PRC invariably followed the Soviet lead in international affairs.

This was not because the PRC wanted to but because it had to. Jung Chang in her biography of Mao suggests that what finally persuaded him to enter the Korean War was not a wish to co-operate with Stalin, but a desire to put pressure on him. 'What Mao had in mind boiled down to a deal; Chinese soldiers would fight the Americans for Stalin in exchange for Soviet technology and equipment.' Yet, whatever gains he might have been hoping for, Mao still had difficulty in persuading his leading military commanders that he had made the right decision. Gao Gang and **Lin Biao** (Lin Piao) argued that the PRC's primary task was to crush its internal enemies and that it did not have the resources to fight in Korea. Mao's counter-argument was that once US troops had entered Korea it would be impossible for China to stay out; if the Americans were to take Korea they would possess a stepping stone to China itself.

China's entry into the war

The Western view of the Korean crisis was that it was the fault of the North Koreans in crossing the 38th parallel and attacking the South. The PRC counter-claimed that the South Koreans had committed the initial aggression. When US forces under the UN flag landed in Korea in June 1950, **Zhou Enlai** (Chou En-lai) condemned it as an imperialist invasion. Organised mass demonstrations took place in China's cities. The principal slogan was 'North Korea's friends are our friends. North Korea's enemy is our enemy. North Korea's defence is our defence.'

Zhou warned that China would be forced to intervene if US troops pushed into North Korea. In fact thousands of PLA soldiers were already fighting alongside the North Koreans as 'volunteers'. In October 1950 US forces under General MacArthur crossed northwards over the 38th parallel. China promptly declared itself to be fully engaged in the war.

China's contribution to the war in Korea

By the end of 1950 a quarter of a million PLA troops under the command of **Peng Dehuai** (Peng Teh-huai) had moved into Korea. That number grew to three million during the course of the 3-year war. Despite China's pretence that all its troops were volunteers, it was a **conscript army** that fought in Korea. It suffered heavily in the fighting. When a truce was called in 1953 the PLA had lost nearly a million men (including Mao Zedong's oldest son, Mao Anying). This was the result of the deadly firepower that the UN aircraft and ground forces brought to bear on the Chinese troops who tended to attack fixed position in concentrated numbers, a tactic that produced great deeds of heroism, but appalling casualty figures.

The UN forces were amazed at how ready the Chinese commanders were to send thousands of their troops to certain death. A young English soldier, Michael Caine, who later became a celebrated film actor, said that what put him off Communism, to which he had been very sympathetic before coming to Korea, was the total disregard which the Chinese and North Korean officers had for the lives and safety of their own men.

Harmful results of the war for China

The outcome of the Korean conflict suggested that Mao had been right in his initial reservations about Chinese involvement. The **Panmunjong truce** which ended the fighting in 1953 left Korea still divided and with no prospect of a Communist takeover of the South. To this political failure could be added other damaging outcomes for the PRC:

- The cost in Chinese lives: although the PRC would not give official figures, calculations by UN and Soviet observers put the number of Chinese deaths at around the million mark.
- The USA pledged itself to the defence of Taiwan and to the continued support of Nationalist China's membership of the UN, a position that was maintained until 1972. This effectively ruled out any possibility of the PRC's reclaiming Taiwan by force.
- The war was a huge drain on the young PRC's economy. Industrial resources earmarked for domestic growth had to be diverted into the war effort. The material losses incurred during the Korean conflict took more than a decade to make good. Mao remarked that China had to pay down to the last rifle and bullet for the Soviet supplies it received during the conflict.

Panmunjong truce
The 1953 agreement that brought the Korean War to an end, but decided little since the two sides simply agreed to recognise the division of Korea at the 38th parallel.

Key term

Benefits the war brought to China

These were obviously serious consequences, but the war did have some positive results for Communist China:

- The government's call for national unity to enable the PRC to surmount its first great crisis helped Mao and the CCP to consolidate their hold over China by crushing the remnants of the GMD on the mainland.
- The 3-year experience of war hardened China's resolve to stand alone in a hostile world.
- Although Stalin had encouraged the war, the USSR chose to play no direct military part. Mao proudly claimed that it was Chinese, not Soviet, comrades who had shed their blood in the cause of international Communism.
- The PRC could justifiably claim that for 3 years it had matched the USA in combat and remained undefeated.

Key question
What were the main effects of the Korean War on the PRC?

The impact of the war on the PRC as a nation

The Korean War left a deep mark on the PRC:

- Plunged within a year of its creation into an exhausting war, the new nation had had to subordinate all its plans to the needs of the struggle.
- The war effort provided a justification for the increasing political and social repression imposed by the government.
- The PRC was obliged to prove itself in war before it had had time to establish itself in peace.

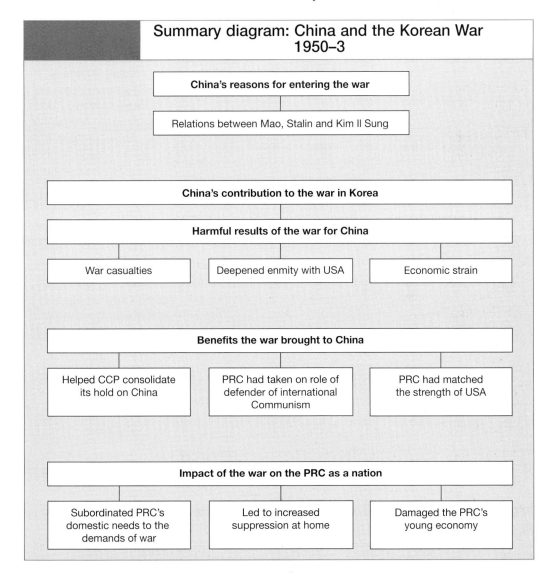

Summary diagram: China and the Korean War 1950–3

China's reasons for entering the war

Relations between Mao, Stalin and Kim Il Sung

China's contribution to the war in Korea

Harmful results of the war for China

War casualties

Deepened enmity with USA

Economic strain

Benefits the war brought to China

Helped CCP consolidate its hold on China

PRC had taken on role of defender of international Communism

PRC had matched the strength of USA

Impact of the war on the PRC as a nation

Subordinated PRC's domestic needs to the demands of war

Led to increased suppression at home

Damaged the PRC's young economy

3 | The Economy: The First Five-Year Plan 1952–6

Mao's aims for Chinese industry

Mao's early attempts to modernise the Chinese economy carried the stamp of Soviet influence. Impressed by the apparent success of **Stalin's Five-Year Plans** in the USSR, Mao wanted the PRC to build on the same model. In 1952 China's first Five-Year Plan was introduced. Its aim was to develop the state-directed growth of **heavy industry**.

A partial basis for this already existed. During their period of government in the 1930s and 1940s, the GMD under Chiang Kaishek had established a National Resources Committee (NRC) which had taken control of industrial investment policy. A large number of NRC managers and over 200,000 of its workforce had stayed on in China after 1949. In addition, a significant population shift had begun with the coming to power of the CCP. Between 1949 and 1957 migration from the countryside to the towns nearly doubled the urban population from 57 million to 100 million.

Thus, as the PRC began its economic reforms it already had available a large potential workforce and considerable industrial expertise. However, the new government's first notable success was scored unaided. In its first 2 years it brought under control the galloping inflation from which China had suffered during the final years of the GMD. From a rate of 1000 per cent in 1949 inflation had dropped to a manageable 15 per cent by 1951. This was largely achieved by:

- slashing public expenditure
- raising tax rates on urban dwellers
- replacing the old Chinese dollar with a new currency, known as the renminbi or yuan.

The first Five-Year Plan 1952–6

Under the plan the areas targeted for increased production were coal, steel and petrochemicals. Attention was also to be given to the development of a Chinese automobile and transport industry. As a morale-boost a number of spectacular civil-engineering projects were undertaken. An outstanding example was the construction of a vast road and rail bridge across the Yangzi (Yangtse) River at Nanjing (Nanking). The degree of success achieved by the plan can be gauged from Table 2.1.

Care has to be taken with these statistics. As in the USSR under Stalin, so in the PRC under Mao, there was a tendency for officials to massage the figures relating to economic performance. All those in the spiral of command from CCP officials and industrial managers down to foremen and workers were anxious to appear to be fulfilling their targets. The presence of party cadres checking on production targets meant that in many areas of industry there was what amounted to a large-scale conspiracy to adjust the figures so that they appeared as impressive as possible.

Key question
What were the objectives of the first Five-Year Plan?

Key terms

Stalin's Five-Year Plans
Between 1929 and 1953, Stalin revolutionised the Soviet economy by a series of government-directed 5-year plans aimed at achieving a massive increase in industrial output.

Heavy industry
Iron- and steel-based products and constructions.

Key question
How far did the first Five-Year Plan achieve its objectives?

Table 2.1: The first Five-Year Plan 1952–6

	1952 Output targets	1957 Output achieved
Gross industrial output (yuan, millions)	53,560	65,020
Particular areas of production		
Coal (millions of tonnes)	113	115
Oil (millions of tonnes)	2,012	1,458
Steel (millions of tonnes)	4.12	5.35
Electric power (billions of kilowatts)	15.9	19.34
Hydroelectric turbines (kilowatts)	79,000	74,900
Machine tools (units)	12,720	28,000
Locomotives (units)	200	167
Freight cars (units)	8500	7300
Merchant ships (tonnes)	179,000	54,000
Trucks (units)	4000	7500
Bicycles (units)	550,000	1,174,000
Manufactured chemicals (thousands of tonnes)	1580	2087

Table 2.2: PRC expenditure (as percentages of national budget)

	1950	1952	1957
Economic development	25.5	45.4	51.4
Education and culture	11.1	13.6	16.0
Defence	41.5	26.0	19.0
Government administration	19.3	10.3	7.8
Miscellaneous	2.6	4.7	5.8
Total (yuan, millions)	**6810**	**16,790**	**29,020**

Yet even allowing for exaggeration, the statistics above, which have been filtered through Western analyses, do indicate a considerable degree of success for the plan, this at a time when the Korean War required China to finance a major war effort.

The plan's scale of success

China's economic growth rate of nearly nine per cent between 1953 and 1957 compared favourably with that of the USSR in the 1930s. In the circumstances of the 1950s it was natural that China should measure itself against the yardstick of the Soviet Union's industrial performance and seek to match its success. At this stage Stalin's USSR was the PRC's political and economic model and mentor. It was, after all, the only country after the 1949 revolution that was willing to offer China economic aid.

Yet this aid was to prove a mixed blessing. In the **Sino-Soviet agreement of 1950** the USSR agreed to provide China with economic assistance, but the bargain was weighted very much in favour of the Soviet Union (see page 139). Soviet aid was not a gift from one brother nation to another; it had to be paid for by commercial concessions. For example, the PRC was required to send a substantial portion of its bullion reserves to the USSR.

Key date

Sino-Soviet Treaty signed: 1950

Key term

Sino-Soviet agreement of 1950
A consequence of Mao's meeting with Stalin in Moscow; the USSR agreed to provide the PRC with vital resources that the PRC would pay back with interest over time.

Furthermore, the 10,000 Soviet economic advisers who went to China came at a price. The PRC had to meet their costs by taking out high-interest loans. Such loans were the predominant form of Soviet aid to China. Only five per cent of the capital sent to China was genuine industrial investment; the rest was in the form of loans. The realisation by the Chinese that they had been exploited rather than aided was a major factor in the later souring of Sino-Soviet relations.

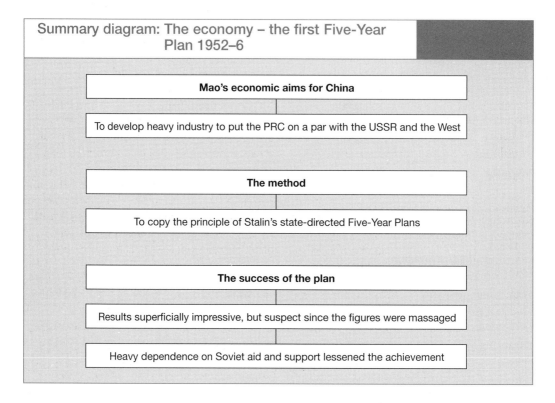

Summary diagram: The economy – the first Five-Year Plan 1952–6

Mao's economic aims for China

To develop heavy industry to put the PRC on a par with the USSR and the West

The method

To copy the principle of Stalin's state-directed Five-Year Plans

The success of the plan

Results superficially impressive, but suspect since the figures were massaged

Heavy dependence on Soviet aid and support lessened the achievement

4 | The Hundred Flowers Campaign 1957

Mao travelled extensively in China during the early 1950s. The rapturous reception he received wherever he went convinced him that he was in touch with the people. In 1956 he informed his government and party colleagues that it would now be an appropriate time to allow greater freedom of expression to those who might wish to comment constructively on how well Communist China was achieving its aim of turning the nation into a proletarian state.

In a widely reported speech on 'Contradictions', given to leading party workers early in 1957, Mao stated his satisfaction with the economic advances made under the first Five-Year Plan, but went on to complain of the heavy-handedness with which some CCP officials were applying national and local policies. He

Key question
What was Mao's motive in launching the Hundred Flowers campaign?

The Hundred Flowers campaign: 1957

Key date

Key terms

Intellectuals
Mao classed intellectuals as those who did not do a proper job, e.g. writers, teachers, artists and lawyers.

Marxist–Leninist
The official Communist ideology based on the theories of Karl Marx as interpreted by Lenin, the Russian revolutionary.

Cult of personality
A reference to the unlimited power that Stalin had taken into his own hands at the expense of the party.

Anti-rightist movement
Rightist had no precise definition; it was applied to anyone Mao wanted to remove.

hinted that the time might have come to allow **intellectuals** a greater say in debate.

This was an unusual twist, since Mao had an abiding distaste for intellectuals. But he had been sufficiently tolerant in 1956 not to give his backing to a campaign against Hu Feng, a writer who had dared to challenge the notion that **Marxist–Leninist** values were the only criteria for judging artistic merit. Hu's argument had brought bitter denunciations from among the upper ranks of the CCP. However, Mao joined Zhou Enlai in suggesting that China had made such progress under the first Five-Year Plan that it could afford to be lenient towards Hu, who was simply confused and mistaken.

Mao's reaction to de-Stalinisation

It is also likely that Mao was influenced by events in the USSR. It was in 1956 that the new Soviet leader, Nikita Khrushchev, shook the Communist world by launching an extraordinary attack on the reputation of his predecessor, Joseph Stalin, who had died 3 years earlier. In a programme of de-Stalinisation, Khrushchev denounced Stalin for his '**cult of personality**' (see page 140). Mao could see how easily this charge could be made against himself in China. His apparent encouragement of criticism from within the party was, therefore, a way of taking the sting out of such a suggestion and preventing the comparison being made between him and Stalin.

Mao invites criticism

Early in 1957 Mao urged Communist Party officials to be prepared to undergo criticism from the people. With the slogan, 'Let a hundred flowers bloom, let a hundred schools of thought contend', he called on critics within the party to state openly where they thought the government and the CCP had gone wrong.

Once they had overcome their initial fear that they might be thought of as being anti-party, members rushed to respond by pointing out the mistakes that had been made. Individuals and policies were complained against on the grounds of corruption, inefficiency and lack of realism. Leading figures in government, education and the arts were heavily censured for their failures. Things even went so far as to include mild criticism of Mao Zedong himself.

Mao changes direction

It was at this point that Mao called a halt to the campaign. Everything now went into reverse; it became a time not of freedom of expression, but of fierce repression. The Hundred Flowers campaign was abandoned and replaced by an **anti-rightist movement**. Those who had been foremost in responding to Mao's call to let a hundred schools of thought contend were now forced to retract their statements. University staff and school teachers, research scientists, economists, writers and artists – many of the best minds and the most able public servants in

China – were obliged to make abject confessions and submit themselves to 're-education'. The party was purged of those members who had been too free with their objections to government and party orders.

Even high-ranking members were vulnerable. Zhou Enlai, despite being one of Mao's most loyal supporters, was obliged to make a humiliating self-criticism in front of a large party gathering. Zhou admitted to having been too slow in putting Mao's industrialisation plans into action. In ordering Zhou to make this statement, which was simply untrue, Mao was showing that nobody in the party or government, no matter how prominent his position, was beyond investigation and criticism.

All the members of the CCP and the government understood the message; if someone as respected as Zhou Enlai could be treated in this way, then nobody was safe. The only way to avoid suspicion, therefore, was to conform absolutely to Mao's wishes.

A victim of the anti-rightist campaign, Zhang Bojun, the Minister of Communications, is humiliated in front of jeering members of his own staff at a rally in Beijing in July 1957. What are the likely explanations for Zhang's being turned on by his staff in this way?

5 | The Key Debate

What were Mao's motives in launching the Hundred Flowers campaign?

Was it a trick?

Many historians have discussed the question of why Mao introduced the Hundred Flowers campaign. Some writers, most notably Jung Chang in her 2005 biography of Mao, argue that the speed with which he reversed his policy was proof that from the beginning the campaign had been a trick on his part. She suggests that, far from being intended as a liberalising measure, it was a deliberate manoeuvre by Mao to bring his critics into the open so that they could be easily exposed, identified and removed. In her words: 'Few guessed that Mao was setting a trap, and that he was inviting people to speak out so that he could use what they said as an excuse to victimise them. Mao's targets were intellectuals and the educated, the people most likely to speak up.'

As Jung Chang sees it, the Hundred Flowers campaign was part of the movement towards a controlled society in which all expression of opinion had to meet the criteria of political correctness as defined by Mao. The way in which the anti-rightist campaign purged the government and party of his critics was of a scale and ruthlessness that anticipated the upheavals of the Cultural Revolution a decade later (see page 89). This is a strongly put case. However, there are other viewpoints equally worthy of attention.

Was Mao genuinely seeking criticism?

Lee Feigon, a US scholar, in a revisionist argument published in 2002 contends that Mao had been genuine in his original appeal for ideas to be expressed. This was not to say Mao was being tolerant. His intention was to undermine the bureaucrats in the government who in the short time that the PRC had been in existence had come to have too big an influence in the running of affairs. Feigon puts it in these terms:

> By giving scientists and engineers the freedom to express their ideas, Mao sought to prevent party bureaucrats from interfering with technical decisions. He wanted intellectuals to expose and attack corruption and bureaucracy. He also wanted peasants, students and workers to speak out and even demonstrate to prevent government bureaucrats from running roughshod over their rights.

Was the campaign simply a muddle?

Jonathan Spence, widely acknowledged by his fellow historians as an outstanding authority on Mao's China, dismisses the idea that the Hundred Flowers campaign was a ruse by Mao to bring his enemies into the open. Spence sees the affair as the confused result of contradictory thinking among the CCP leaders:

It was rather, a muddled and inconclusive movement that grew out of conflicting attitudes within the CCP leadership. At its core was an argument about the pace and development that was best for China, a debate about the nature of the first Five-Year Plan and the promise for further growth. From that debate and the political tensions that accompanied it sprang the Great Leap Forward.

Further points in the debate

In the event, whatever Mao's motives may or may not have been, it was the scale of the criticism that the Hundred Flowers unleashed that took him aback. He had not realised the scale of the dissatisfaction with the party that the campaign had revealed. In practical terms there was little difference as to whether he intended from the beginning to flush out opponents or whether he decided to do this once he had discovered the extent of the opposition. The outcome was the same. Mao crushed those he thought were opposed to him.

There is also the consideration that if Mao had indeed launched the Hundred Flowers out of a fear of being compared with Stalin, the fear greatly lessened from late 1956. In November of that year Khrushchev sent Soviet tanks into Budapest to crush the **Hungarian rising**. That was the Soviet leader's way of making it clear that de-Stalinisation did not mean the lessening of the grip of the Communist Party over the USSR or the weakening of Soviet control over the **Eastern bloc**.

Mao fully approved of the Soviet action for two reasons. In the first place, he believed it was the kind of tough line that Communist governments should take in order to maintain their authority. In the second, he was relieved by the knowledge that the Soviet Union had merely been flirting with liberal ideas. This meant that he did not need to compete with Khrushchev in developing **Communism with a human face**. Neither leader had any intention of relaxing his political control over the people.

It might be wondered why Mao was so sensitive to happenings in the USSR. The answer is that at this early stage of its development, the PRC still regarded itself as being dependent on the economic and diplomatic support of the Soviet Union. It would not be until later that Mao and the Chinese Communists would feel strong enough to throw off Soviet dominance and challenge the USSR for the leadership of international Communism (see page 146).

(see page 146).

Key terms

Hungarian rising An attempt in 1956 on the part of the Communist government of Hungary to break away from Soviet control.

Eastern bloc The countries of eastern Europe which fell under Soviet domination at the end of the Second World War.

Communism with a human face The idea that Marxist governments, without losing their commitment to the Communist ideal, should act in a less authoritarian manner and show understanding of the real needs of ordinary people.

Some key books in the debate:

Jung Chang and Jon Halliday, *Mao: The Unknown Story* (Jonathan Cape, 2005).
Lee Feigon, *Mao: A Reinterpretation* (Ivan R. Dee, 2002).
Philip Short, *Mao: A Life* (Hodder & Stoughton, 1999).
Jonathan Spence, *Mao* (Weidenfeld & Nicolson, 1999).
Jonathan Spence, *The Search for Modern China* (W.W. Norton, 1990).

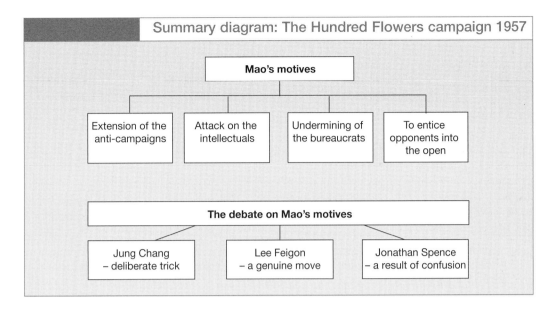

Summary diagram: The Hundred Flowers campaign 1957

Study Guide: AS Questions

In the style of AQA

(a) Explain why Mao launched the first Five-Year Plan in 1952.

(12 marks)

(b) 'The Hundred Flowers campaign of 1957 was a disastrous mistake.' Explain why you agree or disagree with this view.

(24 marks)

Exam tips

The cross-references are designed to take you straight to the material that will help you answer the question.

(a) Look again at page 34. You will need to consider a range of reasons for the plan and it is always a good idea to think of long- and short-term factors when you are asked to explain something like this. The long-term factors would involve comment on the underlying state of Chinese industry, mentioning in particular the developments of the 1930s and 1940s and on the example of Stalin's Five-Year Plans. (You might also find it helpful to look ahead to pages 45–6 for some additional discussion, particularly relating to the ideological and independence factors impelling industrial growth.) To explain the short-term factors, you will need to comment on Mao's political position by 1952, why he felt ready to launch the plan and what he hoped to get out of the development of Chinese heavy industry and the specific reasons for his interest in spectacular civil engineering projects. Another important short-term reason would be the bargain made with the USSR in 1950 (page 35). In conclusion you should show how these factors worked together and try to offer some views on the most important. You should consider, for example, whether Mao was primarily inspired by ideology, economic necessity, need for self-reliance or Soviet pressure.

(b) In this type of question you need to decide on a number of points that can be made in support of the given view and a number which oppose it. When you have done so, you can decide which view you feel is more convincing and argue accordingly in your answer.

In support of the view that the campaign was a mistake, you will need to cite evidence of: how rapidly it was reversed (pages 37–8); its genuine motives (Feigon's view, page 39); how its implementation was muddled (Spence's view, pages 39–40); and the scale of the criticism that it launched (page 40). To oppose the view, you might comment on Mao's motives, his control of what was happening (Jung Chang's view, page 39) and the opportunities it afforded for the exposure and repression of opponents and rivals (pages 37–8).

In the style of Edexcel

How far do you agree that the Hundred Flowers campaign was a trick designed by Mao to trap his opponents? (30 marks)

Exam tips

The cross-references are designed to take you straight to the material that will help you answer the question.

- The key words for you to think about when planning this answer are 'trick' and 'designed to trap opponents'. This is a question about Mao's motives. What prompted him to launch the campaign? You have read that he had a number of possible motives. You will need to reach a judgement about whether a determination to trap his opponents was uppermost in his mind from the start (pages 39–40).
- Select your material with relevance to the question. Avoid becoming involved in a detailed description or narrative about the campaign. Clearly, you will be able to use details of how Mao's critics came out into the open and how they were dealt with, but you should only use those details in support of statements you have made about Mao's motives.
- You could plan to organise your material to consider first the points which support the view that this began as a genuine campaign: the contradiction speech (page 36); the Hu Feng case (page 37); a desire to undermine bureaucrats in the government (page 39); Mao's reaction to de-Stalinisation in the USSR.
- Then you should consider the points which suggest trickery: the anti-rightist movement; the treatment of Zhou Enlai (pages 37–8).
- Another possibility is that Mao began by genuinely inviting debate but then changed his mind (page 40) influenced by the scale of the criticism (page 37) and events in Budapest (page 40).
- Be sure to focus on the key words 'designed' and 'trap' in coming to a balanced conclusion. You should round off your answer by offering your judgement: do you agree or disagree with the statement in the question? If you do decide that you want to argue that Mao genuinely invited debate but then changed his mind, you must also take account of the evidence suggesting that it was deliberate trickery on his part. In that case you might want to plan to deal with those points first in your essay.

Try to form your own judgement, but don't forget you need to provide a balanced answer. There will be points to be made on both sides but your job is to explain why you have adopted the view you have chosen.

3 The Great Leap Forward 1958–62

POINTS TO CONSIDER

The power that Mao had as the leader of a one-party state made him, in effect, an absolute ruler. The problem that such power created was that, since there was no one willing or able to put a check on him, the mistakes he made were magnified. It is a feature of all absolute systems that no one in them tells the truth. The political correctness of the day in China taught that Mao never made errors and was beyond criticism. Hence, nearly everybody either ignored the truth or suppressed it.

The result was that when his industrial and land policies plans proved hopelessly unrealistic and led to the greatest famine in Chinese history the official government response was to pretend that none of it was happening. This remarkable story is the subject of the present chapter, which deals with:

- The reform of industry
- The reform of agriculture
- China's great famine 1958–62

Key dates

1956	Collectivisation began
1958–62	Second Five-Year Plan
	Widespread famine in China
1958	Mao Zedong gave up presidency of PRC
1959	Lushan conference
	Tibetan rising
1962	Panchen Lama's report
	Liu Shaoqi and Deng Xiaoping appointed to tackle the famine

1 | Introduction

Key question
What did Mao mean
by the 'Great Leap
Forward'?

The Great Leap Forward was the term Mao used to describe the second Five-Year Plan of 1958–62. His aim was to turn the PRC into a modern industrial state in the shortest possible time. He believed that by revolutionising China's agriculture and industry the PRC could build an economy that would catch up with those of the major nations and then overtake them.

Mao had led the Chinese peasants to victory in 1949. Yet he was convinced that China's future as a great power actually depended not on the peasants and agriculture but on the workers and industry. It was industrialisation that mattered. He held that history had reached the stage where China, having lagged behind the rest of the advanced industrialised world, would now surpass it purely through the dedicated efforts of the Chinese people led by their inspired Communist government. That was why he used the word 'leap'. China would bypass the stages through which the advanced nations had gone, and go straight from being a rural, agricultural economy to becoming an urban, industrial one.

As he described it, the leap would allow China 'to overtake all capitalist countries in a fairly short time, and become one of the richest, most advanced and powerful countries in the world'. In 1957, while attending a gathering of international Communist leaders in **Moscow**, he said:

> The **imperialists** are like the sun at five o'clock in the afternoon, while we are like the sun at six o'clock in the morning. The East wind is bound to prevail over the West wind, because we are powerful and strong. The problem is that you just cannot decide things with the quantity of steel and iron; rather, first and foremost, things are determined by people's hearts and minds. It has always been like that in history. In history, the weak have always beaten the strong.

It was not by chance that Mao made his announcement while in the Soviet Union. He admired the USSR for what it had achieved economically, and he had also been impressed by the Soviet launching of *Sputnik* in the autumn of 1957. However, he did not enjoy his visits to Moscow and he regretted that the PRC had been so dependent on the Soviet Union since 1949.

He was determined to match the Soviet Union's economic achievement, but he wanted China to do it without slavishly following the Soviet Union's methods. He later explained why he had chosen to change the policy that the PRC had originally followed. He said that in the early days of the PRC:

> The situation was such that, since we had no experience in economic construction, we had no alternative but to copy the Soviet Union. In the field of heavy industry especially, we copied almost everything from the Soviet Union. At that time it was absolutely necessary to act thus, but at the same time it was a weakness – a lack of creativity and lack of ability to stand on our

Key terms

Moscow
The capital of the USSR, the only foreign country Mao ever visited.

Imperialists
The advanced capitalist nations which had become powerful through exploiting weaker countries.

Sputnik
The first Soviet satellite to be successfully launched into orbit around the Earth in 1957.

own feet. Naturally this could not be our long-term strategy. From 1958 we decided to make self-reliance our major policy.

It was in order to achieve that self-reliance that Mao embarked on the Great Leap Forward.

2 | The Reform of Industry

Key question
How did Mao plan to achieve industrial 'lift-off'?

Mao resolved to achieve industrial **'lift-off'** for China by harnessing what he regarded as the nation's greatest resource: its massive population. Mao's conviction was that the Chinese people could achieve two great advances:

- First, the collectivised peasants, working in their communes, would produce a surplus of food that could be sold abroad to raise money for the expansion of Chinese industry.
- Second, the workers would create, literally with their own hands, a modern industrial economy, powerful enough to compete with the Soviet Union and the capitalist West.

'Lift-off'
Increasing output and production at such a pace as to turn China into a modern industrial power.

Key term

Mass effort

Mao assumed that simply by an effort of will the increases in output made under the first Five-Year Plan could be vastly increased. The emphasis was on heavy industry and large projects. Mao, like Stalin, was greatly impressed by the grand project. Size mattered. It was the scale of a construction rather than its economic value that appealed to him. He was convinced that by sheer manpower China could solve all the problems of industrial development.

'The emperor of the blue ants'

It is certainly true that prodigious feats were achieved by manual labour alone during the Great Leap Forward. Mechanical diggers were shunned in favour of the earth being moved by the hands of the workers. Giant span bridges, canals and dams were constructed. These were lauded by the CCP as the visible proof of China's resurgence under Communism.

It became a common sight across China to see thousands of workers, men, women and children, dressed in identical blue uniforms and toiling with only the most rudimentary of tools. The government's propaganda newsreels of the day showed them all gaily smiling and singing as they went about their joyful task of reconstructing China. This was in addition to thousands of prisoners forced to work under the gaze of armed guards. A fitting description was that Mao Zedong had become 'the emperor of the blue ants'.

Tiananmen Square

One particular enterprise that captured the public's imagination was the building of Tiananmen Square in Beijing, which was begun in 1957 and completed within 2 years. This was an enormous project that involved clearing a 100-acre site of its

A young girl hauling a heavy load. In what ways might this 1950s' picture be taken to represent the effort of ordinary people in the Great Leap Forward?

Key term

Ming Tombs
The burial ground of the emperors of the Ming dynasty (1368–1644).

Key question
How accurate was the term 'plan'?

Key date

Second Five-Year Plan: 1958–62

teeming homes, shops and markets and laying a vast concrete-paved level space, open to the south, but with two huge new buildings to the east and west and the Forbidden City to the north. Mao frequently asked about the square's dimensions; he did not relax until he was assured it was larger than Moscow's Red Square.

Mao made it a practice to visit some of the major construction sites. This was as much a propaganda exercise as a genuine desire to mix with the workers. His visits provided the government-controlled press with excellent photo opportunities. One such was at the **Ming Tombs** Reservoir outside Beijing, where Mao delighted onlookers by picking up a spade and joining in the digging for half an hour (see page 48).

The second Five-Year Plan 1958–62

The second Five-Year Plan, the centrepiece of the Great Leap Forward, was introduced in 1958 to great fanfares. Yet there was a sense in which the plan was not a plan at all. It was true that targets and quotas were constantly set and reset, but these were not based on sound economic analysis. Rather they were plucked from the air on a whim. They were acts of faith in Communist China's ability to produce, not a hard-headed assessment of what was realistically possible. That is why the projected figures were changed so frequently. They were usually revised upwards by officials in order to impress Mao that they were responding to his call for a mass collective effort.

The minister of finance, Li Hsien-nien, unwittingly admitted how disorganised the whole thing was when he said in 1958, 'At present the central authorities are compiling targets for the

The Chairman lends a hand in the digging of the Ming Tombs reservoir in 1958. Mao's doctor recorded that this was the only time in 20 years that he had seen him physically exert himself. In what respects might this scene have contributed to the development of the cult of Mao?

second Five-Year Plan, but have not been able to catch up with the swift changes in practical conditions that require upward revision of the targets almost every day'.

'General Steel'

Chinese planners liked to speak figuratively of two great soldiers who would lead the nation to economic victory: 'General Grain' and 'General Steel'. They claimed that just as General Grain was triumphing in the battle to increase China's food supplies, so, similarly, General Steel would win the struggle to turn China into a successful industrial economy.

Backyard furnaces

Mao had a naïve belief that simply by producing masses of steel China would somehow solve all its economic problems. The outstanding expression of this was his insistence on the construction of '**backyard furnaces**'. China would draw its supplies of iron and steel not only from large foundries and mills, but from small family kilns.

Here was a communal activity in which all the people could participate, conscious that by their own efforts they were helping to build the new society. Everybody, peasants as well as workers,

Backyard furnaces Primitive smelting devices that every family was encouraged to build on its premises.

Key term

Backyard furnaces: scenes such as these were widespread across China. Why were so many people so willing to join in the production of steel in this localised way?

young children and old people, could be involved. Enthusiasm not skill was the basic requirement. People would develop successful techniques as they went along. It would be a glorious example of 'learning by doing'.

At Mao's command, the Chinese people rushed to build their little furnaces. It became a national movement. The sky at night was reddened by the flames of millions of kilns. In daytime large areas of China were covered by a pall of smoke that sometimes obscured the noonday sun.

Foreigners in China were amazed by the scale and intensity of the people's response. Roderick MacFarquar, a celebrated writer on Chinese affairs who was then living in Beijing, described the 'seething, clattering frenzy' that had overtaken China. 'People carried baskets of ore, people stoked, people goaded buffalo carts, people tipped cauldrons of white-hot metal, people stood on rickety ladders and peered into furnaces, people wheeled barrows of crude steel'.

Even ministers and their families joined in. In **Zhongnanhai**, hundreds of tiny furnaces were to be found, each one turning out its quota of home-made steel. Excited officials reported back to Beijing on how faithfully and successfully the people of China were answering Mao's call.

Weakness of the campaign

The people may have been faithful but they were hardly successful. Goodwill did not necessarily produce good steel. The only steel suitable for industrial use came from the large foundries. The home-made variety was worthless. Most of it was not steel in any recognisable sense. Smelted from such domestic oddments as pots, pans and bicycles, the peasant' steel ended up

Key term

Zhongnanhai
A building compound off Tiananmen Square that housed the government offices and ministers' residences.

as large, hard blobs, ideal, perhaps, for putting in a gallery as a piece of contemporary sculpture, but unusable in any practical way.

The authorities knew this, but dare not let on. As with agriculture, they went on pretending. The steel continued to be regularly gathered from beaming peasants by beaming collectors, who drove it away and dumped it in deep pits which were then covered over. The fate of the worthless steel could be taken as symbolising the Great Leap Forward itself: lots of energy, noise and endeavour, but little substance.

It should be added that there was also a heavy environmental price to pay; so many trees were felled to supply the backyard furnaces with wood that large parts of China were deforested beyond the point of recovery.

State-owned enterprises

An important feature of the Great Leap Forward was the creation of state-owned enterprises (SOEs). This was an attempt to bring industry under total government direction. Existing firms and companies could no longer operate as private, profit-making concerns. Instead, they would work for the state as designated SOEs. The workers could no longer bargain with employers over rates of pay and conditions. Prices, output targets and wages were to be fixed by the state.

Failings of SOEs

In theory, the SOEs fulfilled the Communist notion of centrally controlled industry. But, in practice, they performed less well than anticipated. This was because they were basically inefficient, largely as a result of their abandoning any idea of incentives. Under the Communist system, the SOEs were given state subsidies and the workers received guaranteed wages. This destroyed any motive for the managers or the workers to show initiative. It did not matter whether an SOE was efficiently managed or not since any surplus it earned went straight to the state. Similarly, no matter whether a worker was conscientious or idle he still received the same pay.

Benefits for the workers

In performance terms, the system was stultifying; it destroyed any sense of endeavour. However, for the workers, the positive side of the system was that they had an '**iron rice bowl**'. Moreover, the SOEs also provided the workers with accommodation and medical and education benefits for their families.

The plan's underlying weakness

There were some apparently impressive increases in output, as Table 3.1 shows. The picture is one of an initial expansion down to 1960 and then a serious falling away in production in the early 1960s. What needs to be stressed here is that, although some of the figures seem impressive, they relate only to the production of materials. They do not reveal how the materials were then used. The fact is that there was no integrated plan for turning what had

Key question
What was the government's aim in introducing SOEs and what were the major flaws?

Iron rice bowl
The system that provided workers with a guaranteed job and protected their wages

Key term

Key question
What prevented Mao from achieving his idea of a Great Leap Forward?

Key term

Manufactured goods
Raw materials turned into sellable products.

been produced into **manufactured goods**. A crippling weakness was that China lacked the following essentials:

- technical skills
- managerial know-how
- efficiently run factories and plants
- an adequate transport system.

Without these, China could not build the modern economy that Mao had promised would overtake the world in a great leap. The failure is evident in Table 3.2. Instead of growing under the Great Leap Forward, the output of industrially produced goods actually fell.

Table 3.1: Production under the second Five-Year Plan

Industrial production	1957	1958	1959	1960	1961	1962	1963	1964
Coal (millions of tonnes)	131	230	290	270	180	180	190	200
Steel (millions of tonnes)	5.4	8	10	13	8	8	9	10
Oil (millions of barrels)	1.5	2.3	3.7	4.5	4.5	5.3	5.9	7
Chemical fertilisers (millions of tonnes)	0.8	1.4	2.0	2.5	1.4	2.1	3.0	3.6
Cotton cloth (billions of metres)	5.0	5.7	7.5	6.0	3.0	3.0	3.5	4.0

Table 3.2: Production of manufactured goods

To an index of 100	1959	1960	1961	1962
Light industrial	100	91.2	78.4	70.0
Heavy industrial	100	90.0	66.4	44.2

What main trends in production are observable from the figures in Tables 3.1 and 3.2?

The limitations of the Great Leap Forward

Key question
What factors prevented the Great Leap Forward from reaching its full targets?

Many of the communal endeavours that took place under the Plan thrilled the Chinese and impressed foreigners, but the plan as a whole did not reach its objective of laying the basis of a modern industrial economy. Among the reasons for this were the following:

- The quality of China's finished products fell a long way short of meeting its domestic industrial needs.
- Political interference made the plan impossible to manage purely as an economic enterprise.
- Officials issued demands and threats aplenty, but hardly any detailed instructions as to how things were actually to be done.
- Despite the setting up of SOEs, so much was left to local initiative that China never really operated an integrated national plan.

Workers constructing a dam in 1958. How does this picture illustrate the notion of Mao Zedong as 'emperor of the blue ants'?

Quality control
The mechanism for monitoring industrial products so that they always meet a consistent standard.

Applied Communism
Planning according to Marxist principles, involving state direction of the economy and the ending of private ownership.

- The result was that effective organisation and **quality control** became difficult to achieve and impossible to sustain.
- The USSR stopped providing technical assistance in 1960. This resulted in the closure of half the 300 industrial plants that the Soviet Union had sponsored in China, including a number of steel mills.

Mao's weakness as an economic planner

The common belief in the CCP was that **applied Communism** would always produce an effective system of production and fair shares for all. This meant that politics always got in the way of proper industrial management. It is remarkable how so much of what passed for planning was really only a set of politically inspired slogans. The reports of the party conferences called to discuss the progress of the Great Leap Forward describe the delegates shouting slogans and counter-slogans at each other instead of addressing the real economic problems.

Key question
What were the major limitations in Mao's economic thinking?

Mao's unwillingness to accept responsibility for failure

Mao would not accept that his policies were at fault. He interpreted the lack of economic achievement not as a failure of Communist planning, but as the result of sabotage by bourgeois elements and backsliders. His invariable reaction to the news of failure was to blame the messenger. The first stage was usually to deny the bad results and then, when they could no longer be disputed, to search for the culprits responsible for administering the policies wrongly, through either incompetence or deliberate sabotage.

Mao's basic misunderstanding of economic processes

There is no doubting the ambition that underlay the economic policies that China followed under Mao Zedong. He aimed to place the PRC on a par with the world's major industrial powers. But ambition was not enough. His economic strategy proved to be flawed and misconceived. He believed that by relying on China's unlimited manpower he could bring about the same advances that the Western industrial nations had made. But Mao lacked the knowledge of agricultural science necessary to understand the reports he received from the countryside.

He was also very limited in his understanding of the industrial process. He accepted that industrialisation was essential, but he had a very imperfect idea of what that meant in practice. He simply believed that by a massive deployment of manpower China could achieve the advanced industrialisation it needed.

China's leaders in January 1962. In one of the few unposed photos of the time, a toothless and anxious-looking Mao is captured in apparently earnest conversation with (from left to right) Zhou Enlai, Chen Yun, Liu Shaoqi and Deng Xiaoping. Why were such photos as this one a rarity at the time?

Mao's reliance on intuition

In no sense was Mao qualified as an economic planner. He admitted as much: 'I only understand social sciences but not natural sciences'. For all his adult life he had been a revolutionary. This is what continued to dominate him and consume his energies. His experience as a political in-fighter and military strategist had in no way prepared him for the task of shaping the economy of a vast nation. His approach was necessarily a series of intuitive leaps. The results were calamitous. His collectivisation programme produced not additional food, but famine; his Five-Year Plans wasted rather than successfully exploited China's vast natural and human resources.

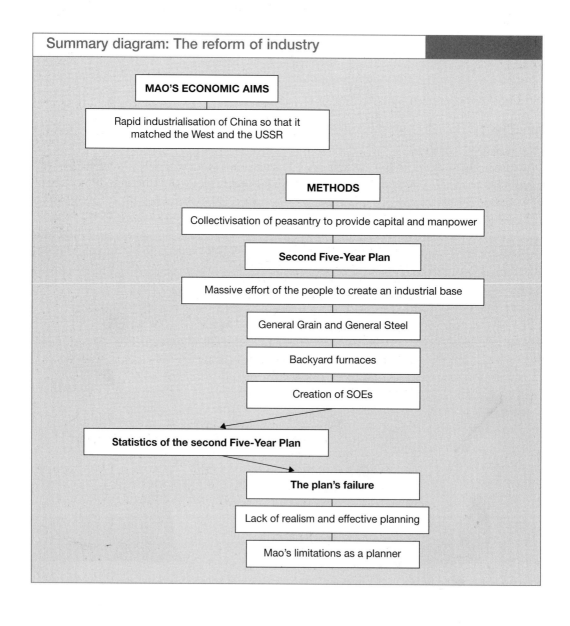

Summary diagram: The reform of industry

MAO'S ECONOMIC AIMS

Rapid industrialisation of China so that it matched the West and the USSR

METHODS

Collectivisation of peasantry to provide capital and manpower

Second Five-Year Plan

Massive effort of the people to create an industrial base

General Grain and General Steel

Backyard furnaces

Creation of SOEs

Statistics of the second Five-Year Plan

The plan's failure

Lack of realism and effective planning

Mao's limitations as a planner

3 | The Reform of Agriculture

Collectivisation

Key question
What was the aim of collectivisation?

The land policy adopted by Mao Zedong has to be seen as a complement to his industrialisation plans. Although he had gained his reputation as leader of a great peasant revolution, he did not allow this to dictate his economic strategy. In his plans for the modernisation of China, the industrialisation programme had priority over all other considerations. By the mid-1950s the organisers of the first Five-Year Plan had become aware that China had a severe labour shortage. Despite the migration from the land that had occurred, those employed in industry were still only a minority of the Chinese working population. The industrial workforce would have to be greatly increased if targets were to be met.

It was also the case that, although the peasants were undoubtedly producing more food, this was not finding its way to the urban workers. The common view among the economic planners was that this was the fault of the peasants: they were indulging themselves by overeating and by having larger families which meant more mouths had to be fed. The authorities were convinced that the peasantry must be brought under strict central control and direction.

Mao himself often became impatient with what he regarded as peasant obstinacy. In one revealing statement he urged his officials: 'Educate peasants to eat less, and have more thin **gruel**. The state should try its hardest to prevent peasants eating too much.'

The PRC's initial land reforms of the early 1950s had been introduced in the euphoria that had accompanied the 1949 revolution. The land had been seized from the landlords and given to the peasants. Yet even at that time the peasants had been urged to pool their resources by joining in farm **collectives**. This was the principle that was now forcibly extended. Between 1956 and 1958 the government directed that the existing 750,000 collectives be amalgamated into a number of large **communes**. In 1958 Mao made this collectivisation process an essential part of the Great Leap Forward:

Key terms

Gruel
A thin, watery porridge.

Collectives
Areas where the peasants farmed communally rather than for themselves individually.

Communes
Organised regions where the collectives were grouped together.

Key date

Collectivisation began: 1956

- China's agricultural land was divided into 70,000 communes.
- Each commune was made up of roughly 750,000 brigades, each brigade containing some 200 households.
- The whole system was under the direct control of PRC's central government; farming methods, the sale and distribution of produce, and the setting of prices were to be dictated from above.
- Private farming would cease to exist.
- The peasants needed internal passports to pass from one commune to another.

A landlord under attack at a public meeting in the 1950s. What opportunities did the anti-landlord campaigns give to the peasants for settling scores and pursuing vendettas at local level?

Mao's attitude towards the peasants

It has been suggested that Mao shared with Stalin a belief that the peasants left to themselves were **'inherently capitalistic'**. John King Fairbank, the US expert on modern China, remarked on the contradiction that lay at the heart of collectivisation: 'the revolutionary state, having established its legitimacy by freeing the peasant from landlordism, now had him boxed in as never before. The state had become the ultimate landlord.'

In public, Mao maintained that collectivisation, far from being forced on the peasants, was a direct response to their wishes. In the summer of 1958 the CCP's Central Committee made the following declaration in Mao's name:

> The people have taken to organising themselves along military lines, working with militancy, and leading a collective life, and this has raised the political consciousness of the 500 million peasants still further. Community dining rooms, kindergartens, nurseries, sewing groups, barber shops, public baths, happy homes for the aged, agricultural middle schools, 'red and expert' schools, are leading the peasants toward a happier collective life and further fostering ideas of collectivism among the peasant masses.

The deceit behind collectivisation

The CCP's claim was a great lie. Collectivisation had been imposed on the Chinese peasantry as part of a massive social

Key question
Why did Mao distrust the peasants?

Inherently capitalistic
Selfish and grasping by nature.

Key term

experiment in which the wishes of the peasants themselves were simply ignored. What is extraordinary about Mao and defies rational explanation is that, although he was himself a peasant and could justifiably claim to have led a great peasant revolution, he had a very low opinion of the class from which he came. In 1959 he declared to a group of government ministers: 'Peasants are hiding food and are very bad. There is no Communist spirit in them! Peasants are after all peasants. That's the only way they can behave.' This disregard for the ordinary people of China was to have the most appalling consequences.

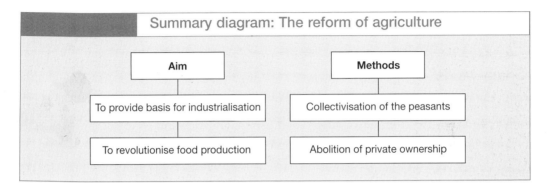

Summary diagram: The reform of agriculture

Aim
- To provide basis for industrialisation
- To revolutionise food production

Methods
- Collectivisation of the peasants
- Abolition of private ownership

4 | China's Great Famine 1958–62

Key question
How far was the famine a man-made disaster?

Key date
Widespread famine in China: 1958–62

Key term
Agronomists
Experts in agricultural science.

The collectivisation programme that began in 1956 entailed a vast social transformation that resulted in the greatest famine in Chinese history. The disruption caused by the ending of private farming was a major cause of hunger since it discouraged the individual peasants from producing food beyond their own immediate needs. But that was only part of the story. Equally significant was Mao's belief that Chinese **agronomists** had made a series of discoveries about crop growing that would revolutionise food production.

Lysenkoism
Chinese scientists were greatly influenced by the theories of Trofim Lysenko, the Soviet researcher whom Stalin had regarded as the voice of scientific truth. Lysenko claimed to have developed techniques that resulted in crops like rice, barley and wheat yielding up to 16 times more food than under traditional methods. It was later realised and admitted that Lysenko's ideas were worthless. His theories about producing such 'super-crops' were wholly fraudulent. But so strong was the influence of the USSR in the early years of the PRC that the Chinese regarded Lysenko as infallible.

A generation of Chinese researchers were trained in the notion that Lysenko could do no wrong. A Beijing doctor recorded: 'We were told that the Soviets had discovered and invented everything, even the aeroplane. We had to change textbooks and rename things in Lysenko's honour.'

Mao made Lysenkoism official policy in 1958 when he personally drafted an eight-point agricultural 'constitution' based on the theories of crop growth advanced by Lysenko and his Chinese disciples, which farmers were forced to follow. The eight headings were:

- the popularisation of new breeds and seeds
- close planting
- deep ploughing
- increased fertilisation
- innovation of farm tools
- improved field management
- pest control
- increased irrigation.

'Sparrowcide'

Taken separately these instructions had some value. The problem was that no attention was paid to the particular conditions and climate in which the crops were planted and grown. The demand that all the instructions be applied everywhere destroyed whatever benefits they might have brought if applied selectively and intelligently.

The most vivid example of the tragic results that followed from unthinking application was in regard to pest control. The whole Chinese population was called on to end the menace of sparrows and other wild birds which ate crop seeds. So, at prescribed times, the Chinese came out from their houses and with any implement they could lay their hands on made as much noise as possible. Clanging plates, metal pots and pans, they kept up a continuous din that prevented the birds from landing, so that they eventually dropped exhausted from the sky. The thousands of dead birds were then publicly displayed as trophies. Villages and regions competed with each other over who could kill the most birds.

The outcome was catastrophic. With no birds now to thin their numbers, insects and small creatures gorged themselves on the grains and plants. The larger birds that would have fed off the smaller ones were no longer around to prey on rats and their kind. Vermin multiplied and destroyed stocks of grain. The absurdity of the enterprise became only too evident in the hunger that it caused, but nobody dared say a critical word publicly since to have done so would have been to challenge Mao's wisdom.

Starvation

The bewildered local peasant communities, whose way of life had already been dislocated by collectivisation, had no means of preventing the famine that followed. Unable to make sense of the orders imposed on them from on high, they became defeatist in the face of impending doom. Those peasants who tried to ignore the new regulations and carry on with their old ways of farming were rounded up and imprisoned as 'rightists'.

China's gaols and forced labour camps (see page 129) were expanded to take in the great numbers of starving peasants who

Table 3.3: China's agricultural record 1952–62

Year	Grain production (millions of tonnes)	Meat production (millions of tonnes)	Index of gross output value of agriculture
1952	163.9	3.4	100.0
1953	166.8	3.8	103.1
1954	169.5	3.9	106.6
1955	183.9	3.3	114.7
1956	192.8	3.4	120.5
1957	195.1	4.0	124.8
1958	200.0	4.3	127.8
1959	170.0	2.6	110.4
1960	143.5	1.3	96.4
1961	147.5	1.2	94.1
1962	160.0	1.9	99.9

What trends in the quantity of food production can be deduced from the table? What clues does the table provide to the character of the famine that afflicted China in this period?

fell foul of the authorities. In these camps, the equivalent of the Soviet **gulags**, hundreds of thousands, possibly millions, starved to death. The bare statistics of the famine are shown in Table 3.3.

The significance of the agricultural record

A careful reading of the figures in Table 3.3 shows a marked reduction in food production from 1958 onwards, the years of the famine. Although the decline does not look especially dramatic, it has to be emphasised that the figures refer to China overall; the food shortages were much more severe in the famine provinces of central China. Nearly every province in China was affected by the famine, but the greatest suffering occurred in central and eastern China. Of the 50 million who died throughout China, the worst death toll was in a great arc of misery that swept through China's rural provinces from Shandong in the east to Tibet in the west:

- Shandong: 7.5 million
- Anhui: 8 million
- Henan: 7.8 million
- Sichuan: 9 million
- Qinghai: 1 million
- Tibet: 1 million.

Hebei (Hopei) and Xinjiang were other areas that experienced terrible suffering. Parents sold their children, and husbands their wives, for food. Women prostituted themselves to obtain food for their families, and there were many instances of peasants offering themselves as slaves to anyone who would supply them with food. The following account of cannibalism in Liaoning province is typical of the experiences that later came to light:

A peasant woman, unable to stand the incessant crying for food of her 2-year-old daughter, and thinking perhaps to end her suffering, had strangled her. She had given the girl's body to her husband, asking him to bury it. Instead, out of his mind with hunger, he put the body in the cooking pot with what little food they had foraged. He had forced his wife to eat a bowl of the resulting stew. His wife, in a fit of remorse, had reported her husband's crime to the authorities. Although there was no law against cannibalism in the criminal code of the People's Republic, the Ministry of Public Security treated such cases, which were all too common, with the utmost severity. Both husband and wife were arrested and summarily executed.

A conspiracy of silence

Key question
How did official attitudes to the famine make it worse?

What deepened the tragedy was that many government advisers were well aware of the facts. They knew that Lysenkoism was nonsense and that people were dying by the million, but they dared not speak out. Indeed, the reverse happened; party cadres and officials reported back to Beijing that production targets were being met and that the Great Leap Forward was on course. Sir Percy Craddock, British Ambassador in China in the 1960s, commented:

> Sycophantic provincial leaders cooked the books; immense increases, two or three fold, were reported; and, in obedience to the bogus figures, an impoverished province such as Anhui delivered grain it desperately needed itself to the state, or even for export abroad as surplus. On his inspection tours Mao saw the close-planted fields that he wanted to see; the local officials moved in extra shoots from other fields and moved them back when he had gone.

Officials often developed a callousness that meant they simply looked after themselves with no thought for the people at large. Dai Wang, a farmer in Jiangsu, decided in desperation to move his family to another province where he had heard that more food might be available. A loyal Communist, he described his bitter disillusion with the party officials to whom he turned for help before setting out:

> At the very last minute I discovered my biscuits, our only food for the four-day journey, had been stolen. In a panic, I went to headquarters to beg for more. The leaders were enjoying a meal with numerous meat and fish dishes, and bread rolls made from flour. Party Secretary Xu, chewing a large mouthful of pork, replied, 'Right now, grain is a big problem in our country. Everyone should take his own responsibility for his food ration.' Left, empty-handed, I thought even the capitalists might not be as hard-hearted as these cadres of a communist country.

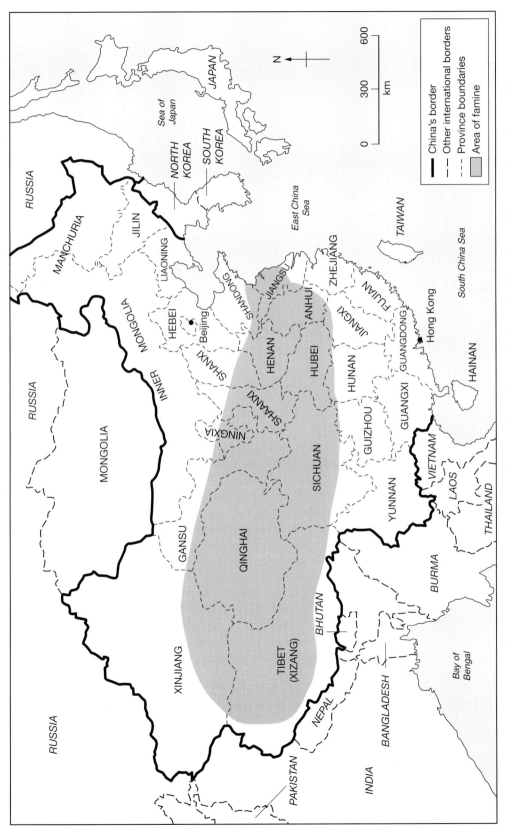

The areas in China worst hit by the famine. How does the map help to explain why the famine might be referred to as an 'arc of misery'?

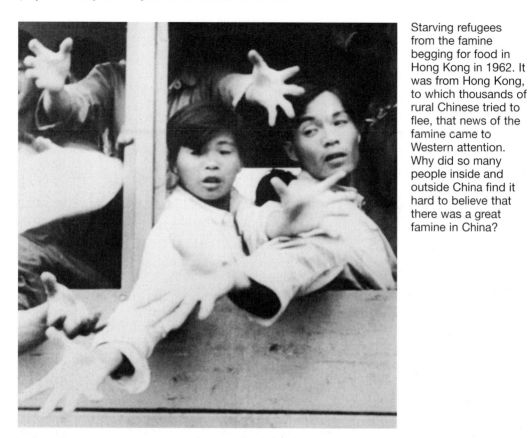

Starving refugees from the famine begging for food in Hong Kong in 1962. It was from Hong Kong, to which thousands of rural Chinese tried to flee, that news of the famine came to Western attention. Why did so many people inside and outside China find it hard to believe that there was a great famine in China?

The Lushan conference 1959

The refusal of those at the top to tell the truth was one of the great betrayals of the Chinese people. Nor can it be said that they were denied the opportunity. At a party gathering in Lushan in 1959, Peng Dehuai (see page 31), fearlessly recounted what he had witnessed on his journey through his own native province of Anhui: 'I saw my people lying dead and dying in the fields and by the roadside'. Here was the moment for the others to back him by confirming the truth of what he had described. But none did.

What made this particularly tragic was that although the Lushan conference had been officially called in order to consider the progress of the Great Leap Forward, all the delegates knew that it had been convened by the party desperate to limit the spreading hunger. The conference had been intended as the first step towards dealing with the famine. Yet when it came to it, the party members did nothing to alleviate the suffering.

Unwilling to offend Mao, the delegates persisted in their slavish obedience to him by denouncing Peng as a troublemaker and dismissing his eye-witness account as a fabrication. They then proceeded to make speeches noting the advances made under the Great Leap Forward and praising Mao for his inspired leadership. Zhou Enlai was so dismayed by the tone of the conference and so ashamed of his own silence that he stopped attending the sessions. Full of remorse, he hid away in his hotel room and drank himself senseless.

Key question
What was the significance of the Lushan conference?

Lushan conference: 1959

Key date

One of the most notorious propaganda photos of the time purported to show children playing on crop leaves that grew so thickly in the field that the youngsters did not fall through. To impress Mao and suggest abundant growth, it was known for crops to be lifted from the fields and placed together alongside the railway track along which Mao's special train travelled. After Mao had passed through the crops were returned to their original fields. Why has this photo been described as notorious?

Key term

Shanghai wing
Between its formation in 1921 and its taking power in 1949, the CCP had undergone a series of power struggles between various factions. One of these was the Shanghai group, renowned for its hard-line Marxism and its ferocity against opponents.

Jiang Qing at Lushan

One of the ironies of the Lushan conference was that Mao had gone to it expecting trouble. He had worried that some members would use the occasion to criticise his economic plans, not openly perhaps, but by implication and by suggesting that there were alternatives to his policies. It was to help him fend off these expected attacks that Mao had brought his wife, Jiang Qing, with him to Lushan. It was the first time he had asked her to play a direct role in political affairs. He judged that her notorious toughness of attitude and her influence with the **Shanghai wing** of the CCP would be very useful if it came to a fight within the party.

Mao's suppression of criticism

In the event, he had no need of Jiang's help. Whatever the original intentions some members might have had before coming to Lushan, once there they allowed themselves to be overawed into submission. In an angry speech Mao ridiculed Peng Dehuai and told the cringing delegates that he was prepared to use the PLA against any in the party who tried 'to lead the peasants to overthrow the government'.

The delegates took this as Mao's way of saying that the supposed famine was really a fiction created by those reactionary peasants who were resisting collectivisation. What Mao had done was to declare that to talk of famine was tantamount to treason against him and the party. It was an unscrupulous move on his part but a clever one, and it worked. Faced with Mao's fierce determination, the party members, with the memories of the Hundred Flowers campaign fresh in their minds, dropped all thought of serious opposition.

The tragedy was that since Mao had declared, in effect, that the famine did not exist, it followed that little could be done in an official, organised way to relieve it. Hence the miseries of the ordinary Chinese were intensified.

Martial law imposed

The members of the CCP party may have been prepared to hide the truth but many of the ordinary people became so desperate that in a number of provinces demonstrations against the authorities began to spread; one of the key demands of the protesters was that the communes be done away with. By 1962 Liu Shaoqi, who held the office of president of the PRC, was so worried that he spoke of a civil war breaking out in China. He ordered preparations to be made to impose **martial law** and asked the PLA to stand by to suppress rebellion. Two factors prevented the crisis reaching the level Liu feared:

- The famine was at its worst in rural China where the people lacked the knowledge and skills to mount an effective anti-government rising.
- The policies that Liu himself and Deng Xiaoping introduced in 1962 began to ease the famine (see page 69).

The famine in Tibet

Relative to the size of its population, Tibet was the province that suffered most during the famine. A quarter of its four million people were wiped out. This figure becomes even more appalling when it is realised that the death toll was intended. The famine in Tibet was a man-made disaster. It was an act of **genocide** by the Chinese government.

The destruction of Tibetan culture

The PRC's treatment of Tibet provides a remarkable insight into the thinking of Mao Zedong and the party he led. Mao seemed to harbour a particular hatred for Tibet. It had been on his orders that the 'reunification' campaign in Tibet in 1950 had been so severe (see page 20). Once the PLA had defeated the Tibetan resistance fighters, the Chinese occupiers set about the

Key terms

Martial law
The placing of the civilian population under military authority and discipline.

Genocide
The deliberate destruction of a people or ethnic group.

Key question
Why was the famine so severe in Tibet?

systematic destruction of the cultural, social and religious identity of Tibet.

What had once been a separate nation was renamed Xizang and forcibly incorporated into the People's Republic of China. The public practice of **Lama**, the traditional Tibetan religion, was prohibited, as were political meetings and the teaching of the Tibetan language and Tibetan history in schools. Those who resisted were arrested and imprisoned. The Chinese aim was simple – to eradicate Tibet as a nation and as a culture.

Imposition of Mandarin

Over the next decade, the Chinese government took a cynical step to speed up this destructive process. It sponsored a mass migration of people from other parts of China to Tibet. Since the new settlers were predominantly Han, the ethnic group that made up four-fifths of the overall population of China, the government's clear purpose was to fill Tibet with people whose alien way of life would swamp the local Tibetan culture. **Mandarin Chinese** was imposed as the official language of Tibet; any Tibetan who wished to keep or gain a position in public affairs had to be proficient in it.

The 1959 Tibetan rising

Despite the pressure it came under, the Tibetan resistance movement was not destroyed. After its defeat in 1950, it went underground. In 1959 it re-emerged to organise what amounted to a national rising against the Chinese occupation. The Chinese authorities responded by sending in PLA units to suppress the demonstrations. Thousands of protesters were arrested and imprisoned and their ringleaders executed.

The Chinese forces made a particular point of attacking Tibetan religion. Priests and nuns were dragged from their ancient Buddhist monasteries, and publicly humiliated and beaten. Many of the monasteries were turned into barracks or administrative offices. Those that were allowed to remain as religious houses had to accept total control by the Chinese state. It became an arrestable offence for ordinary Tibetans even to mention the **Dalai Lama** in public.

The flight of the Dalai Lama

The severity with which the Tibetan rising was suppressed in 1959 by the PLA led to the flight of the Dalai Lama. This was not craven desertion. He chose to leave the country rather than wait for his inevitable removal by the Chinese. He calculated that as an exiled but free man he would be better able to voice the plight of the Tibetan people to the outside world.

In exile, the Dalai Lama became a potent symbol of Tibetan resistance. It was through him that the world's media were kept informed of the continuing severity of the PLA's occupation. Despite angry protests from the PRC, the Indian government granted sanctuary to the Dalai Lama, allowing him to establish a permanent base in Sikkim in northern India.

Tibet's man-made famine

What gave the Tibetan rising in 1959 a terrible twist was that it coincided with the development of famine across China. In one of the most ruthless acts of any government anywhere, the PRC chose deliberately to extend the famine to Tibet. There was no reason in nature for the famine that ravaged Tibet between 1959 and 1962 to have occurred at all. It happened because the Chinese made it happen. The famine that began to take hold elsewhere in China in 1958 was spread to Tibet by the authorities as part of their programme for destroying Tibetan resistance.

Key question
In what sense was the Tibetan famine man-made?

The destruction of Tibetan farming

Traditional Tibetan farming had two main forms: the rearing of **yaks** and sheep by nomadic herders and the growing of barley and oats by farmers. For centuries this had been sufficient to meet Tibet's needs. The people had rarely gone hungry. The Dalai Lama made this point strongly: 'Famine was unknown in Tibet. In Tibet food supplies had been sufficient for centuries. Agriculture was old-fashioned but sufficient.'

Nevertheless, the demand by the Chinese occupiers was that the 'communal and socialist farming techniques created by Chairman Mao' and introduced throughout China must now be adopted in Tibet. It was a demand that was to result in the destruction of Tibet's food production and reduce the Tibetan people to misery, despair and death.

One of the first moves of the self-styled experts who were brought from China to restructure Tibet's farming methods was to insist that the farmers switch from barley to other crops such as wheat and maize. The change proved lethal. The new crops grew only poorly in the Tibetan climate and even when some wheat or maize survived to be harvested it was inedible. It had been the practice of the Tibetans to eat their barley in a digestible form known as *tsampa*. It proved impossible to prepare wheat or maize in the same way. The digestive systems of the local people rebelled against the coarseness of these crops. The result was diarrhoea of such a severe kind that many died from dehydration.

Persecution of the *Khampas*

The official Chinese assault on the traditional methods of the crop farmers was matched by the destruction of the ways of life of Tibet's *Khampas*, who were forbidden any longer to roam the pasture lands with their yak herds. Instead, they were told that they were not nomads now but farmers and were forced to live with their herds in communes.

Even the Chinese officials who were responsible for issuing such orders realised the deadly absurdity of it all. A Chinese report that later came to light, noted: 'The *Khampas* were forced to start farming the high pastures. Old and young were yoked to the plough because their yaks were not domesticated and so could not be trained to plough a field. The officials had to make them do this otherwise they would be disregarding Mao's orders.'

Key terms

Yaks
These are hardy animals, perfectly adapted for the high altitude of the Tibetan plateau. They provide milk, meat and clothing and were thus an essential part of Tibet's rural economy.

Tsampa
A mushy paste made from ground barley.

Khampas
The nomadic yak herdsmen of Tibet.

The *Khampas* were also instructed to follow the socialist science of animal rearing. The Chinese experts announced that the yaks did not need to be grazed over a wide area and, therefore, must not be moved from the communes to summer or winter pastures. The result was that the animals became malnourished and emaciated. The consequence for the Tibetans was that their regular supply of milk, cheese and meat dried up, and the yak hair from which they made clothes and tents became practically useless. The failed experiment was yet another contribution to the hunger and misery that overtook the Tibetan people, hundreds of thousands of whom began to die from malnutrition and cold.

The Panchen Lama's report 1962

Even with the Dalai Lama in voluntary exile, the Tibetan cause still had an effective spokesman and champion. Between 1959 and 1962, the **Panchen Lama** went on a secret tour of Tibet to discover the truth about the famine. He had been led to undertake his enquiry by the realisation that the Communist authorities were churning out lies about conditions in Tibet. A formal statement in 1960 by the National People's Congress in Beijing, which had referred glowingly to 'the wonderful situation prevailing in Tibet today', had alerted him to the way the truth was being suppressed.

The more material he gathered on his journeys the more evident it became how greatly the Chinese had distorted the real picture. In each region that he travelled through, he recorded the number of persons who had been imprisoned, executed or starved to death. His calculations, which he published in a formal report in 1962, showed that:

- 20 per cent of the population had been gaoled: an average of between 80 and 100 for each village
- half of these had died while in prison.

The eyewitness accounts cited in the report formed a series of horror stories, detailing the brutality of the official onslaught on the Tibetan people and their way of life. The Panchen Lama described how, as the whisper went round that he was seeking to find out the truth about the famine, crowds of people put themselves at risk to come out to see him. In tears, they begged him: 'Don't let us starve! Don't let Buddhism be exterminated! Don't let the people of the Land of the Snows be exterminated.'

The report's authenticity

A document as powerful and as disturbing as the Panchen Lama's report will always raise questions about its accuracy. There are two particular factors that give credibility to its findings:

- Originally the Panchen Lama had been sympathetic towards the Chinese in Tibet and had welcomed the PLA into the

Key question
What did the Panchen Lama's report reveal about the causes and character of the famine in Tibet?

Key term

Panchen Lama
Second in spiritual authority to the Dalai Lama.

Key date

Panchen Lama's report: 1962

Key question
How reliable was the report?

region. It was the savagery the Chinese then showed that turned him against them.

- Zhou Enlai later admitted that the report was a fair and accurate portrayal of what the Chinese had done in Tibet.

All the evidence that the Panchen Lama produced at the time and all that has come out since bears out the claims made in the report. It is a story of the deliberate infliction of suffering by Chinese administrators intent on punishing the Tibetan people for daring to cling on to their identity as a culture and their independence as a nation. The result was the unnecessary death of a million people. Of the other three million Tibetans who survived there were few who did not suffer humiliation and degradation as their ancient way of life was destroyed around them.

Mao's response to the report

The Panchen Lama sent a copy of his report directly to Mao Zedong. Unsurprisingly, since it accused the PRC of genocide, Mao dismissed it as a collection of lies and distortions. He had the Panchen Lama, whom he described as a 'big class enemy', arrested, ordered the suppression of the report, and instructed the officials responsible for the PRC's propaganda department to rebut the major claims against the Chinese in Tibet.

The officials did their best. They claimed that the eyewitnesses the Panchen Lama quoted were unrepresentative and reactionary Tibetans trying to prevent their country's march to progress by denying the success of Mao's land policies. The officials' verdict was that:

- the stories of famine and misery were totally without foundation
- the truth was that Tibet had experienced the same abundant harvests as had all the other provinces of China that had embraced collectivisation.

Despite this massive effort of Mao's propagandists to prove that black was white, the reality was that they were guilty of the very charge they levelled against their Tibetan enemies: they were making things up.

Mao's responsibility for the famine in China

So devastating was the famine in Tibet and the other provinces that eventually Mao came to accept that it was happening. But his reaction was characteristic. He refused to acknowledge that the disaster was a result of his policies of collectivisation and applied socialist science. Li Zhisui, his doctor, made a particularly revealing remark about Mao's thought processes, 'the truth had to come to him on his own terms. He could not accept it when it included criticism of him.' Instead of taking the blame on himself, Mao put the famine down to three factors:

Key question
How did Mao explain the famine?

- hoarding of grain by the peasants, which had prevented food getting to the people
- mistakes by local officials who had either misunderstood their instructions or been incompetent in carrying them out
- exceptionally bad weather in the years 1958–61, which had produced both droughts and floods that had destroyed the harvests.

The hollowness of Mao's claims

There was no truth in the first of Mao's explanations, some in the second, and a little in the third. But poor weather does not explain the famine. It is true that 1958 was a bad year, although not particularly exceptional by Chinese standards. However, the weather in the following 3 years was notably mild. Whatever Mao might claim, the famine was not a misfortune of nature; it was a direct and fatal consequence of the decisions he took.

It may well be true that some of the officials made mistakes when implementing the policies they were given. Yet, no matter how blameworthy those lower down in the Communist hierarchy may have been, the responsibility lay with Mao Zedong. It was in pursuit of his instructions regarding the collectivisation of the Chinese peasantry and in accordance with his mistaken notions of science that his officials had set in motion a process that culminated in the horrific deaths of millions of his people.

The evidence suggests that Mao felt that, while his policies had not led to open opposition, his reputation within the party had been damaged. In 1962, he withdrew from the political front line after instructing President Liu Shaoqi and CCP General Secretary Deng Xiaoping to shoulder the task of bringing an end to the rural crisis and restoring adequate food supplies.

Land policy under Liu and Deng

In tackling the problem Mao had left them, Liu and Deng enlisted the aid of **Chen Yun**. Together, the three men concluded that the only workable solution to the food crisis was to allow private farming and markets to operate again; this would provide the peasant farmers with an incentive to produce surplus stocks. The reforms that Liu and his colleagues introduced along these lines were an unspoken admission that the commune system had been a failure.

Unsurprisingly, Mao became uneasy with the methods adopted by Liu and Deng. Their restoration of private ownership of the land undermined the **collectivist principle** on which he had set such store as a Communist revolutionary. When he returned to the centre of things 4 years later, he would make Liu and Deng pay for what they had done (see page 84).

Key dates

Mao Zedong gave up presidency of PRC: 1958

Liu Shaoqi and Deng Xiaoping appointed to tackle the famine: 1962

Key figure

Chen Yun (1905–95) Regarded as the CCP's leading economist.

Key question

What methods did Liu and Deng employ in dealing with the famine?

Key term

Collectivist principle The Marxist notion that social advance can be achieved only by the proletarian class acting together as a body and not allowing individuals to follow their own interests.

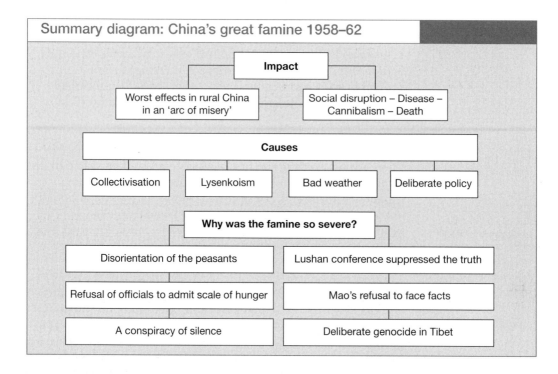

Summary diagram: China's great famine 1958–62

Impact

Worst effects in rural China in an 'arc of misery'

Social disruption – Disease – Cannibalism – Death

Causes

Collectivisation | Lysenkoism | Bad weather | Deliberate policy

Why was the famine so severe?

Disorientation of the peasants | Lushan conference suppressed the truth

Refusal of officials to admit scale of hunger | Mao's refusal to face facts

A conspiracy of silence | Deliberate genocide in Tibet

Study Guide: AS Questions

In the style of AQA
(a) Explain why Mao encouraged the spread of SOEs (state-owned enterprises) after 1958. (12 marks)
(b) 'The Great Leap Forward for industry of 1958 proved only to be a small step.' Explain why you agree or disagree with this view. (24 marks)

Exam tips

The cross-references are designed to take you straight to the material that will help you answer the question.

(a) Re-read page 50. SOEs fulfilled a number of Maoist requirements: they permitted centralised control; they destroyed capitalist practices; they cut industrial disputes; they provided workers with a guaranteed job and wages; workers received education/health services and a home.

Some of these factors link to Communist ideology while others are more practical concerns. In writing your answer, try to differentiate between the factors and show which were the most important. Although you are not asked to discuss the flaws or failures of the SOEs, thinking about these might help you to decide on the most important factors behind their implementation.

(b) Discussing this view is another way of asking you to assess the successes and failures of the Great Leap Forward, so re-read the material on this (pages 51–4). You should be able to prepare a list of points (page 51) that show agreement with the quotation and suggest its success was very limited. In doing so you might consider whether the plan could have ever been more than a 'small step' or if it merely rested on misunderstanding, rhetoric and propaganda.

To balance these points you should also look at ways in which it might be said that 'a Great Leap Forward' had been made. Think about the scale of change, the mass effort, the scale of the people's response to 'General Steel' and the spread of the SOEs. You might want to refer to the statistics on page 51 that show there was a 'leap' between 1958 and 1959 and in some areas the growth continued. Although it would be hard to argue that the plan was a total success, try to offer a balanced appraisal and explain your views carefully ensuring they are backed by specific evidence.

In the style of Edexcel

How far were Mao's agricultural policies responsible for the scale of the great famine in China, 1958–62? (30 marks)

Exam tips

The cross-references are designed to take you straight to the material that will help you answer the question.

- The key words for you to think about when planning your answer to this question are 'responsible for' and 'scale'. This is a question requiring you to explain why there was a famine on such a devastating scale in China, and to reach a judgement about how far it was Mao's agricultural policies that made the famine so severe or whether other factors were more significant.
- Avoid becoming involved in a detailed description of the horrors; it is the causes you have to concentrate on (page 70), and their significance in bringing about this degree of human suffering. No society can control the weather, but was the famine only the result of the impact of bad weather on harvests? Could steps have been taken that would have lessened the famine's impact? And, if so, why were they not taken?
- Each of the following played a part in the scale of the famine: collectivisation (page 55); Lysenkoism (page 57); Mao's distrust of the peasants (page 56); a conspiracy of silence among ministers and officials (page 60); the critical Lushan conference in 1959 that suppressed the truth (page 62); the impact of bad weather on harvests (page 69); deliberate genocide in Tibet (pages 64–8); Mao's refusal to face the facts and his determination to keep control (pages 68–9).

Your task is first to group these into categories and then to decide their relative importance. Which of them relate to Mao's agricultural policies and their impact? Which relate to the nature of Mao's government and control? Which do not relate to Mao personally? Be sure to focus on the key words 'responsible' and 'scale' so as to come to a balanced conclusion. You should round off your answer by offering your judgement – do you agree with the significance attached to the key factor given in the question? A central linking issue around which you might construct your answer could be whether the scale of the famine was man-made and indeed Mao-made. Was it much more than a natural misfortune compounded by the actions of misguided and incompetent officials? How far had Mao's agricultural policies undermined Chinese agricultural production before the onset of the bad weather? Indeed, was the scale of the famine a deliberate policy for enforcing political, social and economic conformity in China?

4 The Cultural Revolution 1966–76

POINTS TO CONSIDER

Between 1966 and 1976 there occurred one of the most remarkable episodes in China's history. It would not be hyperbole to say that in that period China went mad. The PRC became contorted by the Great Proletarian Cultural Revolution, a movement launched by Mao Zedong during which, at his command, the mass of the Chinese people engaged in an orgy of violence. They humiliated, beat and killed anyone suspected of being opposed to Mao and deliberately destroyed the priceless cultural treasures that had adorned China for centuries. This chapter attempts to explain these apparently irrational acts by examining the following themes:

- The prelude to the Cultural Revolution: the power struggle 1962–6
- The Cultural Revolution 1966–76
- The end of the Mao era

Key dates

1962	Mao temporarily withdrew from public life
1963	Mao's Little Red Book became a standard Chinese text
	The Diary of Lei Feng published
1965	The play 'The Dismissal of Hai Rui from Office' came under attack
1966	Creation of the CCRG
	Mao reappeared in public
	First Tiananmen Square rally
	Liu and Deng dismissed
1966–76	Great Proletarian Cultural Revolution
1967–72	'Up to the mountains and down to the villages' campaign
1968–71	'Cleansing the class ranks' campaign
1971	Lin Biao killed in plane crash
1972	'Criticise Lin Biao and Confucius' campaign began
1973	Liu Shaoqi died in prison
	Deng Xiaoping brought back into government
1976	Death of Zhou Enlai
	Tiananmen incident in Beijing
	Death of Mao Zedong

1 | The Prelude to the Cultural Revolution: The Power Struggle 1962–6

Key question
What tensions developed within the CCP between 1962 and 1966?

Key dates
Mao temporarily withdrew from public life: 1962

Mao's Little Red Book became a standard Chinese text; *The Diary of Lei Feng* published: 1963

The Cultural Revolution, which occupied the decade 1966–76, was the climax to a power struggle whose origins went back to 1962. In that year, it had become clear that the Great Leap Forward had failed to meet its industrial targets and had caused a catastrophic famine in the countryside. This had led to Mao's adopting a less prominent place in politics, a decision he came to regret when he saw Deng Xiaoping and Liu Shaoqi, the ministers he had entrusted with ending the famine, growing increasingly popular within the party. Mao never lost his fear that his colleagues, even those who professed the greatest personal loyalty, were ready to remove him from power if the opportunity came. Mao convinced himself that Liu and Deng were using their position to mount a challenge.

Mao had some grounds for his suspicions; in the early 1960s, in the provinces of Gansu and Qinghai, supporters of Liu and Deng took over the local government and began to reverse the collectivisation programme. Many of the details of what happened in the localities remain unclear, but the majority of the provincial leaders appear to have remained loyal to Mao. Nevertheless, Mao judged that he was losing his grip on the party and that a power struggle was looming. He also considered that it had been an error to have largely withdrawn from the forefront of the political scene; his absence had enabled factions to develop. It was to regain his dominance that Mao turned to Lin Biao (Lin Piao). A dedicated Maoist, Lin was a field-marshal of the PLA and had been defence minister since 1959. His reverence for Mao and his leadership of the PLA made him an invaluable ally.

The cult of Mao

Key question
How did Lin Biao help to turn Mao into a cult?

Key figure
Chen Boda
(1904–89) A leading Communist intellectual and the editor of the CCP journal, *Red Flag*.

It was Lin Biao who in the early 1960s collaborated with **Chen Boda** (Chen Po-ta) in compiling the 'Little Red Book'. Formally entitled *Quotations from Chairman Mao Zedong*, the book was a collection of the thoughts and sayings of Mao since the 1920s. Encased in red plastic covers, its 33 chapters ranged over a wide range of subjects and highlighted such topics as 'The Communist Party', 'Classes and Class Struggle' and 'Culture and Art'. The work was prefaced by the exhortation: 'Study Chairman Mao's writings, follow his teachings and act according to his instructions'. Lin Biao made the Little Red Book, the secular bible of China, the source of all truth. A copy was distributed to every soldier and became the basic text used in the study sessions which Lin made a compulsory and daily part of military training. In this way the PLA, the institution with the highest prestige and proudest revolutionary tradition in Communist China, was politicised as a force totally committed to the support of Mao Zedong.

The message soon carried over into the civilian sphere. Mao's slogan 'learn from the PLA' was a way of saying that China's army represented the true revolutionary spirit and was, therefore, the model for all the people to copy. In all, 750 million copies of the Little Red Book were distributed across China. It became the prescribed source for every subject on the curriculum in the schools and universities. In shops and factories, workers began their day and filled their breaks with communal readings from it.

Throughout China it became a social necessity to have a copy of *Quotations from Chairman Mao Zedong* with one at all times; it was the required text, used to define all issues and settle all arguments. When Yang Tang, China's table-tennis champion, was asked by foreign journalists what made him such an excellent player, he did not say his cunning serve, ferocious backhand and lightning speed; his reply was 'the progressive thinking of Chairman Mao as expressed in the Little Red Book'.

The Maoist propaganda campaign made further ground with the publication in 1963 of *The Diary of Lei Feng*. It was claimed that this book was the daily journal of a humble PLA lorry driver whose every thought and action were inspired by his devotion to Mao. The manner in which Lei died, accidentally crushed under

Mao as he appeared on the inside cover of the Little Red Book. This was the most popular image of Mao to appear during his lifetime. The picture was originally painted in 1949 when Mao was 56 years old. It is a magnified copy of this picture that still overlooks Tiananmen Square in Beijing. The original painting by Zhang Zhenshi, which was priceless in Mao's time, was auctioned in Beijing in 2006 for the equivalent of £90,000. Is there anything about the portrait that explains why it became the iconic depiction of Mao?

the wheels of a truck while faithfully going about his assigned duties, was held up as a symbol of martyrdom for the revolutionary cause. Every Chinese person, no matter how humble or humdrum his role in life, should try to reach Lei's level of dedication. That the story was a total fabrication, made up by the government's propaganda department, did not prevent its hero from achieving secular sainthood.

Lei Feng was projected by Maoists as the embodiment of the loyalty of the ordinary Chinese, a loyalty that stood in marked contrast to the time-serving careerism of many of those with soft jobs in the party or government. Lei Feng's *Diary* joined the Little Red Book as an essential text for study in China's schools.

The Wu Han affair

Key question
Why was the play, 'The Dismissal of Hai Rui from Office', so significant in the power struggle?

The central importance of literary and cultural works in the mounting power struggle was especially evident in the furore that developed over a play, 'The Dismissal of Hai Rui from Office', written by **Wu Han**. This work, performed between 1961 and 1965, was set in the days of the Song dynasty (960–1279) and told the story of Hai Rui, a court official, who was demoted and punished after bravely defying the orders of a cruel emperor.

Since Wu Han belonged to a group of writers thought to be critical of Mao Zedong, it was possible to interpret his play as an intended reference to Mao's previous dismissal of Peng Dehuai for opposing the Great Leap Forward and stating the truth at Lushan about the famine (see page 62). It thus provided Lin Biao with a pretext for moving against the anti-Maoist elements in the Communist Party. Beginning in 1965, a series of attacks was made on Wu, charging him with blackening Mao's good name and undermining Marxism–Leninism. A broken man, Wu Han committed suicide 4 years later.

Key figure

Wu Han
(1909–69) A playwright, considered by the Maoists to be a spokesman for the reactionary elements in the CCP.

Divisions in the CCP

Key question
What differences of opinion within the CCP did the Wu Han affair reveal?

The Wu Han affair deepened the divisions that had begun to develop within the CCP and between the CCP and PLA. It was at this stage that Mao's wife, Jiang Qing, a former bit-part film actress in Shanghai, began to play a prominent role. As the chairman's spouse she had an influence that was dangerous to challenge. A fierce hardliner, Jiang denounced the 'reactionaries and revisionists' on the right of the party. She also aimed to undermine the **Group of Five**, whose essential objective was to act as peacemakers to prevent party splits widening. Despite their declared loyalty to Mao, the Group of Five were condemned by Jiang for their moderation at a time when utter ruthlessness was the only proper response.

Key terms

Group of Five
A set of moderate party officials led by Peng Zhen (1902–97), the mayor of Beijing.

Shanghai Forum
A group of hard-line leftist radicals, who believed in the harshest measures being taken against those who opposed Mao.

The Shanghai Forum and the Gang of Four

Jiang Qing was the dominant figure in the '**Shanghai Forum**', a set of Maoists who represented the most hardline element in the CCP. The forum itself was dominated by a group of particularly uncompromising individuals, known as the **Gang of Four**. They were the extreme wing of an extreme movement. The three men in the group, who were feared for their ruthlessness, had risen to prominence in the Shanghai section of the CCP and had become members of the Politburo.

Jiang urged that steps be immediately taken to remove Liu Shaoqi and Deng Xiaoping from their positions in the CCP. She further demanded that Chinese culture should be cleansed of those writers and artists whose attitude betrayed their lack of commitment to Mao's revolution. The severity of her approach so pleased Lin Biao that he asked her to take charge of the PLA's cultural policy.

Key term

Gang of Four
Made up of Jiang Qing and her three male associates, Zhang Chunquiao (1917–2001), Yao Wenyuan 1931–2005) and Wang Honwen (1932–92).

Profile: Jiang Qing 1914–91

1914	Born in Shandong province
1934–7	Worked as an actress in Shanghai
1937	Joined the Communists in Yanan
1939	Married Mao Zedong
1940	Gave birth to daughter, Li Na
1959	Attended the Lushan conference with Mao
1962–6	Led the Gang of Four
1966–76	Hardline controller of the arts during the Cultural Revolution
1976	Arrested in the power struggle after Mao's death
1981	Condemned to death after a show trial
1983	Death sentence commuted to life imprisonment
1991	Committed suicide

Jiang was a film actress in Shanghai until the late 1930s when she abandoned her husband to join the Communists in Yanan. There, she set her cap at Mao, who was so taken with her that he gave up his wife and married Jiang. They stayed together in a stormy relationship until his death. Initially Mao restricted Jiang's involvement in politics, but from 1959 onwards, finding her aggressive public style a very useful weapon against his opponents, he encouraged her to play a much bigger part in public affairs.

An unforgiving woman who bore grudges, and was ferocious in attacking those she believed were deviating from Mao's brand of Communism, Jiang was deeply involved in the infighting that preceded the Cultural Revolution. During that revolution she played a key role as Mao's terrifying cultural enforcer. Having failed to lead the Gang of Four to victory in the power struggle that followed Mao's death, she was arrested and subjected to a show trial. The death sentence she received in 1981 was subsequently commuted to life imprisonment. Unmourned and ignored, Jiang committed suicide in 1991.

Key term

Counter-revolutionaries
Used by hardline Maoists to describe those in the party who favoured more moderate policies.

Asserting that the thoughts of Chairman Mao represented a 'new development of the Marxist–Leninist world outlook', the Shanghai Forum identified the **counter-revolutionaries** who must be struggled against and destroyed:

> China is under the dictatorship of a sinister anti-Party and anti-Socialist line which is diametrically opposed to Chairman Mao's thought. This sinister line is a combination of bourgeois ideas on literature and art, modern revisionist ideas on literature and art and what is known as the literature and art of the 1930s.

The forum's answer was for the PLA, 'the mainstay and hope of the Chinese people', to lead China in rooting out 'anti-socialist weeds' and eradicating all traces of artistic corruption that delayed the achievement of a truly proletarian culture. Lin Biao spoke of an 'imminent and inevitable' struggle against class enemies. Lin's statement proved to be the beginning of a purge of the party. In April 1966, Peng Zhen and the leading members of the Group of Five were denounced for 'taking the capitalist road', as was the playwright Wu Han.

The Central Cultural Revolution Group (CCRG)

Key question
Why was the creation of the CCRG such a significant move?

Key terms

Packing
Controlling the membership of the committees in such a way that they always contained a majority of Maoists.

Central Cultural Revolution Group
A subcommittee of the Politburo, this body was established in May 1966 to direct the Cultural Revolution. Its 17 members included the Gang of Four.

The ground for this attack had been prepared during the preceding 12 months by Maoists' **packing** the key party committees. A striking example of this Maoist control had been the setting up in May 1966 of the **Central Cultural Revolution Group** (CCRG). This body, which was dominated by the Gang of Four, was the instrument through which Mao would run the Cultural Revolution.

Such was the influence of the CCRG that by the early summer of 1966, Liu Shaoqi and Deng Xiaoping found themselves being outmanoeuvred and undermined. Acting on information the CCRG had given him, Mao himself in May 1966 issued a 'notification' to the CCP in which he defined the enemy within:

> Those representatives of the bourgeoisie who have sneaked into the party, the government, the army and various spheres of culture are a bunch of counter-revolutionary revisionists. Once the conditions are ripe, they will seize political power and turn the dictatorship of the proletariat into the dictatorship of the bourgeoisie.

His words were, in effect, an announcement that China had entered that tumultuous and terrifying period of political and social history known as the 'Cultural Revolution'.

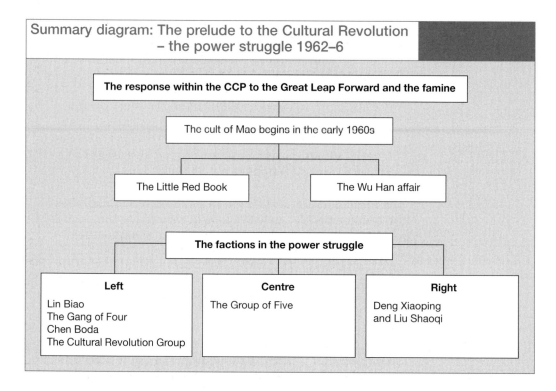

Summary diagram: The prelude to the Cultural Revolution – the power struggle 1962–6

The response within the CCP to the Great Leap Forward and the famine

The cult of Mao begins in the early 1960s

The Little Red Book

The Wu Han affair

The factions in the power struggle

Left
Lin Biao
The Gang of Four
Chen Boda
The Cultural Revolution Group

Centre
The Group of Five

Right
Deng Xiaoping
and Liu Shaoqi

2 | The Cultural Revolution 1966–76

The Cultural Revolution broadened from an internal party purge to a national movement with a poster campaign in the summer of 1966. On Mao's instructions, Lin Biao organised students and radical teachers in the universities to put up wall posters attacking the education system for its divergence from the revolutionary path. The enthusiasm with which the students abandoned their classes and attacked their teachers caused such unrest that Deng Xiaoping and Liu Shaoqi sent special work teams to the campuses in an attempt to contain the trouble.

Zhou Enlai, ever the diplomat, tried to keep the peace between the party factions, between those who wanted to restore order and the Maoist elements who were eager for the disruption to spread. But in an atmosphere of increasing violence even his best efforts were in vain. The work teams were attacked by the students who, in a particularly ominous development, began to take to the streets as 'Red Guards' intent on creating a reign of terror.

Mao's return

It was at this critical stage that Mao Zedong made a dramatic public reappearance. In July 1966, in a stage-managed extravaganza, he was seen swimming across the Yangzi River at Wuhan (Wuchang), the scene of the 1911 Revolution (see page 3). Photos of this feat filled the Chinese newspapers, and television and cinema newsreels carried the pictures into every village.

Key question
How did the Cultural Revolution develop into a reign of terror?

Key question
Why was Mao's Yangzi swim so significant?

Mao had made a great symbolic gesture that excited the whole of China. The Yangzi had been carefully chosen as the site of his return to public view. In Chinese tradition, the nation's greatest river was regarded as a life force. The 73-year-old chairman had proved that he was very much alive and, therefore, still in control of events. The US historian John King Fairbank has suggested that to understand the impact of the incident on the Chinese imagination one needs to think of the reaction there would be in Britain to 'the news that Queen Elizabeth II had swum the Channel'.

Mao exploited the adulation aroused by his spectacular return to tighten his grip on government and party. In August he summoned a special meeting of the Central Committee, at which he condemned the revisionist tendencies in the party and called on members to rededicate themselves to unwavering class struggle. Mao also announced the downgrading of Liu Shaoqi in the party ranking and the elevation of Lin Biao to second in command. This was, in effect, to nominate Lin as his successor.

The August rally 1966

Key question
Why was the August rally so significant in the history of the Cultural Revolution?

The official starting date of the Cultural Revolution was May 1966 when the Central Cultural Revolution Committee came into being. However, the event that first brought the Cultural Revolution to the attention of the Chinese people and to the outside world as a great national movement came 3 months later. On 18 August over a million people, the majority of them in their teens or early twenties, packed into Tiananmen Square in Beijing. Waving their Little Red Books, they screamed themselves hoarse in an outpouring of veneration for their idol. They chanted 'Chairman Mao, may you live for a thousand years!', and sang 'Mao Zedong is the red sun rising in the east'.

Key dates
Mao reappeared in public: 1966

The first Tiananmen Square rally: 18 August 1966

This massive demonstration, which lasted a whole day, was evidence of the organising skill of Lin Biao and Chen Boda, who had made the arrangements for filling the square with such huge numbers of Maoist supporters. So effectively had the cult of Mao been developed that Lin and Chen were able even at short notice to assemble masses of genuinely enthusiastic Maoist demonstrators.

Enlisting the young

It was this ability to manipulate public opinion and behaviour, especially of the young, that allowed Mao to launch the Cultural Revolution, a movement that aimed at nothing less than the creation of a new type of Chinese society. His attempt to do this was to convulse the whole of China for the next decade. Mao had enlisted the youth of China as his instrument for reimposing his will on the nation and reshaping it according to his vision. In August 1966 he presented the students of Qinghua University with a banner inscribed in his own hand, 'Bombard the Headquarters'. It was his way of encouraging China's young people to criticise and attack those ideas and those members in party and government that Mao wanted to remove.

毛泽东同志和林彪同志在天安门城楼上。　　新华社记者摄（传真照片）

我们的伟大领袖、伟大统帅、伟大舵手毛主席在天安门城楼上向群众挥手致意。

我们伟大的领袖、伟大的统帅、伟大的舵手毛主席万岁！

无产阶级文化大革命是共产主义运动和社会主义革命的伟大创举

毛主席同百万群众共庆文化大革命

毛主席和林彪周恩来等同志接见学生代表并检阅文化革命大军的游行队伍

毛主席说："这个运动规模很大，确实把群众发动起来了，对全国人民的思想革命化有很大的意义。"

林彪周恩来同志发表重要讲话，　北京哈尔滨长沙南京等地革命师生也讲了话

The front page of the *Heilongjiang Daily*, 19 August 1966, reports the news of the great rally held in Beijing the day before. The photos show Mao, Lin Biao and the adoring crowds, and the main headline reads 'Chairman Mao celebrates the Great Cultural Revolution with millions of people'. What does the front page indicate about the nature of the political relationship between Mao Zedong and Lin Biao at this point?

The decision to exploit the young in this way was no last-minute thought on Mao's part. In discussions he held with **Kang Sheng** and the Gang of Four late in 1965, he had remarked wryly, but with very serious intent: 'We have to depend on them [the young] to start a rebellion, a revolution, otherwise we may not be able to overthrow the demons and monsters. We must liberate the little devils. We need more **monkeys to disrupt the palace**.'

The attack on the 'four olds'

Key question
What did Mao identify as the targets for attack?

The high point of the rally came in a speech given by Lin Biao. In Mao's name, Lin identified 'four olds' as targets for the young to attack:

- old ideas
- old culture
- old customs
- old habits.

Key figure

Kang Sheng
(1898–1975) Mao's very able, but unbalanced, secret police chief who took a perverse pleasure in terrifying and persecuting people.

There was something bizarre about Mao Zedong, a man aged 73 years, calling on the young to overthrow the old, but at the time the irony went unnoticed by the youngsters. They rushed to do his bidding with a terrifying intensity and ferocity. It is doubtful whether any other society in peacetime has witnessed organised upheaval on such a scale. China had been told that nothing in its past was worth preserving. Hardly anywhere in China, even the remotest regions, would remain untouched. Nearly every family would be affected by what was to happen. Millions would die; many more millions would have their lives irreparably damaged.

The great rallies 1966

Key term

Monkeys to disrupt the palace
Mao's imagery is drawn from the practice in the imperial court of having monkeys as pets. The uncontrolled animals had been notorious for causing mayhem.

Between August and November 1966 there were, in all, eight mass rallies in Tiananmen Square. Mao did not attend all of these; he said he found them exhausting. Nevertheless his was the dominating spirit. Lin Biao, assisted on occasion by Jiang Qing, used the rallies to excite the crowds to ever greater displays of affection and loyalty towards China's leader. Lin appealed to the great throngs to honour Mao Zedong as the outstanding revolutionary genius of the age who was 'remoulding the souls of the people'. It was this very attempt to remould the people of China that was to give the Cultural Revolution its chilling and deadly character.

Mao's reasons for launching the Cultural Revolution

Key question
What were Mao's motives for subjecting his people to the Cultural Revolution?

So massively disruptive was the Cultural Revolution that it raises an obvious question. Why was Mao Zedong willing to plunge into renewed turmoil a nation that had only just emerged from decades of foreign occupation, civil war and famine? At its simplest, the answer is that the Cultural Revolution was to be the means by which Mao would reassert his authority over China and the CCP. He had a number of interlocking objectives:

- to preserve himself in power for the rest of his life by removing all possible sources of opposition
- to obliterate the damaging record of the failure of the Great Leap Forward
- to ensure that his concept of revolution would continue after his death by remoulding Chinese society and culture in such a way that they could never be changed back
- to prevent China making the same mistakes as the revisionist Soviet Union
- to break the power of the urban bureaucrats and restore the peasant character of China's Communist revolution.

Mao's idea of permanent revolution

Mao believed that the revolution, which he had led to victory in 1949, was being betrayed from within. He was convinced that many in the upper echelons of the CCP were infected by '**neo-capitalism**' and a desire for personal power that robbed them of their revolutionary purpose. The Great Proletarian Cultural Revolution, to give it its full title, has, therefore, to be seen as an extension of Mao's belief in **permanent (or continuous) revolution**. He believed that if the Chinese revolution stood still it would cease to be a genuine movement, and he feared that after him the CCP would simply become a self-justifying bureaucracy which would destroy all that had been achieved by the PRC since 1949. To prevent this, he planned to circumvent the party bureaucracy and appeal directly to the Chinese people. In a great populist gesture he would enlist them in a campaign to save and consolidate the revolution. Mao used a memorable paradox to describe his policy; he spoke of 'great disorder across the land leading to great order'; only by a policy of deliberate disruption could the forces of reaction be exposed and destroyed.

Developments in the USSR

Mao had also been disturbed by developments in the USSR, China's great Communist rival. In the late 1950s he had interpreted the Soviet attack on Stalin's 'cult of personality' as a criticism of his own leadership of China (see page 140). The news in 1964 of the fall from power of the Soviet leader, Nikita Khrushchev, gave Mao further concern. The official reason given by the Soviet authorities for their dismissal of Khrushchev was that he had engaged in 'harebrained' economic schemes. Nobody in China had openly dared to use such a term in regard to Mao's policies, but the parallel between the situations in the USSR and China was too close for comfort.

Mao's anxieties went beyond the purely personal. What he observed in the Soviet Union was a party, originally pure in revolutionary spirit, corrupted by its own exercise of power into a self-satisfied élite. Despite his many personal differences with Stalin, Mao had never been willing to accept the lengths to which de-Stalinisation and liberalising had gone in the USSR.

Key terms

Neo-capitalism
A return to the corrupt bourgeois system based on greed, individualism and profit-making.

Permanent (or continuous) revolution
The notion that revolution is not a single historical event, but a continuing and developing process.

Key question
Why was Mao concerned by events in the Soviet Union?

Key terms

Revisionism
Betraying the Communist cause by abandoning basic revolutionary principles.

Détente
A policy aimed at easing relations between the Eastern bloc and Western nations by encouraging mutual acceptance of coexistence.

Mao viewed Khrushchev and his successors as guilty of betraying the revolution by encouraging **revisionism** and by *détente* with the West and he was determined that such developments would not happen in China after him.

Mao's wish to renew the CCP's revolutionary spirit

Mao judged that CCP and government officials were already being seduced by the privileges of power. He had convinced himself that the older revolutionaries who had defeated the Nationalists and established the People's Republic had lost their revolutionary fervour. Consequently, the only way to save his revolution was by waging war against the Communist Party hierarchy itself. It was a time for a new generation of party members to replace the old guard.

Key question
What concerns did Mao have about the younger members of the CCP?

Testing the younger members of the party

However, Mao also judged that the younger members of the party had yet to be tested. They had not undergone the rigours of the legendary experiences of the CCP: the White Terror, the Long March, the anti-Japanese war and the struggle against the GMD (see page 6). They needed hardening in the crucible of revolutionary struggle. Only then would it be certain that they were strong enough to withstand a concerted military attack from the West, an eventuality in which Mao continued to believe throughout the 1960s.

Key question
How did Mao intend to preserve the peasant character of the revolution?

Undermining the bureaucrats and intellectuals

A further aim was Mao's determination to preserve the Chinese Revolution as an essentially peasant movement. It was not that he had a high regard for the peasants as individuals. Indeed, he often expressed contempt for them (see page 56). Nevertheless, he held that as a class the peasants were the main revolutionary force in China. That is why he had built his revolution on them. It was also why he did not want affairs to be run by the bureaucrats and intellectuals in the cities.

A tension had also developed between Mao and the urban intellectuals. It was they who had criticised the Great Leap Forward. Although Mao, judged by his writings and poetry, could be described as an intellectual, he always regarded himself as a man of action. He distrusted the type of political thinker who was more interested in theory than in action. It is possible to interpret his assault on the intellectuals in the Cultural Revolution as an act of revenge on a class that he had always despised.

The attack on Deng Xiaoping and Liu Shaoqi

At a party central committee meeting in August 1966, Deng Xiaoping and Liu Shaoqi were accused of being 'the **spearheads of the erroneous line**'. No immediate action was taken against them since it was reported that Mao had granted them the opportunity 'to correct their mistakes'.

However, 2 months later, following a Red Guard demonstration in Beijing, aimed specifically against them, Deng and Liu were both formally dismissed from their positions in government and party on the grounds that they had adopted 'a bourgeois reactionary line' and had become 'revisionists'. Mao let it be known that he had been offended by the way in which Deng and Liu had previously tried to bypass him. He complained that they had treated him 'like their dead parent at a funeral'.

Wall posters were displayed denouncing both men for their betrayal of Maoist thought. Liu and his wife, Wang Gangmei, were dragged from their government residence and beaten by a jeering mob. Liu was then forced to undergo a series of brutal 'struggle sessions' before being imprisoned in conditions that were deliberately intended to break his health. Suffering from diabetes, he eventually died in 1973 in solitary confinement after being refused proper medical treatment for his condition.

Deng Xiaoping's son, Pufang, was thrown from an upstairs window by Red Guards, an act of gratuitous violence that broke his spine and left him permanently paralysed. Deng himself suffered less harshly but he, too, was forced to undergo public humiliation which involved his being ranted at by 3000 Red Guards. He then disappeared into solitary confinement before being sent to perform '**corrective labour**' in Jiangxi province in 1969.

The growing influence of Lin Biao, Jiang Qing and Kang Sheng

The immediate acceptance by the CCP and the PLA of the dismissal of such prominent figures testified to the power that Lin Biao and Jiang Qing were able to exert in Mao's name. This authority was increased by the appointment of Kang Sheng as head of China's special security forces, the PRC's secret police. Kang, who had a reputation for ruthlessness (see page 8), was a member of the Shanghai Forum and a devotee of Jiang Qing. He became a principal organiser of the purges that continued, at Mao's bidding, to decimate the upper echelons of the CCP throughout 1966 and 1967.

Once it was underway, Mao played little part in directing the Cultural Revolution. He withdrew from Beijing, leaving the officials at Zhongnanhai to the mercy of the Red Guards. Camped outside in Tiananmen Square for months on end, the Guards kept up a constant loudspeaker barrage of insults directed at ministers and officials deemed to be 'rightists'. Anyone trying to break cover and leave the blockaded offices had to run the gauntlet of jeering youngsters who were eager to turn their insults

Key question
Why were Deng and Liu attacked?

Key dates

Liu Shaoqi and Deng Xiaoping dismissed: October 1966

Death of Liu Shaoqi: 1973

Key terms

Spearheads of the erroneous line
Leaders who had tried to persuade the party to follow policies that ran counter to Mao's wishes.

Corrective labour
In Communist theory, a form of imprisonment that brought the prisoner to see the error of his ways.

Wang Gangmei being manhandled by Red Guards. The garland of ping-pong balls has been put round her neck in mockery of her bourgeois habit of wearing expensive jewellery. Although she had been sentenced to death, Wang was reprieved by the personal intervention of Mao Zedong who crossed her name off an execution list on which she appeared. It was one of the few occasions when Mao used his personal influence to save a victim of the Cultural Revolution. However, he made no move to save Liu Shaoqi. This may well have been vindictiveness on Mao's part; he was paying Liu back for opposing him earlier. In what ways does the photo illustrate how the Red Guards behaved in this period?

into blows if given the slightest pretext. Jiang Qing and Lin Biao made sure that the besiegers were kept informed by going down in person to identify the ministers and officials who were to be abused and intimidated.

The role of the Red Guards

Key question
Why did China's young people prove so willing to follow Mao's lead?

The Red Guard movement grew out of prepared soil. Since the Sino-Soviet divide in the 1950s (see page 141), pupils and students had been encouraged to regard themselves as pioneers under Mao Zedong in the advancement of international proletarian revolution. Mass rallies had been used in the Hundred Flowers and anti-rightist campaigns in the 1950s. A student recalled:

The revolutionary fervour was definitely very strong, I think, in the educational system. I think the students and learning classes became much more politicised, and the competition I won with my essay was how to be successful in the revolution. I remember I had all the big rhetoric and empty slogans and everybody loved it. Some people cried and I was very proud. That was 1965, so the education was already gearing up to a very charged class struggle and preparation.

In choosing China's youth to be the instruments of the Cultural Revolution, Mao showed an astute grasp of mass psychology. The young were made to feel that they had a special role to play, not only in the regeneration of the nation, but in the creation of a new socialist world order. As one Red Guard later put it:

Now it was our generation's turn to defend China. China was the only country which wasn't revisionist, capitalist or colonialist. We felt that we were defending China's revolution and liberating the world. All the big slogans made a generation of us feel that the Cultural Revolution really was a war, a war to defend Chairman Mao and the new China.

Mao's hold over the young

The reminiscences of those who had been Red Guards illustrate the extraordinary hold Mao had over them. One described how he believed Mao was a god:

When Chairman Mao waved his hand at Tiananmen, a million Red Guards wept their hearts out as if by some hormonal reaction. Later on we were all conditioned to burst into tears the moment he appeared on the screen. He was divine, and the revolutionary tides of the world rose and fell at his command.

Another recalled how willing he had been to give himself totally to Mao:

I believed in Mao with every cell in my body. You felt you would give Chairman Mao your everything – your body, your mind, your spirit, your soul, your fate. Whatever Chairman Mao wanted you to do you were ready to do it. So we were all there, crying and jumping up and down and shouting ourselves hoarse.

Another recollected how he had become victim to the power of mass suggestion:

When you see the red flags and when you see how emotional everybody was you get carried away with that sort of feeling as well. You just think I should be part of that, I should belong to that because there are millions of people there and everybody worshipped Mao so much that you would question yourself if you didn't feel like that.

This 1974 photograph shows young schoolgirls ecstatically portraying their revolutionary fighting spirit by wearing military-style uniform and carrying mock weapons. Why do you think children as young as these became caught up in the revolutionary spirit of the times?

Another offered a new slant on body piercing:

> I cut a small hole in my chest with a penknife and pinned my Mao badge there. That way I thought that when I put my clothes on no one would be able to see it and I would have Chairman Mao literally engraved on my heart.

The awe in which Mao was held by the young was extreme, but it was not wholly irrational. It was a recognition of what they believed he had achieved for China. The young people who chanted Mao's name saw him as the great hero who had freed China from a century of humiliation at the hands of the foreigner. One of the most popular titles given him was 'the red sun rising in the east', an apt metaphor for the man who had made China a great world power, possessing its own nuclear weapon and capable of displacing the Soviet Union as leader of the international socialist movement.

In a shrewd analysis, Anthony Grey, a British correspondent for **Reuters**, who was imprisoned by the Chinese during the Cultural Revolution, suggested that the worship of Mao illustrated the

Key term

Reuters
An international press agency.

persistence of two remarkable features of Chinese society – emperor worship and the power of conformity:

> The most extravagant and ridiculous language was used all the time about him in the official press. I remember I saw him once on May Day; I was in a crowd in the park and I was talking to members of the crowd and I was saying, 'What were you hoping to see?' they said 'Chairman Mao, we love Chairman Mao'. And they really did say it in a way that made me think of the tendency of young people who want something to idolise, be it pop singers or film stars or in their case only one charismatic individual in a nation. He had managed to work a great spell over the people. I think he used the old admiration for China's emperors and the son of heaven idea which was very strong – inculcated almost into the Chinese nature.

Mao's understanding of the young

Mao knew that the need to conform to the standards of their peers is very powerful among the young, and that this makes

The incident shown in this 1966 photograph, which was of the high points of the first great rally in Tiananmen Square, was celebrated in the Chinese press as the moment when Mao gave his personal sanction to the Red Guards as the main movement leading the Cultural Revolution. The young girl came on to the balcony and to tumultuous applause fitted a Red Guard armband on Mao. When she told him her name was Song Binbin, which means 'gentle', Mao said it would be better as a Red Guard if her name were 'militant'. This story was often quoted as a sure sign that Mao intended the Cultural Revolution to be an essentially violent movement. What does the photo suggest about the veneration in which Mao was held by the young?

them particularly susceptible to suggestion. The more idealistic they are, the more easily led they are. As Anthony Grey hinted, this phenomenon is not restricted to China. There are many examples in the West of the herd instinct taking over from individualism. Peer-group conformity is the explanation for the hold that fashion, in such areas as clothing and music, has over many impressionable young people.

Nor should simple perversity be left out of the account. Marching through the streets chanting slogans is a softer option than working at one's studies. Most students in China were only too willing to believe that by insulting their teachers and burning their textbooks they were in the vanguard of progress.

Red Guard terror

Key question
What methods did the Red Guards use to terrify the population?

The Red Guards became a terrifying and destructive movement. Mao's policies deliberately brutalised China's idealistic young people. By presenting chaos as more virtuous than order, Mao effectively declared that there was no moral restriction on what could be done in the name of the revolution. Students, trained in the Chinese tradition of obedience to parents and teachers, were suddenly told to insult and abuse them. For children to denounce their elders had enormous significance in a society where respect was ingrained. In a reversal of their traditional deference, they behaved with a particular virulence. They were, of course, still being obedient, but this time to a new master.

Anything that represented the corrupt past was labelled under the blanket term, 'Confucius and Co', and was liable to be smashed or torn up. Temples, shrines, works of art and ornamental gardens became obvious targets; many priceless and irreplaceable treasures of Chinese civilisation were destroyed in this wave of organised vandalism. In the words of a Western correspondent:

Key term

Decadent tendencies
Clinging to bourgeois values, the most obvious examples being the wearing of Western-style clothes, jewellery or make-up.

> Mao told the Red Guards: 'To rebel is justified!' They repaid him by crushing almost every semblance of tradition, decency and intellectual endeavour in China, save that of a few protected institutes, where scientific and military-related work continued fitfully in dangerous circumstances.

Self-criticism and struggle sessions

Key question
What tactics were used to break the will of those arrested?

Given free rein, the Red Guards seized public transport and took over radio and television networks. Anyone showing signs of '**decadent tendencies**' was likely to be manhandled and publicly humiliated. An especially vulnerable group were the intellectuals, those whose work or privileged way of life was judged to detach them from the people. Schoolteachers, university staff, writers, and even doctors were prey to the Red Guard squads who denounced them as 'bad elements' and made them publicly confess their class crimes. Those regarded as particularly culpable were forced to undergo 'struggle sessions'.

These ordeals, which became a dominant feature of the Cultural Revolution, were in essence an assault on the individual's sense of self and were aimed at provoking and stimulating guilt. 'Brainwashing' is an appropriate term to describe the terror tactics. To induce guilt the victims were made to study Mao's writings followed by periods of intense self-criticism and confession. The first confession was never accepted; the accused had to dig deeper and deeper into their memory to recall all their errors and sins against the party and the people.

A common practice was for the Guards to force the accused to adopt the 'aeroplane' position; with head thrust down, knees bent and arms pulled high behind the back, the unfortunate victims were made to catalogue their past offences against the people. Those who maintained their innocence were systematically punched and kicked. After days of torment and constant denunciation as 'imperialist dogs', 'lick-spittle capitalists', 'lackeys of the USA' and 'betrayers of the people', few had the physical or mental strength to continue resisting.

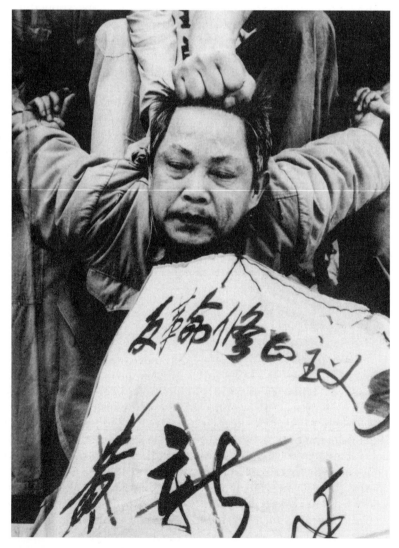

Huang Xinting, the military commander of the Chengdu region, forced by Red Guards into the 'aeroplane' position. The placard around his neck accuses him of being a rightist.

A victim's past achievements in the revolutionary cause offered no protection. Wang Jinxi had been a hero of the resistance in Gansu province against both the Japanese and the Nationalists, and was also renowned for his prodigious efforts to develop the oil fields of the region. He had been personally honoured by Mao in Beijing and had been visited by Zhou Enlai, Deng Xiaoping and Liu Shaoqi. None of this was sufficient to save him. The Red Guards claimed that since Wang had been working in the oil fields at the time they had been controlled by the GMD this made him a 'traitor-worker'. When he would not confess he was beaten and tortured to death over a 3-day period.

Official support for Red Guard terror

Although it often appeared that Red Guard action was spontaneous, it was not only officially sanctioned but was also officially directed. Xie Fuzhi (Hsieh Fu-chih), the Minister for Public Security, in addressing the police forces, revealed both why it was that the Red Guards had such a free hand in their terror campaign and how they were able to target their victims so easily:

> I am not for beating people to death. But when the masses hate the bad elements so deeply that we are unable to stop them, then don't try. The police should stand on the side of the Red Guards and establish contact with them, develop bonds with them and provide them with information about the people of the five categories.

The five categories Xie referred to were defined as:

- landlords
- rich peasants
- reactionaries
- bad elements
- rightists.

The names and whereabouts of all those listed under these headings were passed to the Red Guard detachments who then descended on their victims. In 1996, Ze Rong recalled his behaviour as a 13-year-old Red Guard:

> We found out the names and addresses of the Rightists, landlords and 'bad elements' and drove to their homes in our school truck. When we found the heads of each household, we read out quotations from Mao's Little Red Book. Then we loaded all their valuables into the lorry and carted them off. Some of those whose homes we ransacked were also beaten to death. On a trip to the Babaoshan cemetery, I remember asking the man in charge of the furnaces how many bodies had been burned as the Red Guard terror got under way. It came to a figure of more than 2000 people tortured to death in a period of just 2 weeks.

Leading officials of the Heilongjiang branch of the CCP are publicly humiliated for the crime of 'carrying out Liu Shaoqi's revisionist line'. Why did Liu Shaoqi, despite his high position and status, become a victim of Mao's purge?

Victimisers and victims

As had happened during the **Stalinist purges** in the USSR in the 1930s, so, too, in China's Cultural Revolution, the victimisers became in turn the victims. Revolutionaries struggled to prove their proletarian integrity by becoming ever more extreme. Those who faltered or showed signs of being sickened by the horrors were condemned as reactionaries and found themselves subjected to the savagery that they had recently meted out. Genuine idealism was swiftly corrupted into unthinking brutishness. A young female student recorded:

> One time on my way home I saw some Red Guards arresting a young girl. They said she was a bad element. Whether she was or not was beside the point. Someone said she was a baddie and that was enough. So they were using their belts to beat her up. I was a Red Guard, too, and my first thought was that I must express my revolutionary spirit. I took off my belt and lifted it high as if I too was taking part in the beating. I couldn't actually bring myself to hit her but I knew I had to look as if I was. If you didn't beat people you weren't showing a proper hatred for the enemy or a proper love for the people.

Licensed savagery

The examples of savagery seemed endless. In Beijing itself, in addition to the daily scenes of beatings in the street, theatres and sports grounds became the venues of systematic killings of bound

Stalinist purges During his leadership of the USSR Stalin had introduced a series of fierce purges to crush any opposition that might develop.

Key term

victims. During a 2-day period in Daxing County, north of Beijing, 300 people were clubbed to death in the public square. In Guangxi (Kwangsi) province 67,000 deaths were recorded in the decade after 1966, while in Mongolia, Tibet and Sichuan the figures ran into hundreds of thousands. At the trial of the Gang of Four in 1980 (see page 157), it was charged that the purges they had sanctioned had resulted in the killing of over half a million CCP officials.

Cultural vandalism

The organised terror created a horrifying atmosphere of callousness and brutality. PRC documents record that between 1966 and 1976 in the course of attacking the treasures of China's past, the Red Guards and the other government-sponsored terror squads wrecked, burned or flattened 4922 of Beijing's 6843 'places of cultural or historical interest'. The **Forbidden City** only just survived. Forewarned in August 1966 that the Red Guards planned to destroy it, Zhou Enlai moved in a unit of the PLA to prevent the youngsters running amok.

Arguably the greatest single act of desecration occurred not in Beijing but in Qufu in Shandong province, the home of Confucius. A group of some 200 Beijing University students and teachers went there to join hundreds of local students. Over a four-week period in November 1966, this group committed 6618 organised acts of vandalism. These included the destruction or spoliation of 929 paintings, 2700 books, 1000 statues and monuments, and 2000 graves.

Attacks on foreigners

One of the staggering aspects of the Cultural Revolution was that its victims were not restricted to the Chinese people. In defiance of all the accepted rules of international diplomacy, a total of 11 **foreign embassies** were attacked and their staff assaulted. With only minimal interference from the police, Red Guards were allowed to besiege foreign embassies and terrorise the people who worked in them. Among the examples were:

- the surrounding of the Soviet Embassy by Red Guards who kept up a 24-hour barrage of insults
- besieging the Dutch *chargé d'affaires* and his family in their house for over a month
- seizure of a French commercial attaché and his wife, who were then screamed at for 6 hours by Maoists
- two secretaries from the Indian embassy, being grabbed at Beijing airport before they could board their plane and being badly beaten
- breaking into and burning the British Embassy in Beijing, accompanied by physical attacks on mission personnel.

Donald Hopson, the head of the British Embassy, sent a vivid dispatch to his government describing what had happened:

Key question
What statistics illustrate the scale of the destruction of China's ancient culture?

Key terms

Forbidden City
Beijing's greatest monument, a spacious walled inner city that had been the home and court of the emperors between 1368 and 1911.

Foreign embassies
In international convention, these are specially protected areas which the host nation respects as being immune from local interference.

Outside the crowd broke the glass of the windows, but the bars and plywood shutters held. The mob then started to burn straw at the windows. We threw water through the gaps, but the room began to fill with smoke. We could see the glare of many fires, and it was now clear that the mob would soon be through the wall and there was a danger that we should be burned alive if we stayed. I gave orders for the emergency exit to be opened. We were hauled by our hair, half strangled with our ties, kicked and beaten on the head with bamboo poles.

Most of the staff had similar experiences to my own. Some were paraded up and down, forced to their knees and photographed in humiliating positions. All were beaten and kicked, and the girls were not spared lewd attentions from the prying fingers of the mob. So much for the **morals of the Red Guards**. Most of the staff were eventually rescued by the army and plainclothes police agents.

Chinese attacks abroad

The attacks on foreigners were not confined within China. Disregarding the damage it did to its image abroad, the PRC carried its Cultural Revolution ferociously into other countries. By 1967, Chinese militants had caused violent incidents in over 30 countries around the world. In some of these the local people hit back; in Burma and Indonesia, Chinese expatriates were attacked in retaliation.

Amazing scenes occurred in London in 1967 when scores of staff members, all shouting Mao's name, came out of the Chinese Embassy in Portland Place armed with sticks and machetes, which they waved threateningly at the police. Safe from arrest because of their diplomatic immunity, they demonstrated loudly and went back into their embassy building only after they had caused major disruption in the area.

Trouble in Hong Kong

Mao used the opportunity provided by the Cultural Revolution to make trouble for Britain over its continuing possession of **Hong Kong**. In May 1967, he tried to turn a workers' strike in the colony into an anti-British demonstration in the hope that the police would fire on the demonstrators, thus illustrating the evils of British colonialism in China. When the local police declined to act in this way, Mao instructed Zhou Enlai to send Chinese terrorists into the colony to murder policemen and so create the desired retaliation. In an 8-week period the terrorists killed five policemen and exploded over 160 bombs that caused civilian deaths and extensive damage to property. The Hong Kong authorities still did not resort to the extreme measures that Mao had expected. He had wanted a massacre but he did not get one.

The cynical aspect of the whole affair was that although Mao wished to frighten the British into thinking that the PRC was preparing to take Hong Kong by force, he had no intention of going through with such a plan. He wanted to embarrass the British, but not to push things to the point where he would have to carry out his bluff. He told Zhou Enlai to stop short of actions

Morals of the Red Guards
One of the boasts of the Red Guards was that they had risen above bourgeois thoughts of sex. This was why they dressed in plain unisex blue or khaki uniforms and made themselves look as physically unappealing as possible.

Hong Kong
The Chinese city-port that had been a British Crown colony since 1898 and was not scheduled to return to China until 1997.

that 'might lead to our having to take Hong Kong back ahead of time'.

Reining in the Red Guards

Key question
What role did the PLA play in the Cultural Revolution?

After its first 2 years, 1966–7, the revolution that Mao had unleashed appeared to have got out of hand. The widespread disruption had brought industrial production to a halt and had led to the schools and universities being closed. More immediately disturbing, a series of local civil wars raged in China. The sheer zeal and passion of the Red Guard movement had turned in on itself. Regional groups had begun to clash with one another. Factory workers formed their own units and challenged the claim of the students to be the true leaders of the movement.

The various groups began to go to ever greater lengths to prove the purity of their ideology and the depth of their loyalty to Mao. This convinced the authorities at the top that matters had gone far enough. Orders were given that the work of the Red Guards should be taken over by the PLA.

The role of the PLA

Initially the PLA had tolerated, indeed encouraged, the students and workers in hunting down class enemies, but it was unwilling to share its prestige as the creator and defender of China's revolution. The PLA claimed a special relationship with Chairman Mao and with the Chinese people, which entitled it to take over the Cultural Revolution. Army units travelled throughout China in a campaign to impress on the people the totality of the PLA's loyalty to Mao Zedong. They took over from the Red Guards in hunting down and terrorising 'counter-revolutionaries'.

There is a strong case for suggesting that the anarchy associated with the Red Guards was more apparent than real. They were allowed to run wild only because Mao knew that at any time he could use the PLA to pull them back into line. In all its essentials the Cultural Revolution was directed from the top by Mao and the CCRG. It may often have had the air of spontaneity, and it is true that once started it seemed to generate a momentum of its own, but there were guiding hands behind the marches and the thuggery. Much of it was orchestrated. The Maoists were prepared to let things run to extremes, but always seemed able to call a halt when it suited them. The idealistic youngsters who appeared to lead the Cultural Revolution were pawns in the power struggle in the CCP.

The 'up to the mountains and down to the villages' campaign 1967–72

Key question
How were the energies of the troublesome Red Guards diverted in another direction?

The ultimate control that the government had over China's rebellious youngsters was evident in the ease with which it carried out its decision to redirect the energy and idealism of those who had made up the Red Guard movement. Another great campaign was announced which called on the youngsters 'to go up to the mountains and down to the villages'. They were urged to go into the countryside and live among the peasants; in this way they would both learn what life was like for 80 per cent of the Chinese people and deepen their understanding of revolution.

However, the real motive behind the slogans was much less idealistic. The government's main aim was to rid the urban areas of the gangs of delinquent youths who had threatened to become uncontrollable in the general turmoil. The campaign may also be seen as an extension of Mao's policy for making city intellectuals experience the harsh realities of life that were the common lot of the ordinary Chinese. The notion that people of privilege should learn 'the dignity of labour' was one of Mao's constant refrains.

Key date
'Up to the mountains and down to the villages' campaign: 1967–72

The experience of the young in the countryside

Whatever the ulterior motives underlying the campaign may have been, there was no doubting that it aroused a massive response. Between 1967 and 1972 over 12 million young people moved from the towns into the countryside. Their experience proved to be very different from what they had expected. Most had a very miserable time of it, being wholly unprepared for the primitive conditions they encountered. They had no countryside skills; they did not know how to grow food or rear livestock and the peasants had little food to spare for them.

As to the quality of the contribution the newcomers made to the localities, the peasants were unimpressed. A common complaint among locals was that the students did not really earn their keep and tended to regard themselves as superior beings who were making an act of heroic self-sacrifice in coming to the countryside. It is true that there were words of praise from some villagers for the efforts of the student visitors to raise literacy standards. However, this was small gain to set beside the hunger and deep homesickness most students felt. The idealism of those who made up this great experiment rarely survived the misery and appallingly low standards of living that they met; it is doubtful that more than a small minority felt they had benefited from the experience.

It was this as much as anything that made them doubt what they have never questioned before: the wisdom and goodwill of Mao Zedong. They began to realise they had been used. As one youngster recalled: 'It was only when I went to the countryside that I suddenly discovered the conflict between language and reality and this gave me a profound distrust of the language of all this state propaganda.'

Key question
How did the experience of the young people in the countryside affect their attitude towards Mao and the Cultural Revolution?

The 'cleansing the class ranks' campaign 1968–71

The dispersal of the Red Guards did not mean a weakening of the movement against the anti-Maoists. Indeed, the PLA squads who replaced the Red Guards were if anything even more vicious in their persecution of 'counter-revolutionaries'. The CCRG, with Jiang Qing's Gang of Four playing the most prominent role, developed a new campaign known as

Key question
How was the ferocity of the Cultural Revolution maintained after the dispersal of the Red Guards?

'Cleansing the class ranks' campaign: 1968–71

'cleansing the class ranks'. Committees were established in all the major regions of China and given the task of 'eradicating once and for all any signs of capitalism'. The result was an orgy of killing and destruction as grim as anything perpetrated by the Red Guards. One official described the vicious nature of it:

Pogrom
A state-organised persecution against a particular group of people.

> In some places it became a massive **pogrom** against people of exploiting class background; in some places a campaign of retribution and murder against factional rivals; and in still others a massive campaign of torture and murder to uncover wholly imaginary mass conspiracies that could involve tens of thousands.

The fearful success of the 'cleansing the class ranks' movement as a campaign of terror is evident in the body count:

- Inner Mongolia: 22,900 people were killed and 120,000 maimed
- Hebei province: 84,000 people were arrested, 2955 of whom then died after being tortured
- Yunnan: 15,000 people were 'cleansed'; of these 6979 died from their injuries
- Beijing: 3731 people were killed; these cases were officially classified as 'suicides'
- Zhejiang: 100,000 were arrested and 'struggled against'; of these 9198 were 'hounded to death'
- Binyang county in Guangxi province: 3681 were killed in a mass execution over a 10-day period.

A CCP official later admitted these grizzly details:

> In a few places, it even happened that 'counter-revolutionaries' were beaten to death and in the most beastly fashion had their flesh and liver consumed by their killers. This singular regression to a distant age of primitive savagery in the midst of what called itself the utmost revolutionary 'Great Cultural Revolution' certainly provides plenty of food for thought.

Hangzhou
A town in central China renowned for the beauty of its buildings and gardens.

Mao stepped in at this point and claimed that the excesses that were being reported must be checked. He did this for political rather than humanitarian reasons. He wanted his personal rivals and the nation's class enemies removed, but he did not want damage done to his image as China's great benefactor and champion of his people.

Key question
How much blame attaches to Mao for the horrors of the Cultural Revolution?

The question of Mao's responsibility

It is noteworthy that once Mao had begun the Cultural Revolution, he tended to remain in the background, allowing others to organise it. He spent much of his time away from Beijing, preferring to stay at rather more peaceful places like **Hangzhou**. His absence left affairs in the hands of Jiang Qing and her adherents. He said to his doctor: 'Let others stay busy with politics. Let them handle the problem of the movement by themselves.'

Mao's absence from the political centre of things meant that while the policies were carried out under his authority he was rarely involved in the everyday details. The individual acts of brutality were seldom the result of his specific orders. It may even be that, on occasion, the Cultural Revolution was pushed further than Mao had intended. He himself once said, only half-jokingly, Jiang Qing and the Gang of Four were more Maoist than he was.

But none of this absolves Mao from the responsibility for what occurred. Everything was done in his name. He could have called off the terror any time he wanted, but he chose not to. By leaving Jiang and the extremists in control, he sanctioned what they did to the Chinese people. Mao was the originator of the movement that convulsed China. Without him there would have been no Cultural Revolution with all its attendant horrors.

The fall of Lin Biao 1971–2

By the early 1970s there were signs that many Chinese were becoming disenchanted with the Cultural Revolution. Despite this, there was little open opposition to Mao. Mistakes were blamed on those responsible for implementing Mao's policies, never on Mao himself. The cult of Mao Zedong was by now so well established that, while he lived, there was no realistic chance of undermining his authority.

What happened, therefore, was that the power seekers in the CCP declared their wholehearted loyalty to the **Great Helmsman** and jockeyed for position and influence while awaiting his death which, judging from the rumours that leaked out about his declining health, could not be long delayed.

There was one major exception to the practice of wait and see. In an extraordinary set of events, Lin Biao, the nominated successor to Mao, became a victim of the Cultural Revolution that he had done so much to engineer. As is so often the case with internal Chinese politics, the exact details are difficult to determine. However, in outline what appears to have happened is that by 1971 Mao or those closest to him had become disturbed by the growing influence that Lin Biao and the PLA were acquiring under the Cultural Revolution. Mao remarked with reference to Lin, 'There is somebody who says he wants to support me, elevate me, but what he really has in mind is supporting himself, elevating himself.' As a first step towards removing them, therefore, Lin and other PLA leaders were told that they must submit themselves to self-criticism.

Lin Biao's plot against Mao

Realising that he was a marked man whose time was running out, Lin became a reluctant conspirator in an assassination plot, organised by his son, Lin Liguo, an officer in the Chinese air force. However, when Lin Liguo's sister, Dodo, leaked details of the plan to kill Mao to Zhou Enlai, a full security alert was activated and armed guards hustled Mao away for his own

Key question
In what sense was the Lin Biao affair a turning point in the Cultural Revolution?

Key term

Great Helmsman
One of the terms of adulation in which Mao was described, a reference to his unmatchable skill in steering the 'ship of state'.

Key question
What form did the plot take?

protection. With all chance of the plot's succeeding now gone, Lin Biao made a desperate bid to escape to the USSR. On 13 September 1971 the plane carrying him and his family crashed in Mongolia, killing all on board.

Whether this was an accident or sabotage remains a mystery. Mao insisted that he had not ordered the shooting down of the plane. This may well have been the truth. Mao had expressly rejected Zhou Enlai's suggestion that the aircraft be brought down. 'If we shoot the plane down, how can we explain it to the people of the whole country?' The likeliest explanation is the simplest; the plane, a British-made Trident jet, which had taken off in a great hurry without going through the full checklist, had simply run out of fuel.

Mao's reaction to the plot

Whatever the truth relating to the crash, Mao ought to have been happy with the outcome. The man he regarded as his most dangerous rival had been removed. Yet the affair seemed to depress him. He moped and became unwell. His doctor recorded that Mao 'took to his bed and lay there all day, saying and doing little. When he did get up, he seemed to have aged. His shoulders stooped and he walked with a shuffle. He could not sleep.'

The remains of the plane which crashed in Mongolia, killing Lin Biao and his family in 1971. What chain of events led to Lin Biao's dramatic end?

This may have been because he was a rapidly ageing man, prone to increasing bouts of depression, or it may have been that he truly believed that the thwarted assassination plot was an indication of how widespread the opposition to him in the party had become. It is likely that Mao, after leading his nation for 22 years, was dismayed by the realisation that special security measures were needed to protect him from his people.

The results of Lin Biao's fall

Key question
What consequences
followed from Lin
Biao's disgrace?

The news of the scandal surrounding Lin's fall was not publicly released until a year later in 1972. The announcement came in the form of a 'criticise Lin Biao and Confucius' campaign. The name of Lin Biao 'the great traitor and Soviet spy' was linked with the great reactionary figure of Chinese history. Lin, it was officially declared, had been caught hatching a 'monstrous conspiracy' against Mao and the Chinese people. The memory of his treachery would last 'for 10,000 years'.

'Criticise Lin Biao and
Confucius' campaign
began: 1972

Key date

It was this public denunciation of Lin, a man who only a short while before had been second only to Mao in popular estimation, that led many to question privately whether they could any longer believe the official pronouncements issued by the PRC authorities. Lin Biao, Mao's nominated successor, the compiler of the Little Red Book, the creator and propagator of the cult of Mao, was now to be reviled as a betrayer of his great leader and a traitor to the Cultural Revolution, the very movement that he himself had helped to form. Was this really credible, people asked themselves?

The sudden and baffling changes in the reputation of political leaders created the gravest doubts as to whether any government statement was trustworthy. A party worker later described how she and her husband had reacted:

> The revelations were shattering for me. So many of us had dedicated our lives to the future of our country, but what use were our efforts when the society was being directed by people like Lin Biao? Both my husband and I were disillusioned, aware that something was fundamentally wrong with the system in which we had believed so devotedly. I guessed that we were not the only ones whose faith in the party wavered, but no one could communicate his misgivings.

A Chen villager later admitted:

> When Liu Shaoqi was dragged down we'd been very supportive. At that time Mao Zedong was raised very high: he was the red sun and what not. But the Lin Biao affair provided us with a major lesson. We came to see that the leaders up there could say today that something is round, tomorrow, that it's flat. We lost faith in the system.

At the time, it took a very brave or very foolhardy person to say openly what many CCP members and ordinary Chinese were thinking. One who did speak out was Tu Deyong, a CCP member from Chengdu. Early in 1973, he published 'Ten Indictments against the Great Cultural Revolution', the first one of which read: 'The Great Cultural Revolution has subjected more than 90 per cent of cadres and more than 60 per cent of the masses to mindless attacks of every possible kind, political persecution, sometimes even physical ruin.' He added that the disruption caused by the revolution had damaged China's economy, worsened the people's living standards, and encouraged crime and loose morals among the young.

The inevitable happened; Tu was arrested and sentenced to life imprisonment. At his trial he said tellingly, 'if someone like me, who has really deep feelings for the party and Chairman Mao is now having thoughts like these, one can easily imagine how other people look upon the Great Cultural Revolution'.

The Cultural Revolution runs down 1972–6

Key question
Why did the intensity of the Cultural Revolution lessen after 1972?

Tu Deyong's charges against the PRC's government were powerful, but they could not be admitted by the authorities. Nevertheless, from 1972 to Mao's death in 1976 there was a noticeable lessening of the extremism with which the pogroms and persecutions were conducted. There are a number of explanations for this:

- a general uncertainty in the party about the ailing Mao's true intentions
- the effect of the Lin Biao affair which led to a rethink in the CCP about how severe its policies should be
- an unacknowledged recognition by the party that the points made by critics such as Tu Deyong were an accurate description of the harmful effects of the Cultural Revolution
- the wish to impress the USA, whose president, Richard Nixon, made an official visit to the PRC in 1972 (see page 153).

The return of Zhou Enlai and Deng Xiaoping

Key question
How did Lin Biao's fall benefit Zhou Enlai and Deng Xiaoping?

One important effect of Lin Biao's dramatic end was the enhancement of Zhou Enlai's position in the government and party. Zhou Enlai had played a key part in uncovering the plot against Mao. Zhou was one of the great survivors of Chinese politics. His shrewd sense of political judgement and genuine popularity enabled him to evade the attempts made to bring him down during the Cultural Revolution. It was Zhou who had worked to prevent the fracturing of the party during the power struggles of the 1960s and it was he who became recognised as an outstanding international statesman in the 1970s.

Key date
Deng Xiaoping brought back into government: 1973

Key term

Capitalist roader
Those who wished to see the economy modernised on capitalist lines.

Lin's fall also benefited Deng Xiaoping, another great survivor in the cut-throat world of PRC politics. His earlier dismissal for having been a '**capitalist roader**' now worked to his advantage. In 1973, Zhou Enlai, who had great respect for Deng's detailed knowledge of the workings of the CCP, invited him to re-enter the government. By 1975 Deng had regained his place as Party Secretary. But his rehabilitation did not go unchallenged. Jiang Qing and the Maoists, disturbed by the grip that the moderates appeared to be regaining, turned the 'criticise Lin Biao and Confucius' campaign into an attack on 'the pragmatist clique', a reference to Zhou and Deng.

The return of Zhou Enlai and Deng Xiaoping following the fall of Lin Biao meant that the Cultural Revolution was less savagely enforced after 1973. But it was far from being abandoned. Arrests of suspected persons continued and the prison camps went on expanding. The truth was that as long as the CCRG, dominated by Jiang Qing's hardline Gang of Four, had Mao's support, the Cultural Revolution would continue.

Mao and the Cultural Revolution

It is an obvious truth Mao did not carry out the Cultural Revolution on his own. It needed countless others to implement it. What were the motives of such people? Perhaps the enthusiasm and extremism with which the policy was pursued is explained by long-existing local rivalries and personal vendettas. It is known that Stalin's purges in the USSR could not have been carried out without the willingness of so many to engage in exploitation and terror.

Yet any analysis must focus on Mao Zedong himself. So much of the Cultural Revolution was organised hatred. This began with Mao himself in whom there was a strong element of paranoia. None of his colleagues could relax; even his most devoted supporters fell foul of his suspicions. Mao often spoke of the ruthlessness with which China's revolution had to be pursued. He drew parallels between his own position and that of the ferocious, but effective, Emperor **Qin Shi Huang**.

The comparison was appropriate; Qin had traditionally been described as one of the bloodiest rulers in Chinese history. Li Rui, who had been a personal secretary to Mao in the early years of the PRC, defined the Cultural Revolution as 'Marx plus Emperor Qin'. It was a fitting reference to the continuity between Mao's Communist absolutism and the traditional authoritarianism of the emperors.

Key question
What does the Cultural Revolution indicate about Mao's character and personality?

Qin Shi Huang (ruled from 221 to 210 BC) The emperor whose violent reign brought about the unification of the Han state, often regarded as the birth of China as a nation. His huge terracotta army, which was unearthed at Xian (Sian) in the twentieth century, is one of China's most famous historical sites.

Key figure

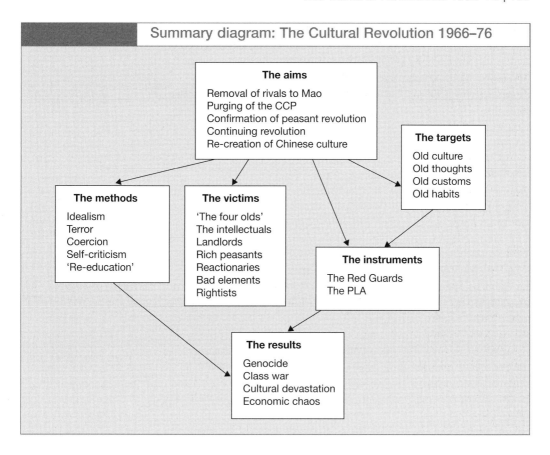

Summary diagram: The Cultural Revolution 1966–76

The aims
Removal of rivals to Mao
Purging of the CCP
Confirmation of peasant revolution
Continuing revolution
Re-creation of Chinese culture

The targets
Old culture
Old thoughts
Old customs
Old habits

The methods
Idealism
Terror
Coercion
Self-criticism
'Re-education'

The victims
'The four olds'
The intellectuals
Landlords
Rich peasants
Reactionaries
Bad elements
Rightists

The instruments
The Red Guards
The PLA

The results
Genocide
Class war
Cultural devastation
Economic chaos

3 | The End of the Mao Era

Key question
How did the Gang of Four try to assert their authority during Mao's final days?

Key dates
Death of Zhou Enlai: January 1976

The 'Tiananmen incident': April 1976

Key term
Heroes Monument
A large shrine, commemorating the great deeds of China's revolutionary past, at the southern end of Tiananmen Square in Beijing.

The influence that Jiang and the Maoists still exercised during the final phase of the Cultural Revolution was evident in the crisis that followed the death of Zhou Enlai in January 1976. (Zhou died from lung cancer after Mao, who had a distrust of surgery, refused to allow him to have an operation.) With his moderating influence now removed, the power struggle took another turn. In April, the memorial service for Zhou, held in the Great Hall of the People facing Tiananmen Square, became the occasion for a large-scale demonstration in favour of the policies that Zhou had advocated. Tens of thousands flocked into the square to lay wreaths and pictures of Zhou around the **Heroes Monument**.

This spontaneous gathering of people was in defiance of an official order that there should be no public displays of mourning. Speeches were made at the monument; these became increasingly bolder in tone, graduating from praise of Zhou Enlai for his wise statesmanship to attacks on the government for its corruption. Fearing that the demonstration might get out of hand, the Mayor of Beijing ordered riot police to remove the flowers and tributes and disperse the crowds. When some of the demonstrators resisted the police used force. Scattered, but violent and bloody, confrontations took place before the police managed to clear the square.

The Politburo condemned this 'Tiananmen incident' as the work of rightist agitators and laid a large part of the blame on Deng Xiaoping, whom they dismissed from his position as Party Secretary. Although he had not been present at the demonstration, Deng chose not to risk defending himself; instead he removed himself from the political scene by hastily leaving Beijing for Guangdong province, from where he would wait on events.

The death of Mao Zedong, September 1976

No clear lead came from Mao Zedong on how to handle the Tiananmen incident for the simple reason that during the final year of his life he was rarely capable of giving a lead. His doctor, Li Zhisui, subsequently revealed that, during the final 3 years of his life, Mao was sustained only by massive injections of drugs that left him comatose for much of the time. The term 'helmsman' has a particular irony, for Mao was quite unable to govern. It was this situation that gave such influence to his close attendants. They became the interpreters of his barely coherent statements.

Yet, even though he was incapacitated his power remained. In an odd way it was actually increased. Since he was so often enfeebled, it became increasingly difficult to know exactly what his ideas and instructions actually were. This had two conflicting consequences:

- it paralysed the fearful into inaction since they were frightened of taking steps that Mao might later condemn in one of his rational moments
- it encouraged those who believed that Mao would never recover to try to manoeuvre themselves into a position from which they could subsequently seize power.

The uncertain situation left Jiang Qing and the Gang of Four in effective control. However, their authority depended wholly on their closeness to Mao. Once he had died everything was at hazard and there was no certainty about what would happen.

Given Mao's god-like status, it was somehow fitting that his death in September 1976 should have been preceded six weeks earlier by what many saw as an omen – a massive earthquake in Tangshan, an industrial city in Hebei province, which caused the death of a quarter of a million of its inhabitants. People recalled that in Chinese folklore earthquakes, 'the speaking of the dragon', denoted the advent of great changes in the state. Mao had been deified in his own lifetime and when gods die the succession – as events were to show – becomes a troubled affair.

Key question
How did Mao's physical decline and death alter the power balance in the PRC?

Death of Mao Zedong: September 1976

Key date

Study Guide: AS Questions

In the style of AQA

Source A

A former Red Guard remembers how he felt at the time of the Cultural Revolution in 1966. Quoted in 'China's Cultural Revolution', BBC World Service broadcast, August 1997.

Now it was our generation's turn to defend China. China was the only country which wasn't revisionist, capitalist or colonialist. We felt that we were defending China's revolution and liberating the world. All the big slogans made a generation of us feel that the Cultural Revolution really was a war, a war to defend Chairman Mao and the new China.

Source B

Anthony Grey, a Reuters correspondent in China, who was seized by the Red Guards in 1966 and confined for months to his cramped one-room flat in Beijing, records the extraordinary influence Mao had over the Chinese people. From Anthony Grey, Hostage in Peking *published in 1970.*

The most extravagant and ridiculous language was used all the time about him in the official press. I remember I saw him once on May Day; I was in a crowd in the park and I was talking to members of the crowd and I was saying, 'What were you hoping to see?' they said 'Chairman Mao, we love Chairman Mao'. And they really did say it in a way that made me think of the tendency of young people who want something to idolise, be it pop singers or film stars or in their case only one charismatic individual in a nation. He had managed to work a great spell over the people. I think he used the old admiration for China's emperors and the son of heaven idea which was very strong – inculcated almost into the Chinese nature.

Source C

A woman recalls how, as a schoolgirl, she was caught up in the violent atmosphere of the Cultural Revolution in 1966. Quoted in 'China's Cultural Revolution', BBC World Service broadcast, published in 1997.

One time on my way home I saw some Red Guards arresting a young girl. They said she was a bad element. Whether she was or not was beside the point. Someone said she was a baddie and that was enough. So they were using their belts to beat her up. I was a Red Guard, too, and my first thought was that I must express my revolutionary spirit. I took off my belt and lifted it high as if I too was taking part in the beating. I couldn't actually bring myself to hit her but I knew I had to look as if I was. If you didn't beat people you weren't showing a proper hatred for the enemy or a proper love for the people.

(a) Explain how far the views in Source B differ from those in Source A in relation to why the youth of China supported Mao's cultural revolution. (12 marks)

(b) How important were Chinese youth to the success of Mao's cultural revolution to 1972? (24 marks)

Exam tips

The cross-references are designed to take you straight to the material that will help you answer the question.

(a) This question focuses on views so you will need to read both sources carefully and come to a conclusion about the standpoints before you begin. When you write your answer you should explain any differences with support from the material within both sources and should also point out any underlying similarities. This will enable you to comment on 'how far' the views differ.

   The perspective in Source B is obviously different from Source A because the writer is looking at events from an 'outsider's' view. He is a British journalist with a grudge against a regime that had imprisoned him and he sees the adulation of youth and a product of the young people's need for 'something to idolise' whereas the 'insider' in Source A – a Red Guard – has an ideological explanation for youth support. It links the Cultural Revolution with a war for China and for Communism. By making comparisons such as these you will be able to show you understand the different perspectives of these sources. However, you can also point out that they both show the great fervour of the young people of China at this time. In both cases, the young are prepared to turn out to support, are almost 'intoxicated' by what is going on and are influenced by propaganda and the charisma of Mao.

(b) To answer this question successfully, you will need to look at the contribution of Chinese youth and to other factors. You will then need to reach a balanced conclusion. Don't forget that you will also need to cite the three given sources as evidence.

In support of the importance of Chinese youth, you should consider the activities of:

- the Red Guards (page 85 and Sources A and C)
- the university students (e.g. page 93 and Source C)
- family members, schoolchildren and others; enlisting the young (page 79); the 'four olds' (page 81); testing the young (page 83).

And examine the part the youth played in:

- the denunciations (pages 89–90)
- savagery and vandalism (pages 92–3 and Source C)
- attacks on foreigners (pages 93–4)
- living among peasants (page 95–6).

You might also want to consider the idealism of youth (Source A) and the power of conformity (Source B).

To balance your answer, try to think of other factors that contributed to the success of the cultural revolution:

- Mao himself
- workers and officials – the CCRG
- the PLA
- propaganda (Source B could be cited again here)
- repression.

You would also need to refer to the way the youngsters were brought under control (pages 95–6).

You will need to decide whether the youth were important on their own account or were merely 'used' by Mao and others. Source C might prove useful here in explaining youth sentiment.

In the style of Edexcel

How far were threats to Mao's position in 1966 from rivals within the CCP responsible for Mao's decision to launch the Cultural Revolution?   (30 marks)

Exam tips

The cross-references are designed to take you straight to the material that will help you answer the question.

The key words for you to consider when planning your answer to this question are 'threats to Mao's position in 1966' and 'responsible for the decision'. This is a question requiring you to explain why the Cultural Revolution was launched and it requires a judgement from you about whether what motivated Mao was something more than a short-term power struggle within the CCP.

- You could plan first to deal with the nature of the power struggle among China's élite and consider whether Mao's position was under threat. The power struggle 1962–6 and divisions within the leadership of the CCP (pages 73 and 75); the role of Jiang Qing (page 76); and the motives for the setting up of the CCRG (page 77) are relevant here.
- However, Mao's objectives can be seen to go further than a desire to gain the upper hand over his rivals in the short term. His objectives relate to his determination to: preserve his legacy and image (page 82); protect the gains of the revolution by instilling a spirit of permanent evolution (pages 82 and 83); prevent the de-Stalinising influence of the USSR from provoking a similar attack on his own leadership in China; remove all possible future sources of opposition (pages 82 and 83).
- Be sure to focus on Mao's key motives when coming to your conclusion. You should round off your answer by offering your judgement – do you agree with the significance attached to the key factor given in the question? You may want to argue that something as wholesale and fundamental as the movement Mao set in train in 1966 had more than short-term objectives.

5 Life in Mao's China 1949–76

POINTS TO CONSIDER
Mao's period of rule had a profound impact on the ordinary people of China. To illustrate this, the following themes have been selected for analysis in this chapter:

- Religion in the PRC
- The status of women and the family
- The reshaping of Chinese culture
- Education and health
- Mao's prison camps: the *laogai*

Key dates

1949–76	Number of women workers quadrupled
	Literacy rate rose from 20 to 70 per cent
1950	Start of the authorities' campaign against religion
	New marriage law
1955	Reform of the Mandarin language
1958	CCP condemnation of the family as the basic social unit
1958–62	Chinese famine
1966–76	The Cultural Revolution
1973	One million barefoot doctors trained

1 | Religion in the PRC

Key question
Why did the Chinese Communists regard religion as a threat?

As a form of Marxism, Chinese Communism considered religious belief and worship to be superstitions that throughout history had been deliberately cultivated by the classes in power to suppress the exploited people. Religion with its promise of eternal happiness in the afterlife was a powerful force persuading the workers to put up with their grim lives without protest; the more they suffered in the here and now the greater would be their reward in heaven.

Mao Zedong expressed his strong personal antipathy to religion by declaring that it was poison and comparing the Christian missionaries in China to the Nazis in Europe. It was logical, therefore, and to be expected that the PRC under Mao would not tolerate religion.

Almost immediately after the Chinese Communists came to power, the attack on religion began. The officially stated justification was since the workers were now in power there was no longer any reason for religion to exist; the triumph of the workers had ended the need for such escapism. For religion to continue openly would be an affront to the new Chinese Communist world. The authorities would not tolerate the people's continuing adherence to a corrupt thought process. Religious worship had now to be replaced by loyalty to the Communist Party and the state.

Start of the authorities' campaign against religion: 1950

Key date

State attacks on religion

Christian churches were forcibly closed, their property seized or destroyed and their ministers physically abused. Foreign priests and nuns were expelled from China. Wall posters, the traditional way by which Chinese governments spread their propaganda, and loud speakers at every corner kept up a running condemnation of religion.

Key question
What measures did the authorities take to suppress religion?

Buddhist monks are paraded to be mocked and humiliated at a temple in Harbin in August 1966. The banners say such things as 'Eradicate the ghosts and demons', 'What are these Buddhist sutras? Just a collection of dog farts'. Why should Buddhism have been selected for special attack by the Communist authorities?

Key terms

Buddhism
An ancient Chinese philosophy, which laid great stress on the individual's gaining enlightenment through meditation.

Slogan-ridden society
The Soviet Union, particularly under Stalin, used mass public propaganda in order to train the people into conformity and obedience.

Confucianism, **Buddhism** and Christianity were denounced as worthless superstitions that had no place in the new nation. Slogans proclaiming the virtues of the new Maoist China were to be seen everywhere. China, possibly even more than the USSR, became a **slogan-ridden society**. The slogans became more than simply a way of exhorting the comrades to ever-greater efforts; they were a means of enforcing solidarity and conformity.

The peasants, the largest and most religious segment of China's population, were the first to be targeted. Beginning in 1950, a sustained campaign was launched to eliminate all traces of religion from their lives. The Chinese traditional faiths, Buddhism and Confucianism, were forbidden to be openly practised, as were the major foreign religions, Christianity and Islam. Priests and monks were prohibited from wearing their distinctive dress; any who disobeyed this order were liable to arrest and imprisonment.

There were cases of the police encouraging bystanders to strip the clothes off the clergy who dared to walk abroad in their traditional distinctive garb. Foreign clergy were expelled from China, and temples, churches, shrines and monasteries were closed down or turned into offices and public buildings. **Ancestor worship** was also condemned as a superstition that was no longer acceptable in the new China.

Attacks on Chinese customs and traditions

Key question
How was propaganda used to undermine traditional ways?

It was not merely the formal expressions of belief that were outlawed. The customs and rituals that had helped to shape the life of the peasants were proscribed. These included the songs and dances they had performed at weddings and festivals, the chants that had accompanied their work in the fields, and the sagas and narratives with which the wandering poets had entertained whole villages. These traditional ways were replaced with political meetings and discussions organised by the party. The huge social experiment of collectivisation that Mao introduced in the 1950s was meant to destroy the time-honoured pattern of rural life.

Key terms

Ancestor worship
The practice of paying respect to the deceased members of the family in a simple ceremony of remembrance. In the West this has sometimes been confused with the Christian practice of praying to the dead to ask for help.

Agit-prop
Short for 'agitation propaganda': the imposition of political ideas through entertainment.

The peasants were now expected to embrace Maoism as their new faith. Troupes of **agit-prop** performers toured the countryside putting on shows and plays which the villagers were required to attend and sit through. The shows were put on in halls and public spaces. Sometimes the players arrived in brightly painted trucks carrying slogans and images extolling the wonders and benefits of the new Maoist world. The sides of the truck could serve as a screen on which propaganda films were projected after dark or they could be removed to convert the truck into a stage.

The message in the propaganda
The message of the films and the live performances was always the same; it hammered home the notion that the old days of cruel landlords and abused peasant farmers had been replaced with a communal way of life in which the peasants, guided by the wisdom of Mao Zedong and the Communist Party, had entered an

era of happy collective endeavour and achievement. The shows were played at knockabout pantomime level; the baddies were always bad, the goodies were always good. The landlords were obviously the worst of the baddies, but religious figures such as scheming Confucian officials and exploiting priests also appeared to be hissed at and jeered.

The patriotic churches

Mao and the authorities were shrewd enough to realise that there could be advantages for them in permitting some forms of public worship to continue. It would give the appearance of toleration. It was laid down that some churches could remain open provided that they 'did not endanger the security of the state'. What this meant in practice was they became state controlled. Known as the 'patriotic churches', the clergy had to profess open support for the Communist regime and accept that the authorities had the right to dictate doctrine and appoint their clergy.

Key question
What was the purpose behind the creation of the patriotic churches?

The PRC's clash with the Vatican

One consequence of the state sponsoring of the patriotic churches was a sharpening of conflict between the PRC and the **Vatican**. The persecution of the Catholic Church in Mao's China, which involved the seizure and closure of churches and chapels and the imprisonment or expulsion of priests and nuns, was condemned by the **Papacy**, which made a particular point of rejecting the notion of the 'patriotic church' as a genuine form of Catholicism. Bishops and priests appointed by the Chinese state would not be recognised by Rome and risked **excommunication**. In 2007, the dispute between Beijing and Rome over this issue had still not been resolved.

Key terms

Vatican
The spiritual and administrative centre of the Catholic Church in Rome, where the Pope has his official residence.

Papacy
The Catholic Church's system of government, headed by the Pope.

Excommunication
Formal dismissal from the Catholic Church.

Religious persecution during the Cultural Revolution

The PRC's decision to allow a semblance of religion to remain was an unadmitted recognition that religious faith was so deep-rooted in Chinese tradition that it would be unrealistic to think that it could be eradicated entirely. Nevertheless, the persecution continued. During the Cultural Revolution, religion was denounced as belonging to the 'four olds' and the attack on it intensified. No public worship or ceremony was allowed and any clergy who had survived the earlier persecutions were rounded up and imprisoned.

Key question
Why was persecution intensified during the Cultural Revolution?

So severe was the repression that it provoked an international outcry. Representatives of the world's major faiths, **denominations** and philosophies called on the PRC to call off the persecutions and show humanity.

Key term

Denominations
Separate groups within a faith, e.g. Catholicism and Protestantism within Christianity.

Campaigns against 'Confucius and Co'

There was little response from Mao's government to the appeals, save to describe them as the product of capitalist distortions and anti-Chinese malice. The suppression of religion continued. Confucianism was denounced as representing all that was worst in

China's past. The name of Confucius was linked to any person or movement that the authorities wished to denounce. 'Confucius and Co' became a standard term of abuse directed at any suspect group or organisation. Significantly, when Lin Biao came under fire during the Cultural Revolution, the slogan coined to attack him was 'criticise Lin Biao and Confucius' (see page 100).

Religion and the movement for regional independence

Key question
How did religion and regionalism overlap in China?

A basic fear of the PRC government was that religion might encourage the breakaway tendencies in the western provinces. From the beginning of its rule in 1949, the PRC let it be known in the most ruthless terms that it would not grant independence to any of its provinces or regions. That is why in 1950 it sent the PLA into Tibet, Xinjiang and Guangdong to enforce its authority (see page 20). It claimed that the strength, indeed the survival, of the People's Republic of China as a nation demanded total unity and obedience to central control.

This had special reference to the PRC's outlying western provinces, Tibet and Xinjiang, areas larger in size than western Europe. It was Tibet's Lama faith, a particular form of Buddhism that inspired Tibetan nationalism in its resistance to Chinese occupation (see page 65). The PRC fretted that religion and nationalism would prove an equally dangerous mix in Tibet's northern neighbour, Xinjiang. Here the majority of the population was made up of the Uighur, Kazakh, Hui and Kirghiz peoples, who were all devoted Muslims.

What added to Chinese fears was the strategic position of Xinjiang, on whose western borders lay Pakistan, Tajikistan and Kazakhstan, all of them strongly Muslim countries. Beijing's understandable and realistic concern was that religious belief would combine with politics to create a dangerous separatist movement in Xinjiang, backed by these border countries.

In a major effort to prevent this, the PRC condemned all independence organisations in China's border regions as 'handfuls of national separatists' with 'reactionary feudal ideas' who were in league with 'hostile foreign forces'; their aim was to split and weaken the Chinese nation itself. The government adopted the same policy that it had in Tibet (see page 65); it tried to dilute the Muslim element in the population by settling large numbers of Han Chinese in the region. This proved only partially successful. At the time of Mao's death in 1976, the Muslim proportion still formed a majority of the Xinjiang population.

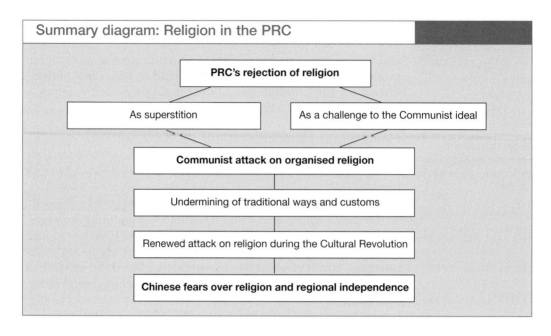

Summary diagram: Religion in the PRC

```
                    ┌─────────────────────────────┐
                    │ PRC's rejection of religion │
                    └─────────────────────────────┘
                       ↙                       ↘
        ┌──────────────────────┐   ┌──────────────────────────────────┐
        │   As superstition    │   │ As a challenge to the Communist ideal │
        └──────────────────────┘   └──────────────────────────────────┘
                       ↘                       ↙
              ┌─────────────────────────────────────────┐
              │ Communist attack on organised religion  │
              └─────────────────────────────────────────┘
                                 │
              ┌─────────────────────────────────────────┐
              │ Undermining of traditional ways and customs │
              └─────────────────────────────────────────┘
                                 │
              ┌─────────────────────────────────────────┐
              │ Renewed attack on religion during the Cultural Revolution │
              └─────────────────────────────────────────┘
                                 │
              ┌──────────────────────────────────────────────────┐
              │ Chinese fears over religion and regional independence │
              └──────────────────────────────────────────────────┘
```

2 | The Status of Women and the Family

Imperial China, the nation in which Mao Zedong grew up, was a **patriarchal** society. Confucius had taught that to be balanced and harmonious a society must follow the rules of the *san gang*:

- loyalty of ministers and officials to the emperor
- respect of children for their parents
- obedience of wives to their husbands.

As a result, it had become traditional for women to be discriminated against in China. To be sure, there were instances of females playing a leading role in public life; one example was **Cixi**. But this was very much an exception. For the most part women played a subordinate role.

Mao and women

Mao Zedong's own story is illuminating. A striking example of how women, and in this case young men, were expected to conform to the *san gang* was Mao's betrothal in 1907, when he was barely 14 years old, to a woman 7 years his senior. Arranged marriages were the practice in rural China. Whether the young couple liked each other or had even met was not a consideration. The arrangement was essentially a financial one between the two families.

Key question
How did Mao's personal experience shape his attitude towards women in China?

Key terms

Patriarchal
Male dominated.

San gang
The three relationships that in Confucian theory held society together.

Key figure

Cixi
(1835–1908) The Empress Dowager who, in effect, ruled for most of the final 20 years of the Qing dynasty.

Key terms

Bride-price
The money paid to the bride's family, based on a calculation of how many children she would have.

Foot binding
The tight bandaging of the feet to prevent their growth. This had two purposes: to hobble the women so that they could not get about and to make them more attractive to men, who traditionally regarded small feet as highly erotic.

In the event, Mao, a natural rebel, who was always at odds with his father, refused to go through with the betrothal, let alone the marriage, even though the **bride-price** had been paid. Mao's stand over this was later used in CCP propaganda as a stirring example of his fight against a corrupt social system in which women were treated as commodities not people.

Mao's fight against the practice of forced marriages

It was as a defender of women's rights that Mao became involved in 1919 in a notorious affair in Changsha, the principal city of his home province of Hunan. A young woman, forced by her family to marry a wealthy man she did not like, waited until the wedding morning, when all the guests had gathered, before cutting her throat and bleeding to death. A furious debate followed in Changsha. Half the people of the city condemned the girl for bringing disgrace on her family; the other half praised her for acting according to her sense of honour.

Mao seized on the incident as evidence of, in his words, 'the rottenness of the marriage system and the darkness of the social system' that had driven a young woman to take her own life. In a series of articles, he condemned arranged marriages as 'indirect rape'. Women, he said, had been 'relegated to the dark corners of society'. He gave bitter descriptions of how they were exploited by China's marriage customs that turned a wife into the slave of her husband and his family.

Key question
How committed to female emancipation were Mao and the Communists?

The CCP and women's rights

Mao's powerful argument suggested that he was a firm believer in women's rights. It was certainly the case that in the Jiangxi and Yanan soviets that he led in the 1930s and 1940s Mao had insisted that women were the equals of men. The party under him formally outlawed the practice of **foot binding** that had survived in parts of China until the 1940s.

However, it has to be said that in practice Mao and the party often failed to respect the principle of female equality. In his personal life Mao tended either to use women or to patronise them. Having been a puritanical young man who was uncomfortable in female company, Mao became a notorious womaniser in his later years. Whatever their official statements, the Chinese Communists operated what was very much a male-dominated system. Few of the important posts in the party organisation went to women. Foreign visitors to the Communist base at Yanan noted how the domestic chores were invariably carried out by the female comrades.

Ding Ling, who had joined the Communists in Yanan, described Mao and the CCP as hypocrites. She asserted that, contrary to their claim to be revolutionaries, they lived comfortable lives at Yanan exploiting the women who worked for them. Although she had been initially supportive of Mao, she came to believe that Mao's brand of socialism did not truly include female emancipation.

Key figure

Ding Ling
(1904–85) An intellectual and China's leading feminist writer, who had so impressed Mao that in 1936 he had written a poem about her which ended: 'Yesterday a literary young lady, Today a warlike general.'

Marriage reform under Mao in the 1950s

Whatever the truth of Ding Ling's accusation, it was to be expected that, in view of his impressive public record in supporting female rights, Mao would support practical measures to help women once he was in power. And so it proved. One of the first acts of the PRC was to introduce a new marriage law in 1950. This laid down that:

- **concubinage** was abolished
- arranged marriages were to be discontinued
- the paying of dowries and bride-prices was forbidden
- women (and men) who had been previously forced to marry were entitled to divorce their partners
- all marriages had to be officially recorded and registered.

In a spirit of great enthusiasm, many women used their new freedom to divorce and remarry a number of times. There were cases of women taking as many as four different husbands in as many years. This threatened to prove so disruptive that a special clause was added to PLA regulations giving the soldiers the legal right to overrule their wives' plea for a divorce.

The impact of collectivisation on the status of women

Further laws passed in the 1950s granted women the right to own and sell land and property. In the land redistribution which followed the seizure of the properties of the landlords, women were actually granted land in their own name. This seemed to be a major advance since it broke the tradition whereby all property dealings had been controlled by the men in the family. However, much of this apparent gain was undermined by Mao's massive collectivisation programme that had ended the holding of private property by either men or women and required people to live in communes (see page 55).

Interestingly, life in the communes did bring women one immediate advantage. The rule now was that everybody should eat in common in mess halls; this meant that women no longer had the daily drudgery of finding food and preparing it for the family. This was described in a poem from a woman that appeared in a magazine in 1958:

> Nurseries, kindergartens, tailor shops,
> You don't do the cooking or feed the pigs the slops.
> Machines make the clothing and grind the flour.
> When you give birth to a baby it's cared for every hour.
> Freed from household drudgery, let's produce more by the day.
> And drive ahead to communism, it isn't far away!

Are there any reasons for thinking that the poem is not to be taken too seriously?

Key question
How did the changes in the marriage laws affect the status of women?

Key date
New marriage law: 1950

Key term
Concubinage
The practice of men keeping women, not as wives but as mistresses (concubines).

Key question
Did women gain or lose from collectivisation?

Key date

Number of women workers quadrupled: 1949–76

Disadvantages balance the gains

Yet for every gain that women appeared to make there seemed to be an accompanying disadvantage. Now that they were officially regarded in Mao's China as the equals of men, they could be called on to do the work of men. Between 1949 and 1976, the proportion of women in the workforce quadrupled from 8 to 32 per cent. This might bring them advantages if the work was suitable, but if it was inappropriate heavy physical labour that they were offered then they were worse off than before.

Ingrained prejudice against women

The hard truth was that social values and attitudes cannot be changed overnight in any country. China was by deep-seated tradition a male-dominated society; no matter how genuine the new Communist regime might be in declaring that the sexes were equal, women were still having to compete with Chinese ingrained notions of female inferiority.

This was clearly evident in the common prejudice against female babies. It was the wish of nearly all Chinese couples to have male children. This desire derived from a mixture of pride and economic interest. The birth of a boy was thought to bring honour on the family, and the promise of another source of income; girls were seen as a drain on resources.

Unchanging peasant attitudes

Peasants complained that the new marriage laws were interfering with the established ways of life. The idea that the female was subordinate to the male was strongly held in all China's rural areas, but especially so in the western provinces where there was a predominantly Muslim culture. In areas such as Xinjiang, families, in accordance with Muslim teaching, were tightly controlled by the men; female members were subject to the orders of husbands, fathers and brothers, and even brothers-in-law, and were likely to be beaten if they disobeyed or showed too much independence of thought.

As late as 2005, Chang Zhen, the representative of the All China Women's Federation described the outlook of Xinjiang's four million women as being like a frog in a well: 'All they can see is a tiny bit of sky, so their outlook is very narrow. A woman is treated as a man's possession. It is the duty of a woman to look after him, whether he is working the fields or in the house.'

Restrictions on women remained

There is also the consideration that, as Ding Ling had earlier suggested, the Communist authorities may not have been as committed to gender equality as they claimed. **Song Qingling**, one of the few women to hold a high position in the PRC government under Mao, later complained that her Communist colleagues did not really treat her as an equal and did not accept that women comrades could play key roles in government and party.

Key figure

Song Qingling
One of a remarkable set of sisters who became prominent in Chinese politics. Qingling had been the wife of the Nationalist leader, Sun Yatsen, while her sister, Meiling, was married to Mao's great rival, Chiang Kaishek.

During Mao's time, women made up only 13 per cent of the membership of the Communist Party. The number of women who became members of the National People's Congress did rise during Mao's period of power (see Table 5.1) but never on such a scale as to suggest that the Communist Party had made a priority of promoting females within its ranks.

Women and the family

In addition to women's being denied a fuller political role, there was a deeper sense in which the policies followed under Mao prevented China's women from making a sustained advance in their status and conditions. If anything, the radical and invariably violent character of the reforms introduced increased their vulnerability.

Collectivisation entailed a direct and deliberate assault on the traditional Chinese family. Mao had already prepared the way for this as early as 1944 when he had stated that 'It is necessary to destroy the peasant family; women going to the factories and joining the army are part of the big destruction of the family.' The prohibiting of ancestor worship, which was part of the attack on religion (see page 109), was intended as a blow against the family as a social unit with its historical roots and deep emotional attachments.

No matter how much women wanted freedom, few of them felt happy that their role as mothers and raisers of families was now to be written off as no longer being necessary. It seemed to go against nature. So determined was the Communist Party to undermine the family that in many of the communes men and women were made to live in separate quarters and allowed to see each other only for **conjugal visits**. An official party statement of 1958 left no doubts over the purpose of such restrictions:

> The framework of the individual family, which has existed for thousands of years has been shattered for all time. We must regard the People's Commune as our family and not pay too much attention to the formation of a separate family of our own.

The same document went on to attempt to elevate the role of women in the new China:

> For years motherly love has been glorified, but it is wrong to degrade a person from a social to a biological creature. The dearest people in the world are our parents, yet they cannot be compared with Chairman Mao and the Communist Party, for it is not the family which has given us everything but the Communist Party and the revolution. Personal love is not so important.

While in some respects this might be considered liberating since women might be freed from the family ties that had restricted them, there was a downside to it. The enforced social change had

Table 5.1: Percentage of women deputies in the National People's Congress

1954	14%
1959	14%
1964	17%
1975	23%

Key question
How did the PRC's undermining of the family as a unit affect women's status?

Conjugal visits
Time set aside for couples to have sexual relations.

Key term

CCP condemnation of the family as the basic social unit: 1958

Key date

happened all too suddenly. The Chinese, a profoundly conservative people, became disorientated; women found themselves detached from their traditional moorings. The famine that struck so many parts of China in the wake of the Great Leap Forward deepened this sense of helplessness.

Key question
Why were women particularly vulnerable in the famine?

Key date

Chinese famine: 1958–62

The impact of the famine on women and the family

It was women who suffered most in the famine that devastated China between 1958 and 1962, as they found themselves trapped in a tragedy that simply overwhelmed them. Circumstances made it impossible for them to remain the providers for their children. The psychological shock suffered by the mothers caught up in the events is frighteningly described in the following extract from an eyewitness account of the famine in Anhui province:

> Parents would decide to allow the old and the young to die first. They thought they could not allow their sons to die but a mother would say to a daughter, 'You have to go and see your granny in heaven'. They stopped giving the girl food. Then they swapped the body of their daughter with that of a neighbour's. About five to seven women would agree to do this amongst themselves. Then they boiled the corpses into a kind of soup. People accepted this as it was a kind of hunger culture.

Divorce and wife-selling

The impossibility of maintaining anything approaching a normal married life in such circumstances was reflected in the divorce figures during the famine period. In Gansu province, for example, the divorce rate rose by 60 per cent. This did not always denote a breakdown of personal relationships, but rather that as the family ran out of food the couple judged it better for the wife to leave and look for a husband elsewhere. Her starving family would at least have the little bit of food that she would have eaten had she stayed. Divorce was an alternative to wife-selling, which became common in the famine areas. As one report stated:

> The poorer the region, the greater the amount of wife-selling. To hide the shame, the wives were called cousins. If the chief family earner died, a teenage daughter might be sold to the highest bidder in a distant place to obtain grain to keep the rest of the household alive.

The family disruption that the buying and selling of wives often caused became clear after the famine had eased by the middle 1960s. Wives often refused to go back to their original husbands, preferring the new life they had made.

In Hebei, Sichuan and Gansu provinces, there was a stream of court cases in which husbands appealed for decisions that would return their former wives to them. In most instances the courts found for the husbands, but this was by no means guaranteed. A number of women resisted being forced to return and were supported by the courts.

The tragic consequences for children

One of the most tragic consequences of the wives' leaving home was that the children of the family were left motherless. This often led to their being sold or abandoned. Youngsters who were old enough to be useful were sold as workers, a practice which was, in effect, slavery.

But at least such children had a chance of survival. It was the very young who suffered most from being deserted. A nurse in Lanzhou, the main city in Gansu, described how on a hospital stairway she came across a tattered cardboard box; inside this crude manger lay a baby girl. Pinned to the dirty rags in which she was dressed was a roughly pencilled note: 'To kind-hearted people, please look after her. From a mother who regrets her faults.'

At first, it was girl infants who were dumped in hospitals, at railway stations, or simply by the road side, but as the famine grew worse boys, too, were abandoned. A Gansu villager described a heart-rending scene:

> The road from the village to the neighbouring province was strewn with bodies, and piercing wails came from holes on either sides of the road. Following the cries, you could see the tops of heads of children who were abandoned in those holes. A lot of parents thought their children had a better chance of surviving if they were adopted by somebody else. The holes were just deep enough so that the children could not get out, but could be seen by passers-by who might adopt them.

Child abuse and prostitution

Even when abandoned children were saved, their lives could then be wretched. A 6-year-old girl was picked up in Anhui by a worker who took her back to his family in Nanjing who treated her so badly, teasing and mocking her and forcing her to work as a skivvy, that her heart broke under the weight of the misery and she killed herself. Abandoned children were obvious targets for exploitation and sexual abuse. One example of a predator was a Communist Party official in Hefei who bought a young girl from a starving family and proceeded to make her his sexual plaything. His behaviour was too much even for a party that was used to ignoring or covering up its members' scandals and he was dismissed.

The party were also involved in the spread of prostitution, which, like wife-selling, became more widespread as the famine bit deeper. In the worst-hit regions women openly offered themselves for sex in return for food. Using the opportunity for exploitation that this provided, CCP workers in Anhui set up a series of brothels reserved for special use by party members.

Key question
What miseries were children exposed to by the social disruption?

Key question
How socially disruptive was the Cultural Revolution?

The impact of the Cultural Revolution on women and the family

Women and society at large had barely had time to recover from the famine when they were plunged into the turmoil of the Cultural Revolution. The rejection of the importance of the individual and the family that came with collectivisation was re-emphasised with particular force during the Cultural Revolution:

- Private property and ownership were now depicted as crimes against Communist society which was engaged in a great collective effort to build a new world.
- The enforced pooling of resources and effort meant that the economic link that held families together was broken.
- Whereas in traditional China the **extended family**, which might in practice be a whole village, had been the main provider of help in difficult times, in Mao's China that role was taken over by the state.
- The provision of social welfare, such as education and medical care, was now to be organised and delivered by Communist Party officials and appointees.

The excesses and absurdities of the Cultural Revolution carried to their terrifying, but logical, conclusion the process of enforced conformity that had begun with collectivisation and the outlawing of private ownership. The traditional **nuclear family** fell into one of the categories of the 'four olds' that the young were set to destroy. Children were told to look on Mao Zedong and the Communist Party as their true parents, and, therefore, deserving of their first loyalty. Normal family affection was replaced by love for Mao. A Beijing student recalled:

> From the first day of my schooling, at 7 years old, I learned 'I love you Chairman Mao', not 'I love you Mamma or Papa'. I was brainwashed for 8 years and looking back I realise that the party was doing everything to keep us pure, purifying us so we would live for Mao's idealism, Mao's power, instead of discovering our own humanity.

The young were urged to inform on those among their relatives who betrayed any sign of clinging, even in the slightest manner, to the decadent values of the past. In such a frenzied atmosphere, it was hard for any semblance of normal family life to survive.

The Red Guards who, after terrorising the nation, were dispersed by Mao and sent 'up to the mountains and down to the villages' to learn the dignity of labour by living with the peasants (see page 95), themselves became bewildered victims. Their bitter experience as they eked out a miserable existence far from home, left them disillusioned and resentful. It proved very difficult for them to pick up the pieces and return to anything approaching normal family life. They have been aptly described as China's lost generation.

Key terms

Extended family
Not just parents and children, but all the relatives, including in-laws.

Nuclear family
Mother, father and their children, considered as a unit.

Population

The social changes described in this section took place against the background of a rapidly increasing Chinese population. During Mao's time the number of people in China almost doubled:

Key question
What major trend in population occurred during Mao's leadership of China?

Year	1953	1964	1976
Population	594,350,000	694,580,000	925,100,000

A later generation of Chinese leaders became deeply worried by this population explosion and brought in compulsory measures to limit the number of births. Interestingly, Mao in his time never saw the expanding population as a problem; on the contrary, he believed 'more people, more power'.

This was in keeping with the notion that had inspired the Great Leap Forward that it was the collective power of the people that was the most important social and economic factor in the regeneration of China. Mao considered that the greater the number of people in revolutionary China, the greater their economic achievements would be and the greater their ability to defend themselves against any external enemy.

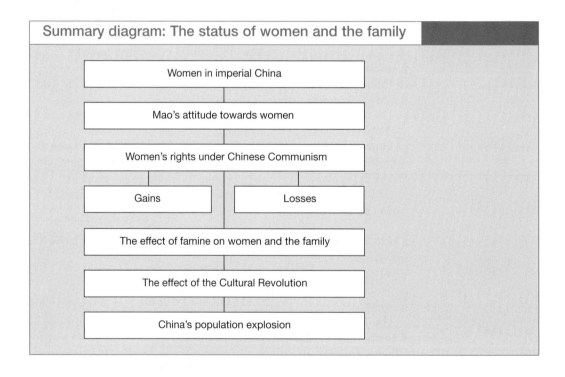

Summary diagram: The status of women and the family

- Women in imperial China
- Mao's attitude towards women
- Women's rights under Chinese Communism
  - Gains
  - Losses
- The effect of famine on women and the family
- The effect of the Cultural Revolution
- China's population explosion

3 | The Reshaping of Chinese Culture

Key question
What did Mao understand by the term culture?

It is important to understand how Mao interpreted culture. For him, it was never a separate, detached aspect of society. Culture was not a matter of refined tastes; it was about the life of the people. From the 1930s on he had taught that:

- Culture was central not peripheral. It was a nation's culture that defined its character.
- Throughout history the culture of every society was the direct product of the values laid down by the ruling class. It was the means by which rulers imposed their control over the people.
- Just as in the time of the **feudal** emperors, Chinese culture had been feudal, so, now that China was a proletarian society the culture had to be proletarian.
- All traces of bourgeois and feudal culture had to be eradicated. This could not be done gently or by persuasion. No ruling class ever gives up its power willingly; it has to be swept aside by force.

Key term

Feudal
The period of history in which the emperor allowed a group of rich lords to hold land in return for their loyalty and service to him. The landlords made the property-less peasants work for them.

Mao had an expression for this policy of ruthless suppression: 'the more brutal, the more revolutionary'. No genuine revolutionary in clearing away the feudal and bourgeois clutter that hindered the march of the People's Republic of China should ever be deterred from action by the thought of having to deal ruthlessly with class enemies. Mao put this in a well-known saying of his: 'A revolution is not a dinner party, or writing an essay, or painting a picture, or doing embroidery. A revolution is an insurrection, an act of violence by which one class overthrows another.'

Mao's notion of the role of the creative artist

Key question
What did Mao require of China's artists?

Mao demanded that all creative artists – writers, painters, musicians, film-makers, etc. – must accept that their first duty was to serve the people. Their works must further the cause of revolution. Mao had no time for artistic self-expression for its own sake. He asserted that there was 'no such thing as art for art's sake, art that stands above classes, art that is detached from or independent of politics. Proletarian literature and art are part of the whole revolutionary cause.'

The role of Jiang Qing

Key question
What means did Jiang Qing use to carry out Mao's instructions?

In a remarkable move, Mao decided that his wife, Jiang Qing, was to be the creator-in-chief of the new Chinese culture he desired. He gave her the responsibility for turning his general denunciation of China's 'four olds' into a definite programme for the suppression of traditional Chinese society. Mao instructed her to become the 'cultural purifier of the nation'. Believing that her former career as an actress ideally qualified her for such a task, Jiang applied herself to the job with fanatical zeal:

- She imposed a rigid system of censorship which denied a public showing or performance of any work that did not meet her criteria of revolutionary purity.
- Only those writings, works of art, broadcast programmes and films which had directly relevant contemporary Chinese themes were permitted.
- Western music, both classical and pop, was banned.
- Traditional Chinese opera was ruled out and replaced by a repertoire of specially commissioned contemporary works.

The works which Jiang commissioned were a set of opera-ballets, all concerned in the most naïve fashion with the triumph of the proletariat over its class enemies. They were an exact expression of Mao's demand that Chinese culture must be relevant and meaningful to the people by having as its only theme the struggle of the heroic masses. Grindingly tedious though they were, the opera-ballets were loudly applauded by the privileged audiences who dared not reveal their true feelings. In his memoirs President Nixon confessed that after sitting through a performance of one of them during his visit to Beijing in 1972 (see page 153), he was bored rigid by the utter tedium of it all.

An open-air performance in Harbin of 'The Red Woman Troop', one of Jiang Qing's specially commissioned opera-ballets in 1975. How is the size of the crowd to be accounted for?

Key terms

Political correctness
A requirement that people conform to a prescribed and restricted set of opinions and vocabulary when expressing themselves to show that they have accepted the ideology of the leaders of society.

Conservatoire
A specialist music college.

Key question
What impact did Jiang have on Chinese culture?

Jiang's demand for conformity

Jiang Qing's rejection of all non-proletarian culture was **political correctness** in its most extreme form. This was an intellectually and emotionally destructive process that aimed at the systematic undermining of all sense of tradition. In accordance with Mao's saying, 'the more brutal, the more revolutionary', children were urged to knock the heads off flowers in order to show their rejection of bourgeois concepts of beauty. Zhou Guanrun, a professor of music, recalled how Jiang's edicts against bourgeois culture terrorised the staff at the Beijing **Conservatoire** into silence.

> No music sounded any more. The conservatoire was silent. Everybody was just learning and doing self-criticism or accepting criticism from students. So we had to come every day, every morning at the time of office hours and sit there and read books and then do criticism. We had to analyse our mistakes in our work, our teaching or performing, because we performed a lot of classical or Chinese traditional music. We thought that we popularised the bad things to the young generation.

The consequences of Jiang's cultural terrorism

By the early 1970s Jiang Qing's assault on traditional culture had begun to produce an artistic wasteland. Musicians, painters and writers who showed reluctance to embrace the new rigidities were denounced and sent to 're-educational' labour camps where they were treated in brutal ways. One example was the denial of tools to the musicians who were sent to work in the fields; pianists and string players were made to scratch at the ground with their hands so that they would lose the vital sensitivity in their fingers and never be able to play well again.

Lack of resistance to Jiang's orders

There were rare attempts to question Jiang Qing's suffocating political correctness. On one occasion Deng Xiaoping dared to suggest that culture was about entertainment as well as indoctrination. He remarked caustically, 'After a hard week's work people want to go to the theatre to relax, but they go there and watch Jiang Qing's pieces and find they are on an effing battlefield'.

However, Deng apart, none of the leading politicians was prepared to challenge Jiang's policy of cultural barbarism. They, like the majority of artists, opted publicly to approve her great cultural experiment while privately hoping that her power would be broken once the rapidly ageing Mao had died. One of the most distressing features of Mao's China was the failure of the intellectuals and natural leaders of community to protest against the crimes of the regime. A mixture of moral cowardice and an understandable fear of what might be done to them and their families led them to accept the unacceptable without complaint.

Disastrous consequences

Jiang's stranglehold on the arts remained for the whole of the decade between 1966 and Mao's death 10 years later. By then it was clear that the result of this artistic persecution had not been the creation of a new culture but merely the near destruction of the old one. Writers and artists had been frightened either into inaction or into producing politically correct dross that would not fall foul of the censors.

Describing the profound damage done to China by the artistic destruction, Yan Yen, a poet, commented: 'As a result of the Cultural Revolution you could say the cultural trademark of my generation is that we have no culture.' Twenty years after the events, Deng Xiaoping's son, Pufang, reflected: 'The Cultural Revolution was not just a disaster for the party, for the country, but for the whole people. We were all victims, people of several generations. One hundred million people were its victims.'

Key question
What was the outcome of Jiang's system of censorship?

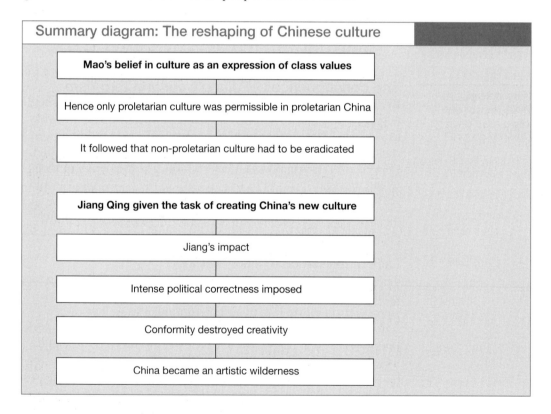

Summary diagram: The reshaping of Chinese culture

Mao's belief in culture as an expression of class values

Hence only proletarian culture was permissible in proletarian China

It followed that non-proletarian culture had to be eradicated

Jiang Qing given the task of creating China's new culture

Jiang's impact

Intense political correctness imposed

Conformity destroyed creativity

China became an artistic wilderness

4 | Education and Health

The PRC began with high hopes of raising the educational levels of the Chinese people. In 1949, the majority of the peasants were illiterate or barely literate. They could read a little, but write almost nothing. It had been one of Mao's contentions that, under Communism, China would see a major spread of education among the people and a sharp decrease in illiteracy. He kept his word.

Key question
How did the Communist authorities tackle the question of basic literacy?

By the middle 1950s a national system of primary education had been set up; its success is evident from the figures.

Key dates

Literacy rate rose from 20 to 70 per cent: 1949–76

Reform of the Mandarin language: 1955

Literacy rates (percentage of population with basic reading and writing skills)

1949 – 20%; 1960 – 50%; 1964 – 66%; 1976 – 70%

Language reform

One fascinating aspect of this was the reform of the Chinese language adopted by the PRC. In 1955, a new form of Mandarin, the language of 80 per cent of the Chinese people, was adopted. Up to that date there was no standardised form of written Mandarin that everybody could understand. This was because of two factors:

- The pronunciation of Mandarin varied widely from area to area; visitors from one place often could not understand or be understood by speakers in another.
- Mandarin had no alphabet. Whereas all the words in every European language are made up from a basic alphabet (English, for example, has 26 letters), written Mandarin was made up of **ideograms**, not letters. This made writing Mandarin extremely difficult, since all its words had to be learned separately.

Key terms

Ideograms
Literally pictures; Mandarin symbols had begun as pictures of the ideas they described.

Pinyin
A modernised form of Mandarin.

To solve the problem, the PRC hit on the idea of introducing a written form of Mandarin that all speakers and writers of it could recognise and use. The result was the adoption of *pinyin*: in this all the sounds in Mandarin were given a particular symbol. This greatly eased the learning process since all Mandarin speakers could now express the words they said in a standardised, recognisable written form. Here is an example:

Mandarin Chinese: 三个孩子都上学
Pinyin: sān gè háizi dōu shangxué
English: All three children go to school.

Failures in educational policy

There was no doubt that through such initiatives Mao's leadership of China saw major advances in education by the middle 1960s. However, during the final decade of Mao's life the gains that had been made were largely squandered. A census compiled in 1982, 6 years after Mao's death, contained the following revealing figures:

- fewer than 1 per cent of the working population had a university degree
- only 11 per cent had received schooling after the age of 16
- only 26 per cent had received schooling between the ages of 12 and 16
- only 35 per cent had received schooling after the age of 12.

Educational standards of CCP members

An embarrassing revelation for the Communist authorities who succeeded Mao in the late 1970s was that among the officials responsible for running the party and the government only 6 per cent had been formally educated beyond the age of 16. That the PRC under Mao had had such a poorly educated workforce and administration indicated how unrealistic his dreams had been for turning China into a modern state. It is notable that when Deng Xiaoping began to reform China after 1978, one of his major priorities was the improvement of education which had been so neglected under Mao.

Reasons for lack of educational progress

The principal reason for the sharp decline in qualified youngsters was the disruption caused by the Cultural Revolution. Between 1966 and 1970, 130 million of China's young people simply stopped attending school or university. Nor was it simply a question of numbers. Education itself as an ideal was undermined. The deliberate creation of disorder and the encouragement of pupils and students to ridicule or attack their teachers, tear up the curriculum and reject all forms of traditional learning had the all too obvious consequence of undermining the purpose of education itself.

Key question
Why had educational progress been so disappointing under Mao?

Table 5.2: Number of universities and higher education colleges operating in China 1949–85

Year	Universities
1949	200
1957	205
1958	229
1959	791
1961	1289
1965	434
1970	434
1972	434
1976	434
1982	598
1984	805
1985	1016

What main trends are indicated in Table 5.2? How is the contrast between the figures for 1961 and those from 1965 to 1976 to be explained?

Schoolchildren parading in Harbin, Heilongjiang province, 1 October 1966. How is the children's enthusiasm for marching and demonstrating to be explained?

Everything became politicised. Nothing was regarded as being of intrinsic worth any longer. Learning and study were dismissed as worthless unless they served the revolution. It was more important to train loyal party workers than it was to prepare China's young people to take their place in a modern state. That was why having used the young as the instrument for waging the Cultural Revolution, Mao then sent 12 million of them not back to school and college, but 'up to the mountains and down to the villages' (see pages 95–6).

Health provision in Mao's China

Mao and the Communists began with high hopes of providing the people with health care. From 1949 on, based on their experiences in Jiangxi and Yanan, they introduced a series of programmes, called '**patriotic health movements**'. Teams of party workers went into the countryside to explain in simple terms the connection between dirt and disease. The local populations were enlisted in great communal efforts to drain swamps and eradicate the bugs, rats, mosquitoes and flies that carried the **dysentery**, **malaria** and other various **endemic** diseases that afflicted the peasants.

Successes

It was the government's policy in the early years of the PRC to train many more doctors and nurses, with the specific aim of providing direct medical care in the remoter parts of China. In the 1950s large numbers of Chinese people were treated by a qualified doctor for the first time in their lives.

Failures

However, the number of qualified doctors never reached the original targets because here, as in so many areas of social life, politics intervened. As with education, so with health, the original good intentions of the Communists were undermined by the self-inflicted disruption caused by the Great Leap Forward and the Cultural Revolution.

China's doctors attacked

During the 'anti-movements' (see page 22) and the Cultural Revolution doctors came to be included among the professional classes who were condemned as living off the backs of the workers. It was said that the doctors' long years of training had prevented them from learning the dignity of labour and had left them as privileged people who used their special skills to make money which they then spent on a selfish bourgeois lifestyle.

While it may have been true that there were doctors who exploited their position, to attack the whole medical profession on the grounds that it was corrupt was part of the madness that Mao's increasingly irrational ideology created. The consequence was that to survive, doctors had to subordinate medical considerations to political ones. This produced

Key term

Patriotic health movements
Government-sponsored schemes for providing Chinese people with basic information on health and hygiene.

Key question
Why were the PRC's original plans for providing health care only partly successful?

Key terms

Dysentery
Severe diarrhoea and dehydration, often fatal.

Malaria
A debilitating feverish condition, caused by parasites passed on by mosquito bites.

Endemic
A disease constantly present in particular communities.

Key question
Why did the medical profession come under attack?

absurdities such as surgeons cancelling operations in order to show their solidarity with the workers by sweeping floors and cleaning toilets.

Caught up in the politically correct atmosphere, some doctors decided that since showing pain was a bourgeois reaction and that bearing things without flinching was a sign of revolutionary purpose, they would no longer use anaesthetics and analgesics. China's maternity wards resounded to the groans of women in labour as, denied any painkillers, they struggled to suppress their agonised cries.

The barefoot doctors

Despite the denigration of the medical profession on political grounds, Mao remained aware of the propaganda value of effective health provision. He knew what a boost for the regime it would be if access to medical treatment could be made a basic right of the Chinese people under Communism. It was such thinking that lay behind the crash programme for training doctors that was introduced by the late 1960s.

In keeping with the ideological notion that it was their long period of academic study that had detached the doctors from the people and encouraged their bourgeois ways, the new system was based on short practical courses. Instead of long years of preparation, covering all aspects of medicine, the trainees would now engage in 6-month periods of intensive study with the emphasis wholly on the practical. Once trained in the basics, the new doctors would be sent to work among the peasants. It was very similar to the way in which the ex-Red Guards had been dispersed into the countryside (see page 95).

The scheme had its undoubted successes. By 1973, over a million new doctors had been trained. They contributed greatly to the improvement of the lives of the peasants. Known colloquially as **barefoot doctors**, these idealistic young general practitioners travelled around rural China providing treatment, often free of charge.

One of them, Dr Liu Quan, later recalled, 'In Chairman Mao's time, you could see a doctor whether you had money or not. We would carry out disease prevention, like injections.'

But impressive though such dedicated doctors as Liu were, often performing minor miracles, with limited equipment, in primitive conditions, they were a stop-gap. They could not provide the full national medical service that a modern state requires.

Key question
What was the role of the barefoot doctors?

Key date
One million barefoot doctors trained: 1973

Key term
Barefoot doctors
The teams of swiftly trained medics who were sent into China's countryside to provide a rudimentary health service.

Summary diagram: Education and health

```
                          Education
        ┌─────────────────────┴─────────────────────┐
```

Aims

Mass literacy
Language reform
University development

Results

Largely achieved by 1976
Successfully operating by 1976
Initial growth but then decline

```
                           Health
        ┌─────────────────────┴─────────────────────┐
```

Aims

Eradication of endemic disease
Patriotic health movement
Barefoot doctors

Results

Partial success
People trained in health care
Impressive individual efforts,
    but limited success overall

5 | Mao's Prison Camps: The *Laogai*

It was a feature of the major totalitarian sates of the twentieth century – Hitler's Germany, Stalin's Soviet Union and Mao's China – that they rested ultimately on terror. In each case the principal means of enforcing that terror was by the creation of prison camps in which the conditions were deliberately made so wretched that they broke the body and spirit of the inmates. In order to enforce conformity and obedience in China, Mao created a vast network of labour camps in which those who opposed him or were suspected of opposing him were imprisoned.

The theory behind the camps

As the name *laogai* suggested, the official theory was that the camps were not places of punishment, but of re-education. The fiction was maintained that the mass of the people were happy and contented in the Communist state created by Mao, and that those who were dissatisfied with things and protested against the system were the exceptions, who were not so much bad as misguided. It was the state's duty, therefore, to help them towards the truth by putting them in camps where they could be trained to see things in an enlightened way.

Key question
What in theory was the purpose of the *laogai*?

Key term

Laogai
Meaning 're-education through labour'. It came to be used to describe the vast prison-camp system established under Mao.

The practice in the camps

In reality, the camps became places where the harshest means were used to dehumanise the prisoners, who were forced to do humiliating and backbreaking work while being systematically starved. The camps were to be found throughout China, but many of the worst were deliberately built in the most inhospitable parts of China where the bitter cold of winter or the searing heat of summer made life a torture for the prisoners. To obtain even the bare minimum ration of food, prisoners had to make a full confession of their crimes. Those who persisted in claiming that they were innocent were interrogated, deprived of sleep, held in solitary confinement, beaten and starved until they broke down and conformed.

Very few prisoners had the physical or mental power to resist such treatment for very long, and even those who had exceptional reserves of strength tended to buckle when told that their families would suffer if they did not give in. The desperate state to which the prisoners were brought by their hunger was described by a doctor who visited the camps:

> I noticed on many occasions a very strange wound at the back of the thigh of many of the dead. First of all I dismissed it as a gunshot wound at close quarters, but after seeing a few more I asked a friend and he told me that many of the prisoners were cutting chunks out of the bodies to eat. On my next visit to the mortuary I actually saw a prisoner whip out a knife, cut a portion of the leg of a dead body, and put it quickly into his mouth.

Statistics relating to the camps

The figures relating to the *laogai* make fearful reading:

- The average number of prisoners held in the camps each year during Mao's time was 10 million.
- Over 25 million prisoners died during that period, the number being comprised of those who were officially executed, those who died from hunger and ill-treatment, and those who committed suicide. Even in death prisoners were treated with contempt. The term used by the prison authorities to describe those who took their own lives was 'alienating themselves from the party and the people'.
- By the time of Mao's death in 1976, there were more than 10,000 labour camps spread across China.

The economic significance of the camps

In the early 1950s, when setting up the camps, Mao's officials received help and advice on the running of them from Soviet officials who were operating the *gulag* in Stalin's USSR. A key factor in the management of the camps was that they were not simply prisons; they were economically important in that they provided an inexhaustible supply of slave labour. Much of the mass workforce used in the Great Leap Forward on hazardous

Key question
What was the reality of life in the camps?

Key question
How did the camps contribute to Chinese industry?

projects such as clearing malarial swamps and mining in dangerous areas were prisoners from the camps.

The broader purpose of the camps

Key question
In what ways were the *laogai* used as a means of political control in China?

For the Chinese government, the *laogai* performed a function that went beyond simply the punishment of particular dissidents. The existence of the camps effectively terrified the whole population. Even when prisoners were released after completing their sentence they remained under constant threat of being rearrested. There was always the feeling that what had happened to them could happen to anybody. The families of prisoners were also regarded as guilty by association and were shunned by their neighbours.

This was more serious than merely being ostracised; shops would not sell them goods, homes and jobs became impossible for them to obtain or keep and their children were denied places in school. An inhuman practice that developed in regard to executed prisoners was for the authorities to send the dead man's family the bullet that killed him together with a bill for the cost of it. The organs of executed prisoners were often extracted and sold for transplantation without the families' permission.

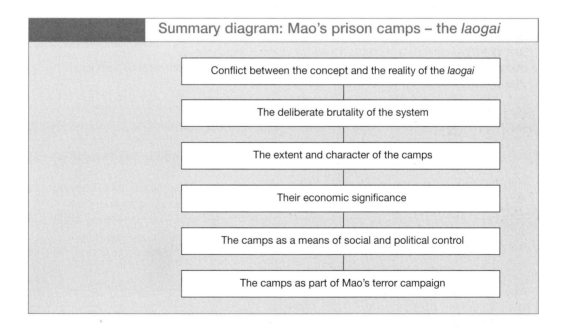

Summary diagram: Mao's prison camps – the *laogai*

Conflict between the concept and the reality of the *laogai*

The deliberate brutality of the system

The extent and character of the camps

Their economic significance

The camps as a means of social and political control

The camps as part of Mao's terror campaign

Mao's impact on the Chinese people

Key question
Why was the period of Mao's rule of China, 1949–76, such a troublesome one for the ordinary Chinese people?

When he took power in 1949, Mao seemed genuinely to have wanted to improve the conditions of the people. Yet, whatever social and economic gains may have been made between 1949 and his death in 1976, the truth remains that his policies were essentially destructive rather than creative. From the beginning he used coercion to enforce his vision of the new Communist society on the people. His great schemes for the regeneration of

China, which began with the Great Leap Forward, became increasingly extreme, culminating with the deliberately created mayhem of the Cultural Revolution.

In a society directed by a leader who embraced turmoil as a means of achieving his political goals, there was little chance of the real interests of the people being a priority. As a revolutionary Mao thought of people in the abstract; individuals counted for little. It was the notion of the proletariat as a revolutionary class, not as individual peasants and workers, that was all-important. It was this abstraction that made it possible for him to treat the Chinese people with such disdain.

Study Guide: AS Questions

In the style of AQA

(a) Explain why Mao introduced marriage reform laws in the 1950s. (12 marks)

(b) 'The position of women deteriorated in Mao's China.' Explain why you agree or disagree with this view. (24 marks)

Exam tips

The cross-references are designed to take you straight to the material that will help you answer the questions.

(a) To answer this question you should re-read pages 112–14. Remember this question requires that you find a variety of explanatory factors. Start by reflecting on the long-term factors. You will need to explain the inferior position of women in Imperial China and women's position in society before the 1950s. You should also refer to the development of Mao's own attitudes to women and forced marriages and to Communist ideology. A further relevant comment would be to relate the laws to the consolidation of Communist power (as covered in Chapter 2) and to consider what Mao hoped to gain from their passage. Although you are not asked to describe what the laws said, by thinking about their terms you should be better placed to assess why they were introduced. In your conclusion you should show how your factors inter-relate and provide some overall comment about the most important.

(b) This is clearly a provocative quotation and you will need to find evidence that both supports and opposes it. When you have done so, you should form your own judgement as to whether you agree or disagree. You will need to argue a case throughout your answer, but don't forget that your final essay should show both sides of the argument and lead to a balanced and supported conclusion.

In support of the quotation you might refer to:

- the impact of collectivisation (page 114)
- peasant attitudes (page 115)
- the undermining of the family (pages 116 and 119)
- the impact of the famine
- divorce and wife-selling (page 117)
- child abuse and use of children to support the cultural revolution (pages 117–19).

In disagreement with the quotation you might refer to:

- the marriage reform laws (page 114)
- equality in the law and other practices (page 114)
- liberation from family ties (pages 116–17)
- welfare provision.

Try to balance the gains against the losses and remember that you should try to judge developments in the context of the time and place rather than from a Western twenty-first century viewpoint!

In the style of Edexcel

How far did the position of women improve in China in the years 1949–65? (30 marks)

Source: Edexcel specimen paper, 2008

Exam tips

The cross-references are designed to take you straight to the material that will help you answer the question.

The key words for you to think about when planning your answer to this question are 'position of women' and 'improve'. This is a question requiring you to analyse the changes that affected the role of women in China and it requires you to reach a judgement about the extent to which these changes constituted improvements. Be careful not to simply detail Chinese government policies. You need to make links between the government's measures and the effects they actually had on women.

- You could plan first to deal with those aspects that could be seen as suggesting attempts at improvement: Mao's support of the principle of women's emancipation and liberation (pages 112–13); change in China's marriage and divorce laws and land reform in the 1950s (page 114); greater employment opportunities for women in Mao's China (page 115).
- You could then balance this with evidence that suggests restricted progress or ways in which government policies had negative effects on the position of women: the restricted part played by women in the Communist Party and government (page 115); the evidence of unchanging attitudes (page 115); the impact of collectivisation on land-holding (page 114); the negative impact of collectivisation and the famine on women's roles within the family (page 117); the social disruption of the Cultural Revolution (page 119).
- Be sure to focus on 'improvement' for women when coming to your conclusion. You should round off your answer by offering your judgement. You should have identified in the body of your essay clear criteria by which to measure 'improvement'. Clearly Chinese society changed radically during this period from what it had been like at the beginning (page 112), but to what extent had the subordinate role of women changed? And had their position in Chinese society got any better as a result of the changes to the traditional Chinese family way of life?

6 Mao's China and International Relations

POINTS TO CONSIDER

No modern state can exist in isolation. It has to live with its neighbours and the wider world. How the PRC handled the problems of its foreign relations tells us much about Mao Zedong himself and the new China he had created. The topic is studied under the following major themes:

- China's international relations under Mao
- Mao's China and the Soviet Union
- The PRC and the United States

Key dates

1917	Russian Revolution
1950	Mao visited Moscow
	Sino-Soviet Treaty
1953	Death of Stalin
1956	Beginning of de-Stalinisation
1957	Mao attended Moscow Conference
1958	Khrushchev met Mao in Beijing
1961	Soviet advisers withdrawn from PRC
1962	Sino-Indian War
	Cuban Missile Crisis
1963	Mao attacked Soviet policy of coexistence with the West
1963–75	Vietnam War
1964	China produces its own atom bomb
	Khrushchev dismissed in USSR
1967	China produces its own hydrogen bomb
1968	Soviet crushing of Prague spring
1969	Lowest point in Sino-Soviet relations
1971	PRC replaced Taiwan in UN
1972	Visit of US President Nixon to China

1 | China's International Relations under Mao

In 1917 Russia had been the first great nation to undergo a successful **Marxist revolution**; China in 1949 was the second. The PRC's triumph left it with a dual aim: to develop China into a modern nation and to lead the rest of the world towards

Key question
How did Mao's China see its role in the world?

Key term

Marxist revolution
In October 1917, the Bolshevik (Communist) Party led by Lenin, seized power in Russia.

international proletarian revolution. The pursuit of this second aim created huge questions for China:

- Was it realistic for it as an economically backward nation to attempt to play such a role?
- Would an aggressive revolutionary attitude towards the capitalist world leave China friendless and unable to obtain essential resources?
- Where did the young PRC stand in the world Communist hierarchy? Was it merely to follow the Soviet Union or did it have an equal right to interpret Marxism for itself?

There was a sense in which it was the last of these questions that presented the greatest difficulty. The PRC was formed in 1949 just after the Cold War had begun to take shape. This meant that as a Communist state it would naturally line up with the USSR against the USA and the capitalist world. But while it was certainly the case that at the beginning the PRC 'leaned to one side', Mao's term for its alliance with the Soviet Union, things were never as simple as that. Mao and the Soviet leaders as people, and the PRC and the USSR as nations, had a strained relationship.

Key question
What factors explain the tensions between the PRC and the USSR?

2 | Mao's China and the Soviet Union

Deep differences between the Soviet Union and the PRC were present from the beginning. They were sometimes submerged, but they were never far below the surface. After 1949 there were occasional periods of apparent harmony when the two Communist powers seemed to represent a solid front towards the West, but the prevailing relationship was one of suspicion, which at times degenerated into warlike hostility.

Border disputes
The reasons for the strains between the PRC and the USSR went back well before 1949. The 7000-km border between China and Russia had made the two neighbours very wary of each other in tsarist times. The Bolshevik Revolution in 1917 did nothing to alter this. In 1919, Lenin's Bolshevik government seized Outer Mongolia, a province which the Chinese had traditionally regarded as their own. At the end of the Pacific War in 1945, Manchuria, which had been occupied by the Japanese, was returned to China, but only after the withdrawing Soviet forces had stripped the region of its industrial resources, depriving China of over $2 billion worth of plant and machinery. Even after the PRC had been established in 1949, border disputes continued to sour Sino-Soviet relations for decades. It was an aspect of their mutual jealousy as great powers.

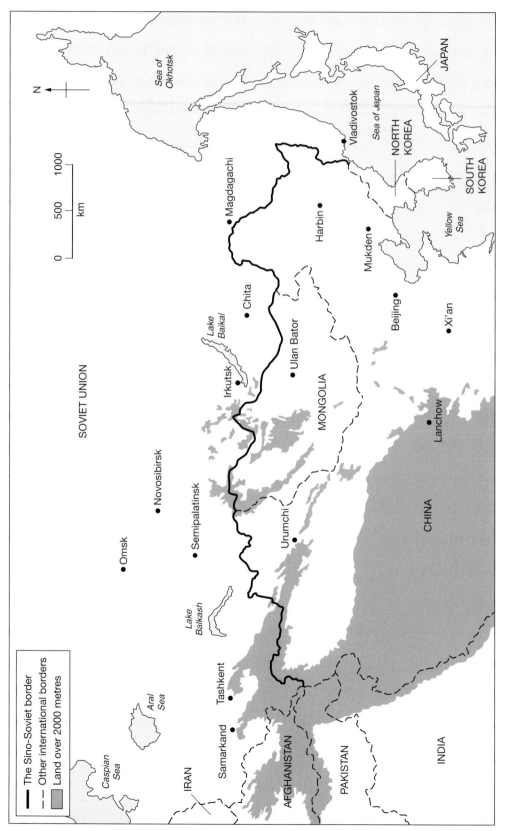

A map showing the Sino-Soviet border.

Figure 6.1 A visual representation of the Marxist notion of the workings of the dialectic. How does the diagram help to explain why Chinese and Soviet Communists disagreed over their interpretation of revolution?

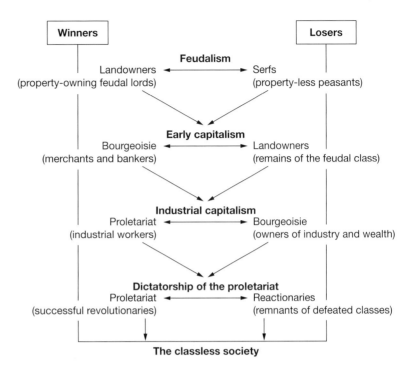

Ideological differences

It has to be stressed that the Chinese Communists did not regard Marxism simply as a political movement. For Mao, Marxism was a means by which the regeneration of China as a great nation was to be achieved. The Marxist dialectic (see Figure 6.1) provided a programme for achieving revolution in China, but it was vital that the Chinese revolutionaries interpret that programme in their own terms. Mao had a crude peasant expression for this: 'the Chinese', he said, 'must plant their backsides on the soil of China'. His approach was essentially nationalist; he insisted that Communism in China must take its character from the Chinese situation. Revolutionaries outside China could not dictate to the Chinese how they should conduct themselves:

> China's revolutionary war is waged in the specific environment of China and so it has its own specific circumstances and nature ... Some people say that it is enough merely to study the experience of revolutionary war in Russia. However, although we must value Soviet experience ... we must value even more the experience of China's revolutionary war, because there are many factors specific to the Chinese revolution.

Such a **Sino-centric** view of Marxism and revolution was bound to cause friction between Communist China and the Soviet Union, which, as the country of Lenin and Stalin, regarded itself as the only true interpreter of the **Communist faith**. These differences of attitude within the international Communist movement were often as fierce as the conflict between Communism and its

Key terms

Sino-centric
Having Chinese interests at the centre of things with all other considerations secondary.

Communist faith
The intensity with which Communists held their beliefs in revolution may be legitimately compared to the conviction that inspires the followers of a dogmatic religion.

political enemies. Sino-Soviet relations after 1949 often descended into a battle over who represented true Communism: the Soviet Union or Maoist China.

Differences over the meaning of Marxism and how it should be applied in China had bedevilled relations between Mao and Stalin since the 1920s. Stalin had been unwilling to accept that a peasant-based movement such as Mao was leading could be genuinely revolutionary. For him, the Marxist rules of the dialectic dictated that true proletarian revolution had to be urban based.

Stalin's insistence on this point convinced Mao that what the Soviet leader wanted was a disunited and divided China which would leave the USSR as the dominant force in Asia. This was why Mao found it hard to accept the USSR, despite its revolutionary pedigree, as the true voice of international Marxism. He came increasingly to believe that what motivated the Soviet Union was not Communism, but national self-interest. He later reflected:

> After the success of our revolution, Stalin feared that China might degenerate into another Yugoslavia and that I might become another **Tito**. I later went to Moscow [in 1950] and concluded the Sino-Soviet Treaty of Alliance. This was the result of a struggle. Stalin did not wish to sign the treaty; he finally signed it after 2 months of negotiations.

Mao and Stalin: a clash of personalities

The treaty to which Mao referred was the first formal agreement between China and the USSR. Despite Stalin's earlier doubts about the ability of the CCP to survive, the establishment of the PRC in 1949 was officially welcomed by the Soviet Union. Stalin calculated that China, as a newly formed Marxist state in a hostile capitalist world, would look to the USSR, the first great Communist nation, for guidance and protection. Indeed, the US State Department referred to the Sino-Soviet alliance as 'Moscow making puppets out of the Chinese'. However, events were to show that Mao Zedong and China were far from regarding themselves as mere creatures of Stalin and the USSR.

Mao's official visit to the USSR in 1950 confirmed his doubts concerning Stalin's attitude. Mao was offended by the superior air adopted by the Russians and by Stalin's offhand treatment of the Chinese delegation. Mao complained that he had been dumped in a poor-quality villa outside Moscow with a wonky table-tennis table as the sole means of recreation. His hosts had made no arrangements to entertain him beyond the formal round of official meetings and banquets. His only other outing was to the Bolshoi Theatre.

Mao, who was on his first visit abroad, felt slighted. Biographers suggest that the two leaders disliked each other as people and this may explain why Stalin was reluctant to meet Mao, except formally. Their personalities conflicted because they were so similar in type. Once Mao had negotiated the treaty,

Key figure

Josip Broz Tito (1914–90) Communist leader of Yugoslavia who defied Stalin by keeping his country independent of the Soviet-dominated eastern bloc.

Key question
What lay at the root of the mutual suspicion between Mao and Stalin?

Key date
Mao visited Moscow: 1950

which was the sole purpose of his visit, he left the USSR as quickly as possible.

The Sino-Soviet Treaty 1950

Key question
What did the PRC gain from the treaty?

Key dates

Signing of Sino-Soviet Treaty: 1950

Death of Stalin: 1953

It soon became apparent that Mao had good reason for distrusting Stalin. The Chinese realised soon after the 1950 treaty had been signed that the Soviet Union was intent on exploiting the agreement in its own favour. This was in spite of Mao's initial belief that the hard-won treaty had obliged the USSR to provide China with expertise and aid at low cost. Its wording, which spoke of 'friendship and equality' and 'economic and cultural co-operation', had appeared to promise much. But Stalin had struck a hard bargain. Under the terms of the treaty:

- the $300 million Soviet advance was a loan not a gift; the PRC had to undertake to repay the full amount plus interest
- the upkeep of the 10,000 Soviet economic and military advisers who went to China had to be paid for fully by China
- China had to give the bulk of its bullion reserves to the Soviet Union.

Key figure

Nikita Khrushchev
(1894–1971)
Emerged from the power struggle that followed Stalin's death to become the Soviet leader between 1956 and 1964.

Nikita Khrushchev, a later Soviet leader, admitted that the treaty had been 'an insult to the Chinese people. For centuries the French, English and Americans had been exploiting China, and now the Soviet Union was moving in.'

Mao's realisation that China had been exploited put the barely formed Sino-Soviet partnership under great stress. The tension was felt as early as the Korean War which began in 1950 (see page 28). Mao remarked that China had to pay 'down to the last rifle and bullet' for the Soviet *matériel* it received during that conflict. There were also suggestions that Stalin deliberately prevented an early armistice being reached in Korea in order to exhaust the Chinese. It was certainly the case that almost immediately after Stalin's death in 1953 Zhou Enlai was able to negotiate a truce.

The PRC's dependence on the Soviet Union

Key question
Why did Mao, in spite of his deep reservations about Stalin's motives, allow Soviet influence to impose itself on China?

The Soviet planners and engineers who came to the PRC in its early years left a marked imprint on China's physical appearance. Over 200 construction projects were undertaken by the USSR in China during the 1950s. New public buildings and squares bore the Soviet stamp. In Beijing many of China's most delicate and antique structures were razed to be replaced by Soviet-style functional eyesores, which most Chinese loathed as an aesthetic affront. But, as Mao saw it, this was the price that had to be paid for the material aid that China needed from the USSR. Soviet scientific techniques were also adopted in China.

Even when these, in contrast to Western methods, were dated and cumbersome they were deemed to be superior since they represented 'socialist science'. One tragic example of the folly in allowing ideology to have precedence over fact was the disastrous effect of China's commitment to the pseudo-science of

Lysenkoism during the Great Leap Forward of the late 1950s (see page 57).

The USSR's military assistance was also judged to be necessary, at least for the time being. Despite the great feats of the PLA, the hard fact was that China's international isolation meant that it could not easily obtain resources and expertise from anywhere other than the Soviet Union. This remained the situation until the 1960s when China was able to mount its own independent nuclear-research programme (see page 147).

China and de-Stalinisation

Since it had principally been Stalin's uncompromising manner that had caused disharmony between Moscow and Beijing, it was reasonable to expect that after the Soviet leader's death in 1953 relations would ease. This appeared to happen at first; something of a Sino-Soviet honeymoon period intervened in the mid-1950s. The new Soviet leaders were willing to provide China with further loans and technology. But even as better relations developed, events undermined the possibility of a genuine partnership.

Key question
Why was Mao disturbed by the Soviet policy of de-Stalinisation?

Key date
Beginning of de-Stalinisation: 1956

Mao's worries over the 'cult of personality'

In February 1956, Nikita Khrushchev staggered the USSR and the Communist world by launching a detailed attack on Stalin for his 'crimes against the party'. A particular charge that rang alarm bells in China was that Stalin had put himself above the party by engaging in a 'cult of personality' (see page 37). While Mao had had profound differences with Stalin, he was deeply disturbed by the ferocity of this assault upon Stalin's record. He read the denunciation of the cult of personality as an intended criticism of his own style of leadership in China.

Mao's concerns over the Communist bloc

Mao was also disturbed by the political developments that occurred in the Communist (Eastern) bloc in the wake of the de-Stalinisation programme. Greater freedom appeared to be offered to the **Soviet satellites** to criticise their Communist governments and to question their subordination to the USSR. This had not been Khrushchev's intention, as he was quick to demonstrate by ordering the suppression of the anti-Soviet rising in Hungary in November 1956. But for Mao, the Hungarian rising and those that had occurred in Poland and East Germany were the direct result of the Soviet Union's relaxation of its ideological grip. Mao was angered by the failure of the post-Stalin leadership to control what he regarded as the reactionary forces within the Communist bloc.

Key term
Soviet satellites
The various countries that had fallen under Soviet control between 1945 and 1948.

Mao's concerns over Soviet revisionism and *détente*

Mao was equally offended by the softening of the Soviet attitude towards the West. Moscow now seemed to accept that there were alternative ways of achieving revolution in the modern world other than by armed struggle. Khrushchev had by the late 1950s

Key question
Why was Mao opposed to the Soviet Union's pursuit of better relations with the West?

Key term

Superpowers
The description given to nations which possess advanced nuclear weapons.

concluded that in a world of nuclear **superpowers** the Marxist–Leninist notion of a final violent conflict between the international proletariat and the forces of capitalism was no longer acceptable. He said that had comrade Lenin lived in a nuclear age he would have adjusted his views.

This was rejected by Mao as heresy. He believed that the final struggle was unavoidable and that it was the duty of all revolutionaries not only to prepare for it but also to hasten its coming. For Mao, Khrushchev's policy of de-Stalinisation was clear evidence that Soviet Communism had taken the revisionist path.

Mao's second visit to the USSR 1957

Key question
What deep differences between China and the USSR were revealed during Mao's visit?

Disturbed by the murmurings in the Marxist camp, Khrushchev in 1957 convened a conference in Moscow of the world's Communist parties. His broad aim was to repair the differences between the USSR and the other Marxist countries. His particular hope was that he could lay Stalin's ghost by bringing Tito and Yugoslavia back into the Soviet fold. However, at the last moment Tito declined to attend. This disappointed Mao, who had agreed to revisit the Soviet Union only because he thought Tito would be there. Nevertheless, since the arrangements were too advanced to cancel, Mao swallowed his irritation and went to Moscow.

Key date
Mao attended Moscow Conference: 1957

At the meeting, Mao was still prepared to recognise the USSR's unique place in Communist history. He also approved a Sino-Soviet declaration that expressed China's readiness to co-operate. But at the same time Mao let it be known that he regarded Moscow's approach to the West as too accommodating. He called on the Soviet Union to abandon revisionism and return to the true Marxist–Leninist path. Rather than making concessions to capitalism, it was the Soviet Union's revolutionary duty to fight the class war by fully supporting the liberation movements world-wide. This could not be done by extending peaceful overtures to class enemies: the imperialist Western nations.

Mao's suspicions towards the Soviet Union

What prompted Mao's words was his suspicion that the Soviet Union was following a policy of *détente* with the West in order to leave China internationally isolated. Mao's chief spokesman at the Moscow meeting was Deng Xiaoping, who excelled himself in putting over the Chinese version of international revolution. Deng argued powerfully that the proletarian world revolution was achievable only through armed struggle; capitalism had to be overcome by force. In a tense series of exchanges he got the better of the leading Soviet political theorist, Mikhail Suslov, and won the admiration, if not the open support, of many of the other delegates. The Soviet hosts were embarrassed and angered by Deng's performance.

Mao and Khrushchev

Despite Mao's strong words about the Soviet Union, Khrushchev made another attempt to improve relations with the PRC. In 1958, following the mishandling by Pavel Yudin, the Soviet Ambassador in China, of negotiations regarding a joint Sino-Soviet naval programme, Khrushchev flew to Beijing to meet Mao again. He came to assure Mao that Yudin had given the wrong impression by suggesting that China's navy must be brought under Soviet control.

Khrushchev humiliated

Mao, however, was not disposed to listen. In a tit-for-tat for the poor treatment he had endured during his visits to Moscow, Mao deliberately set out to make Khrushchev uncomfortable. He arranged for the Soviet delegation to be put up at a hotel without air-conditioning; the Russians sweltered in Beijing's fierce summer heat and were plagued by mosquitoes.

In one notorious incident Mao insisted that a round of talks take place in his private pool. Mao was a regular swimmer; Khrushchev hated the water. Nonetheless, to humour his host Khrushchev agreed. In a pair of baggy shorts and squeezed into a barely-buoyant rubber ring, the rotund Soviet leader desperately floundered and splashed while interpreters raced round the pool's edge trying to make sense of his gurgled replies to Mao's questions. The talks were not a success.

Key question
Why did Mao get on no better with Khrushchev than he had with Stalin?

Khrushchev met Mao in Beijing: 1958

Key date

Mao and Khrushchev together in China in 1958. Why might their happy smiles towards each other be regarded as misleading?

PRC accuses USSR of 'chauvinism'

The failure of the Moscow talks was not simply the result of the swimming-pool farce. Deng Xiaoping was again let loose to savage the Russian delegation as he had in Moscow. He attacked the USSR for its 'great nation, great party **chauvinism**', in acting as if it was the only true interpreter of Marxist theory. Deng repeated Mao's accusation that the technical advisers sent to China by Moscow were in fact Soviet spies. He charged the Soviet Union with betraying the international Communist movement. It has been suggested that it was Mao's remembrance of Deng Xiaoping's brilliant onslaught on the USSR that saved Deng from harsher treatment at the time of his disgrace in the Cultural Revolution in 1966 (see page 84).

The Taiwan issue

In 1958 the simmering Taiwan issue provided another test of the genuineness of Sino-Soviet sympathies. Without consulting Moscow, Mao ordered Chinese forces to make ready for full-scale assault on the Nationalist-held island (see page 7). The USA responded by preparing for war with mainland China. In the event, Mao held back from a direct attack on Taiwan. It is doubtful that Mao really intended to attack, but the reason he gave for not doing so was that the USSR had declined to offer China even moral support.

Khrushchev countered by saying that he was unwilling to put the USSR at risk by recklessly 'testing the stability of the capitalist system'. He denounced Mao and the Chinese as '**Trotskyists**' who had lost all sense of political reality. The resulting deterioration in relations led the Soviet Union to withdraw its economic advisers from China and to cancel its commercial contracts there.

Soviet reaction to China's Great Leap Forward

Sino-Soviet relations were not helped by Moscow's response to China's Great Leap Forward. In 1959, Mao was enraged by the news that the Soviet Union had dismissed his attempt to revolutionise the Chinese economy as a total blunder. He was particularly angered by rumours that one of his own chiefs-of-staff, Marshal Peng Dehuai, had passed on to Moscow details of the widespread starvation that the Great Leap Forward had caused (see page 62).

Sino-Soviet rivalry over Albania

China had condemned de-Stalinisation for the encouragement it had given to reaction and counter-revolution in the Eastern-bloc countries. Yet, when the Chinese leaders saw the chance to embarrass the Soviet Union by supporting the socialist countries hostile to the USSR, they took it. In retaliation for what Mao saw as the Soviet Union's attempt to undermine China's standing among the Communist nations, the PRC gave support to those countries which defied the USSR. An especially clear example was **Albania**.

Key term

Chauvinism
Exaggerated and aggressive belief in the value of one's own nation.

Key question
How did the question of Taiwan further divide the PRC and the Soviet Union?

Key terms

Trotskyists
Followers of Stalin's great rival, Lev Trotsky, who believed in the necessity of world revolution at any price.

Albania
Run by an oppressive neo-Stalinist regime, it was the only Communist state in Europe to recognise China rather than the Soviet Union as the leader of the international revolutionary movement.

Key question
How did Mao exploit the Albanian issue to hit back at the Soviet Union?

In 1961, the Soviet Union, angered by the Albanian government's refusal to accept dictation from Moscow, withdrew its financial aid. The PRC immediately stepped in to supply Albania with money and technical assistance. It did not matter that the country was only a minor player on the socialist stage. It was enough for the Chinese that it was on bad terms with the USSR.

China's walkout from the 1961 Moscow Conference

It was the Albanian question that brought matters to a head and led to the severing of diplomatic relations between the Soviet Union and the PRC. The occasion was Zhou Enlai's walkout from the 1961 Moscow Congress of the Communist Party of the Soviet Union, to which China had been invited as an observer. Khrushchev's speech at the congress, abusing the Albanian Communist leaders for their backward Stalinist ways, was interpreted by the Chinese as a deliberately offensive attack on themselves. Having expected such an onslaught Zhou and the Chinese delegation quit the hall in accordance with a rehearsed plan. This dramatic gesture was the climax to a decade of Sino-Soviet recrimination.

Key dates

Soviet advisers withdrawn from PRC: 1961

Sino-Indian War: 1962

Sino-Soviet name calling

The collapse of diplomatic relations encouraged the Soviet and Chinese leaders to be still more offensive in their personal references to each other. Khrushchev abused Mao as an 'Asian Hitler' and 'a living corpse'. Mao responded by dismissing his Russian adversary as 'a redundant old boot' that ought to be thrown into a corner.

Border disputes

One result of this flurry of insults was the sharpening of the local disputes between the USSR and China along their common border. Throughout the 1960s and 1970s there were frequent and sometimes violent confrontations. During this period, the USSR committed nearly 50 Red Army divisions to defend its Asian frontiers. China angrily asserted that the refusal of the USSR to return the Chinese territories that Russia had acquired by the 'unequal treaties' of the nineteenth century made it as guilty of imperialism as the original tsarist land grabbers. Beijing's news agency spoke of the 'anti-Chinese atrocities of the new tsars'.

The Sino-India War 1962

The Chinese were especially incensed by the USSR's attitude during the **Sino-Indian War** that broke out in 1962. The Soviet Union was formally neutral, but it provided India with fighter-planes and its moral support was all on India's side. Mao regarded the offer by Kosygin, the USSR's foreign minister, to act as mediator between the PRC and India as hypocrisy. He rejected it as yet another attempt by the Soviet Union to undermine China's international standing.

Key term

Sino-Indian War
In 1962 a long-running territorial dispute, compounded by India's granting sanctuary to the Dalai Lama, led to an outbreak of fighting between Indian and Chinese troops on the Tibetan border.

Key question
What was Mao's view of Soviet actions over Cuba?

Key dates

Cuban Missile Crisis: 1962

Mao attacked Soviet policy of coexistence with the West: 1963

The Cuban Missile Crisis 1962

A dramatic Cold War episode in 1962 provided China with the opportunity to ridicule the Soviet Union's claim to the leadership of world revolution. In October of that year the USSR exploited its influence over **Communist Cuba** to install rockets and nuclear warheads on the island. Since Cuba stood only 150 km off the coast of the USA, President Kennedy demanded the withdrawal of the weapons.

After a tense stand-off, Khrushchev complied. The two superpowers then made a compromise settlement in which the USSR agreed to withdraw all its weapons and installations in Cuba in return for the USA's promise never to invade the island and to withdraw its own nuclear weapons from Turkey.

China scorned Moscow for its original 'adventurism' in siting detectable nuclear warheads in Cuba and for its subsequent 'capitulationism' in abjectly bowing to the US threat to retaliate. Was this, China asked contemptuously, the way to inspire the world's struggling masses in their fight against American imperialism?

Sino-Soviet disagreement over coexistence with the West

Key question
How did the PRC and the USSR differ over the issue of coexistence with the non-Communist world?

The broad response in the West to the ending of the Cuban Missile Crisis was to congratulate both Kennedy and Khrushchev for their statesmanship in drawing back from the brink of war. Khrushchev was praised for putting his policy of **coexistence** into practical effect.

That was not how the Chinese saw it. For them, coexistence was a betrayal of the revolution. Instead of achieving peace, the policy simply played into the hands of the imperialist powers by settling issues on their terms. Genuine coexistence could exist only between equal nations. But, in Marxist theory, all pre-revolutionary states were in subjection to the exploiting capitalist power. In a formal statement in 1963, Chinese Communists explained the fallacy of coexistence and why they would not engage in it:

Key terms

Communist Cuba
In 1959 Communist guerrilla forces led by Fidel Castro had taken power in Cuba.

Coexistence
A willingness among nations with opposed ideologies to live and let live.

> Only after victory in the revolution is it possible and necessary for the proletariat to pursue the policy of peaceful coexistence. As for oppressed peoples and nations, their task is to strive for their own liberation and overthrow the rule of imperialism and its lackeys. They should not practise peaceful coexistence with the imperialists and their lackeys, nor is it possible for them to do so. It is therefore wrong to apply peaceful coexistence to the relations between oppressed and oppressor classes and between oppressed and oppressor nations.

The Soviet reply was to accuse the Chinese of total irresponsibility. It was arrogant and dangerous of them to claim to speak for the international working class: 'We might ask the Chinese: What right have you to decide for us questions involving our very existence and our class struggle? We too want socialism, but we want to win it through the class struggle, not by unleashing a world thermonuclear war.'

At the time of his fall from power in the USSR in 1964, Khrushchev was still trying to convince the rest of the Marxist world that the Maoist brand of Communism was heretical. His policy of isolating China was continued by the collective leadership that superseded him. In the fierce Sino-Soviet propaganda war each side accused the other of a long list of crimes against Communism. The USSR resurrected the spectre of the '**yellow peril**'. The Cultural Revolution that began in 1966 was cited as an example of China's raging fanaticism, a fanaticism that threatened to destroy the world.

Key term

Yellow peril
A term first used in the nineteenth century to suggest that China's vast population was preparing to spread out of Asia to swamp Europe, with Russia as the first victim.

Key question
How did Mao interpret China's revolutionary role?

Mao's concept of continuing revolution

Mao Zedong responded to the Soviet insults by describing the USSR's leaders as the corrupters of true Communism. He condemned their reforms of the Soviet economy as a return to capitalism and their moves towards coexistence as collusion with the imperialist West. Mao called on Communists in all other countries to reject the USSR's lead and develop their own form of true Marxism along Chinese lines.

The vital concept for Mao was that of 'continuing revolution' (see page 82). Fierce ideological battles over this notion had been fought earlier within the Soviet Union. Trotsky, Stalin's arch opponent in the 1920s and 1930s, had made 'continuing' or 'permanent' revolution the essence of Marxism–Leninism. For Trotsky, revolution was not an event, but a continuing process that guaranteed the ultimate victory of the international proletariat. Revolutions which regarded themselves as complete, or that were confined to individual countries, would cease to be revolutions and would fall prey to reaction. Mao Zedong's own definition of continuing revolution corresponded to Trotsky's:

> Our revolutions come one after another. Starting from the seizure of power in the whole country in 1949, there followed in quick succession the anti-feudal land reform, the agricultural co-operativisation, and the socialist reconstruction of private industries, commerce, and handicrafts. Our revolutions are like battles. After a victory, we must at once put forward a new task. In this way, cadres and the masses will forever be filled with revolutionary fervour.

Rivalry over the leadership of international Communism

The dispute between the USSR and China over the meaning of revolution raised the demanding question as to which nation was the real leader of the Communist world. Was it the USSR, direct heir of the great 1917 revolution, or Mao's China, whose peasant-based revolution in 1949 offered an inspiring model for all oppressed peoples?

In strict Marxist theory, true proletarian revolution could occur only in an urban, industrial society. According to Soviet political scientists, China, being a preponderantly rural, peasant society, could not be a fully developed Communist state. They asserted that Mao had distorted Marxism to make it fit the Chinese context. The CCP's theorists retorted that the Soviet Union was betraying the cause of world revolution by pursuing a suicidal policy of *détente* with the West.

The nuclear issue

The controversy over whether coexistence was compatible with Marxism–Leninism was at its fiercest in the Sino-Soviet dispute over the **Test Ban Treaty** of 1963. Mao dismissed the treaty as another betrayal by the USSR of its revolutionary role. Instead of confronting imperialism, it was collaborating with it: 'Soviet revisionists are uniting with the running dogs of capitalism'.

Khrushchev's rejoinder was that, rather than seek peace, the Chinese wished to see East and West destroy themselves in nuclear war, leaving China free to dominate what was left of the world. What gave particular irony to Khrushchev's charge was that China was only a year away from exploding its own atomic bomb.

Ever since the early 1950s Mao Zedong had been unhappy with the attitude of Stalin and successive Soviet leaders towards the nuclear question. Moscow's position was that if China wanted Soviet assistance in its nuclear programme it must give the USSR a controlling hand in the PRC's defence policy. This was too much for Mao. The Soviet demand redoubled his determination to make China a superpower by achieving nuclear status unaided.

In 1959 a particularly low point in Sino-Soviet relations was reached when the USSR decided to withdraw its scientists from the PRC. Nonetheless, China, undeterred, pressed on with its own research programme. Chinese nuclear physicists painstakingly pieced together the records that the Soviet advisers had shredded before their hurried departure.

Such efforts brought their reward. In 1964, to great rejoicing with massed crowds singing 'The East is Red' in Mao's honour, Communist China detonated its first atomic device. Three years later it became a superpower when it produced its first hydrogen bomb. China's remarkable feat allowed it to mock the USSR's refusal to assist. The first Chinese bomb was codenamed 59/6, a reference to the year and month in which the Soviet technicians had withdrawn from China. Mao recorded gloatingly:

> Modern weapons, guided missiles, and atom bombs were made very quickly, and we produced a hydrogen bomb in only 2 years and 8 months. Our development has been faster than that of America, Britain and France. We are now in fourth place in the world. Guided missiles and atom bombs are great achievements. This is the result of Khrushchev's 'help'. By withdrawing the experts he forced us to take our own road. We should give him a big medal.

Mao's willingness to contemplate nuclear war

China's emergence as a superpower frightened the world. China seemed not to have the same awesome fear of nuclear war that the West and the Soviet Union had. Mao referred to atomic weapons as '**paper tigers**'. He told Khrushchev at one of their

Key question
Why were the Soviet Union and China so divided over the question of nuclear weapons?

Key terms

Test Ban Treaty
Signed in 1963 between the USSR and the Western nuclear powers, in which the parties pledged to end their atmospheric testing of atomic weapons.

Paper tigers
One of Mao's favourite expressions; anything or anyone whose power, he believed, was more apparent than real.

Key dates

China produces its own atom bomb: 1964

China produces its own hydrogen bomb: 1967

meetings that despite the awesome destructiveness of atomic weapons, the PRC was quite willing to contemplate nuclear war with its enemies. To Khrushchev's amazement, Mao casually informed him that China's population was so big that it would soon make up any losses it suffered, no matter how great the disaster.

This was in keeping with an earlier CCP statement, which indicated China's belief that it could successfully survive a nuclear war, 'On the debris of a dead imperialism, the victorious [Chinese] people would create very swiftly a civilisation thousands of times higher than the capitalist system and a truly beautiful future for themselves.' Mao believed that China's emergence as a superpower and its refusal to be frightened of paper tigers had confirmed its position as the true champion of the oppressed peoples of the world:

> The success of China's hydrogen bomb test has further broken the nuclear monopoly of United States imperialism and Soviet revisionism and dealt a telling blow at their policy of nuclear blackmail. It is a very great encouragement to the revolutionary people of the whole world.

Mao and Brezhnev

The dismissal in 1964 of Nikita Khrushchev as Soviet leader and his replacement in the late 1960s by Leonid Brezhnev did little to improve Sino-Soviet relations. Brezhnev, who was to remain at the Soviet helm until 1982, was a Stalinist hardliner in foreign policy and is best remembered for the attitude that bears his name, the '**Brezhnev doctrine**'. In 1968, in an example of this doctrine in practice, Soviet tanks rolled into the Czechoslovak capital to suppress the '**Prague spring**'.

While Mao had no time for counter-revolution in Communist states he was unwilling to accept the right of the USSR, by his reckoning itself a socialist **apostate**, to impose Soviet authority on the members of the Marxist camp. From the outset, therefore, it was unlikely that Mao would have any better relations with Brezhnev than he had had with Stalin and Khrushchev – and so it proved.

Sino-Soviet confrontation 1969

In 1969 Brezhnev called an international Communist Conference in Moscow with the aim of outlawing China. However, the Soviet invasion of Czechoslovakia in the previous year had weakened the USSR's moral leadership and the conference was largely a failure from Brezhnev's perspective; he did not get the outright, unanimous condemnation of China that he had wanted.

The fact was that international Communism had seriously fragmented. The year 1969 marked the **nadir** in the relations of the two Communist superpowers. Serious border incidents threatened to turn into full-scale war. In an extraordinary development the PRC and the Soviet Union repositioned their nuclear-armed rockets so that they now faced inwards towards

Key terms

Brezhnev doctrine
The demand that all Communist states toe the Soviet line. If they failed to do so they must be disciplined by the other Marxist states acting as 'a socialist community' under the leadership of the USSR.

Prague spring
The attempt of the Czech Communist government in 1968 to assert its independence of Soviet control.

Key question
What effect did the emergence of Brezhnev as Soviet leader have on the USSR's relations with China?

Key terms

Apostate
A person, group or nation that abandons its original political or religious beliefs.

Nadir
The lowest point.

Key term

Social fascism
First used by Stalin to denote those Communists and socialists who were willing to compromise with their political enemies.

each other rather than outwards towards their Western enemies. This may have been bluff and counter-bluff, but there was no doubting that Sino-Soviet relations had reached their lowest point. This was powerfully expressed in Lin Biao's 1969 denunciation of Brezhnev and the Soviet 'revisionists':

> Since Brezhnev came to power, the Soviet revisionist renegade clique has been practising **social fascism** more frantically than ever. In order to justify its aggression and plunder, the Soviet revisionist renegade clique trumpets the so-called theory of 'international dictatorship' and the theory of 'socialist community'. What does all this stuff mean? It means they will exercise 'international dictatorship' over you – dictatorship over the people of other countries, in order to form the 'socialist community' ruled by the new czar.

Key question
What approach did Mao's successors adopt towards the Soviet Union?

The impact of Mao's death on Sino-Soviet relations

Mao's death in 1976, which was soon followed by the overthrow of the fanatically anti-Soviet Gang of Four, effectively removed the immediate danger of Sino-Soviet nuclear confrontation. Despite the previous difficulties, the new leaders of the PRC, Deng Xiaoping in particular, adopted a much more tolerant line towards both the USSR and the West. Deng adopted Zhou Enlai's accommodating style as an international statesman. He deliberately toned down the aggressive anti-Soviet approach that he had shown while serving under Mao. The possibility of nuclear war between China and either the USA or the USSR became increasingly remote.

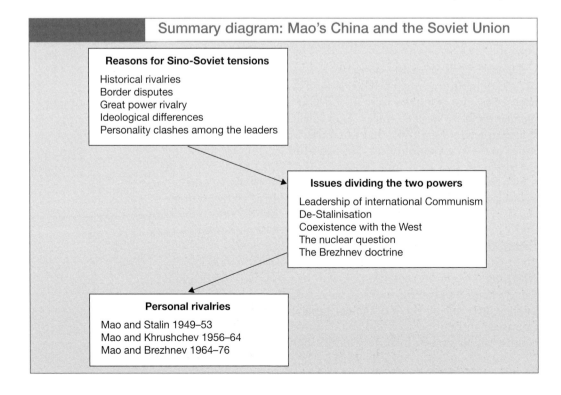

Summary diagram: Mao's China and the Soviet Union

Reasons for Sino-Soviet tensions

Historical rivalries
Border disputes
Great power rivalry
Ideological differences
Personality clashes among the leaders

Issues dividing the two powers

Leadership of international Communism
De-Stalinisation
Coexistence with the West
The nuclear question
The Brezhnev doctrine

Personal rivalries

Mao and Stalin 1949–53
Mao and Khrushchev 1956–64
Mao and Brezhnev 1964–76

3 | The PRC and the United States

Key question
What were the roots of Sino-American hostility?

For a generation after 1949, relations between the PRC and the United States were tense and bitter. The specific reasons are not hard to find:

- American anger at the fall of China to Mao's Communists in 1949
- the USA's protection of Taiwan
- the USA's refusal to grant diplomatic recognition to the PRC
- conflict in Korea
- US Central Intelligence Agency (CIA) involvement in Tibet
- development of Chinese atomic weapons in the 1960s
- Mao's China was not directly involved in the **Vietnam War**, but it gave moral and diplomatic support to the USA's enemies
- the underlying ideological divide between the capitalist and Marxist systems they each represented.

Vietnam War: 1963–75

From 1950 the PRC had mounted a continuous propaganda attack on 'American imperialism' which included the ritual daily chanting by China's schoolchildren of, 'Death to the American imperialists and all their running dogs'. The campaign reached new levels of intensity during the Cultural Revolution and the Vietnam War into which the USA was drawn between 1963 and 1975.

Vietnam War
Between 1963 and 1975, the USA fought unsuccessfully to prevent South Vietnam being taken over by the Communists of North Vietnam.

Mao's Third Line

Key question
What anxieties led Mao to construct the Third Line?

Although official Chinese Communist propaganda made great play of Mao Zedong's mockery of the USA and its nuclear weapons as 'paper tigers', Mao's public bravado belied his private disquiet. From the time of the Korean War onwards he was convinced that the USA was planning a retaliatory attack on China.

There was a remarkable similarity between Joseph Stalin and Mao Zedong in this regard. They shared an abiding fear that their respective countries were in constant danger of a strike against them by Western forces. Mao calculated, as Stalin had done earlier in the USSR, that when the West was ready it would move to destroy Communism. His anxieties led him to devise a defensive strategy for China, known as the 'Third Line'. This was a plan for a vast network of fortifications, installed above and below ground, so strongly built as to be capable of withstanding the heaviest bombardment.

Deng Xiaoping's role

To organise this great defensive system Mao turned to Deng Xiaoping, who undertook the task with his customary dedication. Deng planned to use the existing bases, which had been created by the GMD during the war against Japan, to establish a series of industrial and military settlements that would be defensible against US air strikes, including atomic bombing.

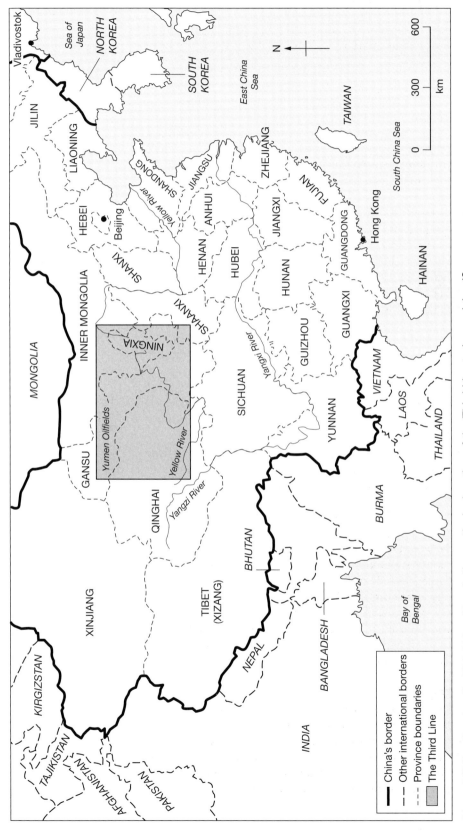

Map of China showing the Third Line. How is the particular location of the Third Line to be explained?

Reasons for the particular siting of the Third Line

The Third Line was to be located in the remoter regions of central China into which, in the event of an American attack, the population and industries of the vulnerable eastern and southern provinces could be withdrawn. Deng aimed to overcome the remoteness of the designated areas by creating a communication network capable of sustaining the projected military-industrial complex. As planned, the schemes entailed a massive relocation of Chinese industry and labour. Although the Third Line was never fully completed, the many constructions that were finished became a model for the large-scale industrial projects which were later to provide the basis of Mao's economic strategy for China.

The parting of the bamboo curtain

Mao's fears that had led to the creation of the Third Line hardly suggested that there was any likelihood of an easing of Sino-American rivalry. Yet this is what began to happen in the early 1970s. A major factor was the USA's reversal of its position on Chinese representation in the United Nations (UN); in 1971 it formally recognised Red China's right to replace Taiwan in the UN.

This important diplomatic gesture encouraged the PRC to soften its approach to the USA. While Mao was alive the fear that he had bred into the Chinese people of an American military attack would never entirely disappear, but following the USA's formal recognition of the PRC it was suspended sufficiently to allow talks to begin in 1971.

Mao's aim of undermining the USSR

It has to be stressed that China's willingness to improve its relations with the USA had a deeper purpose than merely a desire to be on better terms with the West. The softening of China's previously hard line was part of its strategy to undermine the Soviet Union. The Chinese particularly resented the Soviet policies of *détente* and coexistence. They saw this attempt to draw closer to the Western powers as a Soviet tactic to leave China internationally isolated. The PRC decided to outplay the USSR at its own game by achieving a Sino-American *détente*. Given the Cold War tensions, the USA was equally eager to see the USSR embarrassed in this way.

The role of Zhou Enlai and Kissinger

The initial diplomacy was conducted by Zhou Enlai and **Henry Kissinger**. A gesture that caught the headlines on both sides of the Pacific was the PRC's invitation to the US table-tennis team, then touring Japan, to play in China. It was this that gave the name 'ping-pong diplomacy' to the negotiations. The talks between Zhou and Kissinger prepared the way for Richard Nixon's visit to Beijing in February 1972.

Key question
Why did the early 1970s see a marked improvement in the relations between the PRC and the USA?

Key term

Bamboo curtain
A figurative way of describing China's hostile and suspicious attitude towards the non-Communist world; it is similar to the notion of the iron curtain.

Key dates

PRC replaced Taiwan in UN: 1971

Visit of President Nixon to China: 1972

Key figure

Henry Kissinger
President Nixon's special adviser on foreign affairs.

Photo showing Mao and Nixon shaking hands in Beijing in 1972. Why might this photograph be described as iconic?

Key question
Why was Nixon's visit such a major event in East–West relations?

The significance of the Nixon visit

That Nixon's visit took place at all made it a momentous event. For the leader of the USA, 'the number one enemy nation', to be invited to China would have been unimaginable only a few years earlier. The ailing Mao seemed to take an almost boyish delight at the thought of meeting the President of the United States, arguably the most powerful man in the world. The two men genuinely took to each other; their talks and those between their officials went very well. Overall, the visit was certainly a major diplomatic success. A joint communiqué was issued in which the two nations expressed:

- the hope that there would be continuing Sino-American contacts
- the desirability of commercial, cultural and educational exchanges
- their joint agreement to give further consideration to ways in which the previously intractable Taiwan issue could be resolved.

Nixon's visit was more than merely symbolic. As their communiqué showed, the PRC and the USA remained guarded in their approach. But the visit had indicated that after the upheavals of the Cultural Revolution China was prepared, if not to lift the bamboo curtain, at least to part it.

The Chinese were undoubtedly assisted in this by the more understanding approach of the Americans and by their mutual readiness to do down the Soviet Union. Relations continued to improve during Mao's remaining years and beyond; they reached a high point in 1979 with the establishment of full diplomatic relations between the two countries. Much remained to divide the two nations. But the machinery for diplomatic contact and trade had been put in place.

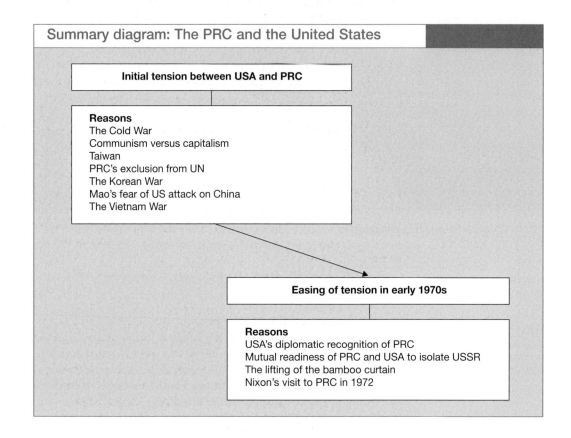

Summary diagram: The PRC and the United States

Initial tension between USA and PRC

Reasons
The Cold War
Communism versus capitalism
Taiwan
PRC's exclusion from UN
The Korean War
Mao's fear of US attack on China
The Vietnam War

Easing of tension in early 1970s

Reasons
USA's diplomatic recognition of PRC
Mutual readiness of PRC and USA to isolate USSR
The lifting of the bamboo curtain
Nixon's visit to PRC in 1972

China After Mao: The Deng Revolution 1978–97

POINTS TO CONSIDER

Soon after Mao's death, Deng Xiaoping emerged as the leading figure in Chinese politics. Without ever openly denouncing his predecessor, Deng set about changing Mao's policies and directing China on a new path. So important were the changes he introduced that they merit being called a revolution. Deng's impact is studied in this chapter under the following themes:

- The abandonment of Maoism
- Deng's economic reforms
- The pro-democracy movement 1979–89

Key dates

1976	Gang of Four arrested
1976–8	Deng returned to prominence
1978	Third Plenum convened
1979	Pro-democracy movement began
	Wei Jingsheng imprisoned
1981	Sentencing of the Gang of Four
1986	Protests in China's leading universities
1989	Death of Hu Yaobang
	Mikhail Gorbachev visited China
	Pro-democracy demonstration crushed in Beijing
1997	Death of Deng Xiaoping

1 | The Abandonment of Maoism

Key question
What were Deng's aims in post-Mao China?

Within 2 years of Mao Zedong's death in 1976, Deng Xiaoping, having survived denunciation and exile during the Cultural Revolution, had returned to become the dominant force in China. By the time of his death in 1997, Deng would prove to have been as remarkable a leader as Mao. Believing that Mao's economic policies had been fundamentally mistaken, Deng restructured Chinese agriculture and industry in such a way that he laid the basis for China's development as a modern nation, capable of competing commercially with the advanced nations of the world.

Deng's victory in the power struggle after Mao's death 1976–8

Key question
Why had Deng emerged as Mao's successor by 1978?

Between 1976 and 1978 Deng was able to outmanoeuvre the other contenders for power, principally the Gang of Four, who were arrested and imprisoned. By July 1977, he had resumed his role as CCP General Secretary. A year later, at a full party meeting, Deng was acknowledged as China's outstanding spokesman. Deng's return to prominence rested on a number of strengths that his opponents could not match:

Gang of Four arrested: 1976

Deng returned to prominence: 1976–8

Third Plenum convened: 1978

- his long experience at the heart of Chinese politics
- exceptional political skills
- genuine popularity within the CCP
- support among leading party officials at the centre and in the provinces
- contacts with key military leaders
- success in ending the famine in the early 1960s
- an impressive record as an economic planner, working with Zhou Enlai in the 1970s in drafting a major programme for national economic recovery
- his standing as an international statesman, having been foreign secretary Zhou Enlai's principal assistant for much of the period 1949–76.

The Third Plenum 1978: the PRC's turning point

Key question
In what ways was the Third Plenum a turning point in post-Mao China?

The first major meeting of the Chinese Communist Party to gather after Mao's passing became known as the Third **Plenum** of the Central Committee of the CCP. Convened in December 1978, it proved to be a landmark in China's post-Mao reformation. The decisions reached at the plenum meant a new departure for the People's Republic of China:

- The resolution 'to restore party democracy' began the process of rehabilitating those who had been wrongly condemned during the Maoist purges of the 1960s and 1970s.
- The plenum confirmed Deng's leadership of China by appointing him chairman of the People's Political Consultative Conference (PPCC), an organisation that was given the principal responsibility for economic reform in China.
- The plenum accepted Deng's '**four modernisations**' as the basis for China's development.

Plenum
A full, formal, authoritative gathering.

Four modernisations
Plans for the reform of agriculture, industry, defence and education, which Deng had been working on since the 1960s but could not introduce until Mao had gone.

These resolutions of the Third Plenum clearly meant that the Cultural Revolution had been abandoned. Deng Xiaoping's personal success at the plenum, in obtaining the full support of the CCP for his proposals, also showed that he was now the outstanding figure in Chinese politics. This was soon recognised by the CCP by its conferring on him the honorary title of 'paramount leader'. This had no specific functions attached to it but was all the more powerful because of that. He feigned humility by declining to accept formal positions while knowing that he had the influence and connections to remain in control of developments. He was now in a position to begin what was to become known as the Deng revolution.

Dealing with Mao's legacy

Key question
How did Deng plan to undermine Mao's policies and reputation?

Since the early 1960s, when he had tackled the famine in China (see page 69), Deng had regarded the policies of the Great Leap Forward as basically wrong; he believed they had produced not growth but stagnation. Now that he was in power he was resolved to remove the remnants of Maoism that stood in the path of China's economic progress.

However, Deng was very conscious that Mao's impact had been so powerful that if it were to be suddenly denounced it would bewilder and disrupt China. Deng judged that the Chinese people would not be able to understand an attack on the 'Great Helmsman', the leader who had come to be regarded as a god. In the USSR, Stalin's record and reputation had become reviled within 3 years of his death in 1953. But there was to be no equivalent to de-Stalinisation in China. Any criticisms of Mao would have to be muted and subtle.

The Central Committee resolution 1981

Deng was also well aware that any attack on Mao would by implication be an attack on those who had served him. This would include all the current leaders of the government and the party. Far safer, therefore, to subject Mao's reputation to the **drip effect**. A CCP Central Committee resolution of 1981, drafted by Deng Xiaoping himself, revealed the compromise the party was obliged to seek. It observed that Mao Zedong had indeed been a great leader in his day, but one who had made errors which China was now entitled to correct: 'It is true that he made gross mistakes during the Cultural Revolution, but, if we judge his activities as a whole, his contribution to the Chinese Revolution far outweighs his mistakes'.

Key term

Drip effect
Letting a reputation gradually erode rather than formally attacking it.

The party then declared that Mao in his policies had been 70 per cent right and 30 per cent wrong. This subtle mathematical formula left Deng and the government free to abandon Mao's policies while still appearing to be loyal to his memory.

The trial of the Gang of Four 1980–1

This key resolution came after another event that provided Deng and the reformers with a very convenient opportunity to condemn the old Maoist ways while still appearing to honour Mao himself. In November 1980, over 4 years after their arrest, the Gang of Four were at last put on trial. The aim was to use them as scapegoats to explain why China had gone wrong. The general accusation was that they had betrayed Mao and the Chinese Revolution. Among the specific charges against them were that during the course of the Cultural Revolution they had been individually and collectively responsible for the deaths of 35,000 people and that they had 'framed and persecuted' a further three-quarters of a million.

Key date

Sentencing of the Gang of Four: 1981

Jiang Qing, the principal defendant, remained totally defiant, refusing to accept the charges against her and shouting abuse at her accusers. She asserted repeatedly that she had had Mao Zedong's support in everything she had done and that the Cultural Revolution had been carried out in accordance with his wishes. At one point she cried out: 'I was Mao's bitch. Whoever he told me to bite, I bit.'

Jiang's spirited resistance throughout her 3-month trial embarrassed the court, but it did not save her. The trials ended in January 1981 with guilty verdicts on all those charged. Jiang was sentenced to death. Subsequently, the sentence was commuted to life imprisonment in order to give her 'time to repent'. But she was not the repenting kind; at the time of Jiang's death 10 years later in 1991 she was still angrily proclaiming her innocence.

Whatever their weakness as a public relations' exercise, the trials marked a fitting final closure of the Great Proletarian Cultural Revolution. The sentencing of the Gang of Four was the new regime's way of admitting that Mao's extraordinary political and social experiment had been a ghastly and deadly failure.

Key terms

Market
The system of allowing the economy to run freely according to the play of supply and demand without interference by the state.

Socialist concepts
The structuring of the economy by the government with the aim of spreading equality.

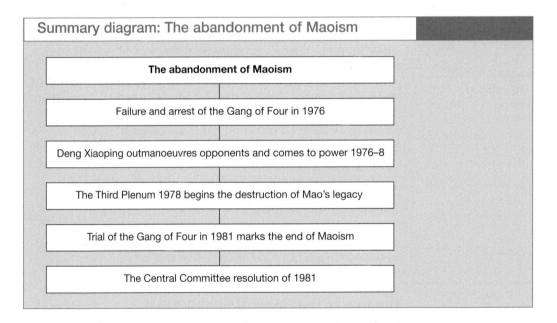

Summary diagram: The abandonment of Maoism

The abandonment of Maoism

Failure and arrest of the Gang of Four in 1976

Deng Xiaoping outmanoeuvres opponents and comes to power 1976–8

The Third Plenum 1978 begins the destruction of Mao's legacy

Trial of the Gang of Four in 1981 marks the end of Maoism

The Central Committee resolution of 1981

2 | Deng's Economic Reforms

Throughout the 1970s, Deng had urged that realism, not theory, ought to prevail in the planning of China's economy. If a plan worked, keep it; if it did not, scrap it. If the **market** produced better results than rigid adherence to **socialist concepts**, then let the market operate freely. If contact with the capitalist West increased China's trade and commerce, then encourage such contact. This essentially practical approach was summed up in Deng's favourite saying: 'It does not matter whether a cat is black or white, so long as it catches mice'.

Key question
What was Deng's basic approach in economic matters?

During Mao's time, such apparent disregard for strict socialist planning was thought too extreme and was one of the reasons why Deng had become politically suspect. But with Mao dead and the Gang of Four, who had fiercely opposed the liberalising of the economy, dead or imprisoned, the time to apply Deng's ideas had come. In 1982 he defined China's economic aims as:

- invigorating China's domestic economy
- opening Chinese trade to the outside world
- allowing the development of individual enterprises
- encouraging joint ventures with both Chinese and foreign investment.

Deng's 'hands off' policy

Key question
In what sense was Deng's policy a 'hands off' approach?

Deng's approach to economic reform was to be an essentially 'hands off' policy. The state would not entirely detach itself from economic planning. The state-owned enterprises (SOEs) that had been set up in Mao's time (see page 50) would remain the basic form of industrial organisation, but much greater freedom and initiative would be granted to managers and experts on the spot. **Dogma** would give place to practicality. Purely administrative concerns would not be allowed to overrule economic considerations. Bureaucracy would be the servant not the master of the Chinese economy.

In explaining his reforms to the party, Deng stressed that the various adjustments he was pressing for all rested on two essential changes:

Key terms

Dogma
Rigid, unchanging beliefs.

Xiang
Village or township.

- restoration of the market as the chief mechanism by which the Chinese economy operated
- opening of China to foreign trade.

The reforms themselves divide into two key sections and periods. Between 1978 and 1984, the main emphasis was on the improvement of the rural economy. After 1984, attention shifted to the development of industry and commerce.

Agriculture

Key question
What major changes took place on the land?

In the countryside, the commune was abandoned and replaced by the *xiang*. The *xiang* would still be required to meet food production output quotas, but, instead of these being achieved by the former collective work units, individual peasants and their families would contribute their due share under a new 'household responsibility system'. Provided the peasants paid their taxes and contributed to the local quotas, they were left free to sell any surplus produce for private profit. As Table 7.1 overleaf shows, this policy of privatisation had notable success in the early 1980s.

Table 7.1: China's agricultural record 1978–89

Year	Grain production (millions of tonnes)	Meat production (millions of tonnes)	Index of gross output compared to base of 100 in 1952
1978	304.8	8.6	229.6
1979	332.1	10.6	249.4
1980	320.6	12.1	259.1
1981	325.0	12.6	276.2
1982	354.5	13.5	306.8
1983	387.3	14.0	330.7
1984	407.3	15.4	373.1
1985	379.1	17.6	385.7
1986	391.5	19.2	398.9
1987	404.7	19.9	422.0
1988	394.1	21.9	438.5
1989	407.8	23.3	452.0

Problems

The undoubted benefits that the ending of collectivisation brought the peasants were offset by the continuing uncertainty about their property rights. The great majority of farmers in China still held their farms on a 15-year lease. In most cases privatisation did not grant permanent ownership. The legal position was that after 15 years the land would revert back to the state. It is true that the government promised to consider extending the leases, but the bitter experiences of the Chinese peasants in the twentieth century had taught them to distrust government promises.

Doubts about the security of their land holding deterred the peasants from improving their farms or investing for long-term growth. Hence, the traditional, but inefficient, methods continued to prevail at the very time when the government believed its land reforms would lead farmers to embrace modernisation and expansion.

Key question
What problems did the land reforms create?

Industry

Educational changes

The relative success that had been achieved in agriculture by the mid-1980s enabled Deng and the government to turn their attention to industry. With the aim of promoting industrial growth and scientific education, the universities were greatly expanded in size and number. The plan was to train a million technical students to become the managers and administrators of the new economy. The same objective underlaid the schemes for sending thousands of Chinese students to study abroad; this was the means by which China would gain direct knowledge of Western technology and industrial expertise.

Key question
What steps were taken to modernise China's industry?

Special Economic Zones

The intention was that the students would then return to China to apply their training and experience to the development of the **Special Economic Zones** (SEZ). The first four SEZs were Shantou

Special Economic Zones
The areas, containing China's main export industries and companies, which were earmarked for immediate and concentrated development.

Key term

(Swatow) and Xiamen (Amoy) in the north, and Shenzen (Shentsen) and Zhuhai (Chuhai) in the south. The SEZs became China's chief commercial outlets. They were given regional autonomy and granted special tax concessions and financial freedoms to enable them to fulfil Deng's plea that the nation open up its commerce to the world.

The SEZs proved to be one of modern China's success stories. Between 1978 and 1989 China's international trade flourished; exports grew by over 500 per cent and foreign investment in China quadrupled (see Table 7.2).

Table 7.2: China's imports and exports balance 1978–89 (in US$ billions)

Year	Imports	Exports
1978	10.9	9.8
1979	15.7	13.7
1980	20.0	18.1
1981	22.0	22.0
1982	19.3	22.3
1983	21.4	22.2
1984	27.4	26.1
1985	42.3	27.4
1986	42.9	30.9
1987	43.2	39.4
1988	55.3	47.5
1989	59.1	52.5

Key terms

Pragmatism
A way of tackling problems that is based on the actual situation rather than on abstract theory.

State subsidies
A scheme of payments, introduced in Mao's time, to supplement workers' or businesses' low income.

Key question
What difficulties were attached to the development of the SEZs?

Deng's **pragmatism** in economic matters was evident in all this. He had observed that where the younger and more progressive party officials had been allowed to put their ideas into practice the results had been strikingly successful. Two particular provinces, Sichuan and Guangdong, had witnessed major increases in productivity and output. Deng was greatly impressed by the way the young managers in these regions had achieved greater output and improved quality of product by introducing wage incentives to encourage the workers to develop efficient work practices and attain higher skill levels.

Problems

It was in regard to incentives that a major problem arose for Deng's reformers. Although the methods followed in Mao's SOEs had not encouraged genuine growth, they had provided the workers with an 'iron rice bowl' (see page 50). Deng's changes, however, meant that workers and companies no longer enjoyed guaranteed incomes. Freedom from state control also meant the end of **state subsidies**. The SOEs were now expected to become efficient and competitive. Cost-saving schemes were to be introduced as a means of achieving higher and cheaper output. New short-term contracts that were aimed at improving

productivity meant that employees would now be paid according to performance and would retain their jobs only if they contributed genuinely to the enterprise. There were no guaranteed jobs any longer.

Resistance from the SOEs

Not surprisingly, the modernisation schemes met strong resistance from the SOEs. No matter how much the reformers emphasised the virtues of the new proposals, the workers were unwilling to put their 'iron rice bowls' at risk and were slow to co-operate. This reluctance meant that the intended reforms took far longer to implement than had been planned. It took until 1986 to get a modified **labour-contract scheme** operating and then it applied only to new employees not to established workers. The government offered further concessions in the form of unemployment insurance, but 6 years later the scheme covered barely one-fifth of the 80 million employees in the SOEs.

Such resistance to new ideas did not prevent progress towards industrial modernisation, but it did slow it down. This indicated that in a country the size of China, with its conservative attitude among the workers and its regional variations, centralised economic planning would always be difficult to achieve. The actual success is evident in Table 7.3.

Productivity
The efficiency with which an article is made, measured by the time and cost involved in its production.

Labour-contract scheme
An agreement between employers and workers, based on the principle of higher wages in return for greater effort and higher productivity.

Table 7.3: China's industrial performance 1979–89

Year	GDP* (in billions of yuan)	Annual GDP growth rate (%)	Annual inflation rate (%)	Annual manufacturing output growth rate (%)
1979	732.6	7.6	6.1	8.6
1980	790.5	7.9	−1.5	11.9
1981	826.1	4.5	7.0	1.6
1982	896.3	8.5	11.5	5.5
1983	987.7	10.2	8.3	9.2
1984	1130.9	14.5	12.9	14.5
1985	1276.8	12.9	1.8	18.1
1986	1385.4	8.5	3.3	8.3
1987	1539.1	11.1	4.7	12.7
1988	1713.1	11.3	2.5	15.8
1989	1786.7	4.3	3.1	4.9

* Gross domestic product is the total value of goods produced in a year.

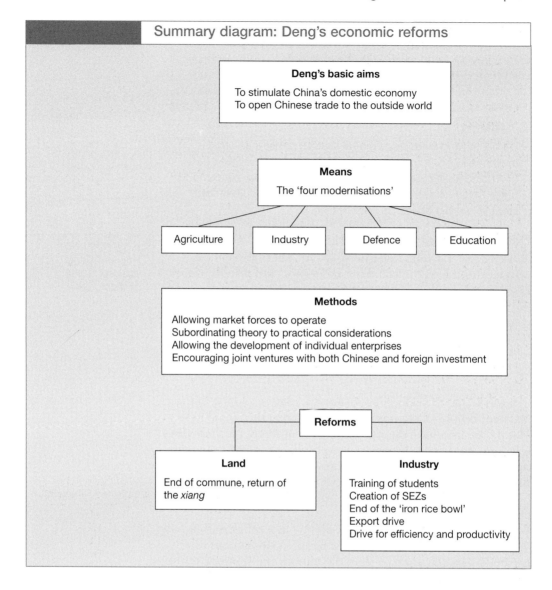

Summary diagram: Deng's economic reforms

Deng's basic aims

To stimulate China's domestic economy
To open Chinese trade to the outside world

Means

The 'four modernisations'

Agriculture | Industry | Defence | Education

Methods

Allowing market forces to operate
Subordinating theory to practical considerations
Allowing the development of individual enterprises
Encouraging joint ventures with both Chinese and foreign investment

Reforms

Land

End of commune, return of the *xiang*

Industry

Training of students
Creation of SEZs
End of the 'iron rice bowl'
Export drive
Drive for efficiency and productivity

3 | The Pro-democracy Movement 1979–89

Deng Xiaoping's opposition to political reform

An important point to stress is that Deng's programme for regenerating China was as much concerned with political conservatism as it was with economic progress. He had emphasised this strongly when introducing his reforms. Deng balanced the 'four modernisations' with his 'four cardinal principles', which he defined as:

- 'keeping to the socialist road'
- 'upholding the people's democratic dictatorship'
- 'upholding leadership by the Communist Party'
- 'upholding Marxism–Leninism and Mao Zedong Thought'.

Key question
Why was Deng so determined to resist political reform in China?

Key date
Beginning of pro-democracy movement: 1979

What is noticeable about these principles is that, unlike the 'four modernisations', they were not a formula for change but for the maintenance of the existing political structure. They were essentially a restating of the concept of democratic centralism, the idea that the Chinese Communist Party as the voice of Marxist correctness was entitled to the absolute obedience of the people (see page 27).

> We are striving for socialist modernisation, rather than other modernisations. To preach bourgeois liberalisation will lead our country to the capitalist road. We should take a clear-cut stand to uphold the Four Cardinal Principles and carry out a protracted struggle against bourgeois liberalisation.

Deng's political aims for China

As Deng saw it, China's first need was for internal stability; without this the nation could not modernise and take its proper place in the world. He said that China, having just gone through the bitter experience of the Cultural Revolution, needed a rest from politics. He meant by this that China should move away from debate and discussion and devote itself to the task of making itself a powerful economic nation. 'Our task is to build up the country, and less important things should be subordinated to it.'

It was Deng's thinking that inspired a 1980 resolution of the National People's Congress which condemned the liberal view that the people 'have the right to speak out freely, air their views fully, and hold great debates'. China could not afford to indulge in popular democracy along Western lines. It would merely cause distraction and disruption.

Deng's basic political attitude

It is broadly correct to see Deng Xiaoping as a reformer, but only in the economic sphere. In politics, he was a Communist hardliner. His aim was to restore the morale and standing of the CCP after the disruptive decades of the Great Leap Forward and the Cultural Revolution. He wanted to show that the Communist Party was still capable of governing China and had the right to the loyalty of the people.

Like Mao Zedong, he was part product, part creator, of the turbulent history of China through which he had lived since the 1920s. His belief in the authority of the CCP as the only legitimate shaper of China's destinies was unshakeable. It was this conviction that made a major showdown between the old-guard CCP and the supporters of democracy increasingly likely.

The 'democracy wall'

In the Avenue of Eternal Peace, near Tiananmen Square, there used to stretch a 200-metre brick wall. In the late 1970s the avenue became a common gathering place for students, who established the practice of affixing to the wall a mass of literature from small personal letters to large posters. The writings covered

Key question
How did Deng interpret China's political needs?

Key question
What form did the protests take?

Key date

Wei Jingsheng imprisoned: 1979

every conceivable subject and gave an obvious opportunity for the expression of anti-government and anti-party feelings. Periodically, the government forbade the 'democracy wall' to be used in this way; it ordered the posters to be torn down and had the more outspoken of the critics arrested.

Wei Jingsheng

One such occasion occurred early in 1979 when Wei Jingsheng (Wei Ching-chen), a former Red Guard, used the wall as part of his personal campaign to call the government to account for its failure to introduce real democratic freedoms into China. He was particularly critical of the PRC's recent foreign policy blunders. When Wei sought to reveal details of China's disastrous showing in **Vietnam** he was arrested and sentenced to 15 years' imprisonment.

Key question
What was the movement's basic demand?

Key term

Vietnam
In 1978, Chinese forces actively supported a Cambodian invasion of Vietnam. PRC government propaganda portrayed this as a great military success. In fact, the Chinese forces were heavily defeated and forced to withdraw.

The democracy movement

Wei may be regarded as the first martyr in what became known as the 'democracy movement'. This was never an organised party and its numbers and strength fluctuated, but it broadly represented those intellectuals who saw in Deng's reforms the opportunity not only to modernise the economy but also to liberalise the political system.

The democracy movement did not initially challenge the authority of the CCP. What it urged was that Deng and the government should honour the Communist principles that they supposedly espoused. In particular it asked that the party's commitment to the rule of the people should not merely be a slogan, but should be genuinely upheld by extending Deng Xiaoping's 'four fundamentals' to include a fifth: the adoption of democracy.

For long periods the democrats were broadly tolerated, but they were always likely to be turned on whenever the government felt objections had gone too far. This explains the severity of Wei Jingsheng's punishment. It was intended as a salutary warning to those intellectuals and journalists who mistakenly believed that it had become permissible in post-Mao China to criticise the party and government.

Key question
Why was the government particularly sensitive on the question of corruption?

Charges of corruption against the government

The charge which most disturbed the authorities was that government in China had become corrupt. In the late 1970s a notorious case of racketeering came to light in Heilongjiang (Heilunkiang) province when it was revealed that the managers of a state-owned fuel and power company had been diverting large sums of public money into their own pockets. The chief embezzlers were put on public trial and executed.

The government expected to gain credit from this widely publicised example of its resolute response. Yet the fact was that the scandal had come to light only through the tenacity of an investigative journalist whose exposé forced the authorities to take action. Furthermore, the chief culprits in the Heilongjiang case were all leading members of the provincial CCP. Critics began to ask just how widespread was corruption within the party.

Demonstrations spread

The belief that there was something implicitly corrupt about the CCP's management of China underlay the series of student demonstrations that occurred sporadically throughout the 1980s. The common demand of these protests was for greater political democracy and economic opportunity. Major disturbances occurred in 1986 in universities in Hefei, Wuhan and Shanghai. Thousands of students followed Fang Lizhi (Fang Li-chih), who was both a professor at Hefei and a CCP member, in calling for the open government and democracy that the authorities continually talked of but never delivered.

The government quelled the disturbances by dismissing Fang, arresting the ringleaders, and dismissing the troubles as the work of an anti-social minority. But how deeply the government had been shaken was evident in its removal of **Hu Yaobang** (Hu Yao-pang), the CCP General Secretary. The party blamed Hu for having encouraged the student troubles by criticising the slow pace of political change.

Deng's rejection of democracy

After the crushing of the 1986 protests, Deng thought it appropriate at this point to restate his rejection of 'bourgeois liberalisation'. He defined this as the mistaken notion that had developed among some party members since the defeat of the Gang of Four that modernisation involved moving towards Western-style democracy. Deng spelled out why genuine democracy was not an option for the Chinese. It was essentially a matter of practicalities:

> China is such a huge country, with such an enormous population, so many nationalities and such varied conditions that it is not yet possible to hold direct elections at higher levels. Furthermore, the people's educational level is too low. So we have to stick to the system of people's congresses, in which democratic centralism is applied. Without the leadership of the Communist Party, there can be no building of socialism.

Deng's statement captured the fundamental difference of outlook between the CCP hardliners and the **progressive thinkers** who made up the pro-democracy movement. What Deng was declaring was that there was no need for greater participation by the people in Chinese politics; the uninformed people should be content to let their enlightened government lead them. For Chinese progressives this was no longer an acceptable attitude; as they saw it, developments in China had shown that left to itself the government was incapable of providing those advances that they had come to expect and to which they believed they were entitled.

Key question
Why were significant numbers of students to be found among the protesters?

Protests in China's leading universities: 1986

Key date

Key question
For what reasons did Deng reject Western-style democracy for China?

Hu Yaobang (1915–89) A protégé of Deng Xiaoping, he had been a prominent figure in the party until his dismissal for being too sympathetic to the dissident students.

Key figure

Progressive thinkers
Those with a forward-looking attitude who in the 1970s were beginning to demand that power and privilege in China should not be the monopoly of the leaders of the CCP.

Key term

Key question
Why did so many
Chinese people feel
let down by Deng's
economic reforms?

Mounting frustration

For many Chinese people, the reforms introduced by Deng in the period 1979–89 proved deeply disappointing. This was the result of a number of factors:

- After the initial economic spurt of the early 1980s there had been a serious downturn in agricultural and industrial production.
- The ending of the subsidy system had created uncertainty and anxiety among the workers and had removed the shield that had protected the urban dwellers from high prices.
- Inflation had reduced the workers' real wages.
- The growing population and the continuing movement of people from the countryside into the urban areas had led to severe overcrowding in the major cities.

These developments had undermined the improved standards of living that had been experienced in the early years of Deng's reforms. It seemed that aspirations had been raised only to be dashed. Students and intellectuals felt that, despite the promise of progress and reform held out by the modernisation programme, the Communist Party under Deng Xiaoping had failed to deliver.

Anger over lack of employment opportunities

Poor job prospects were a particular anxiety among the students. In the late 1970s, in accordance with the 'four modernisations' programme, there had been an explosion in the numbers entering higher education. But a decade later it was evident that employment opportunities had failed to keep pace with the rising number of graduates. There was resentment that such jobs as were available were reserved for party members and their children. It was this grievance that fuelled the anger over government corruption.

Key question
Why was the
massacre such a
significant event for
China?

The Tiananmen Square massacre, June 1989

In Beijing, in the summer of 1989, a tragedy took place that shocked the world: the shooting on government orders of thousands of unarmed demonstrators in Tiananmen Square. The massacre was a violent climax to the tensions that had been building up since Mao's death. It was a product of basic problems in China that Deng's reforms, far from solving, had intensified.

The path to the massacre

On 15 April 1989 the death of Hu Yaobang focused the minds of all those who were unhappy with the economic and political system as it was operating under Deng Xiaoping. Hu had not always been sympathetic to the demands for greater democracy, but all that was forgotten at his passing. What was remembered was his removal from government in 1987 for daring to support the student protests. He had been forced to undergo self-criticism and had undergone such harsh treatment that his health had

Key date
Death of Hu Yaobang:
April 1989

broken. Posthumously he was elevated by the students into a symbol of resistance whose death from a heart attack was blamed on the harassment he had suffered for having upheld democratic values.

Hu's memorial service

By the time of Hu's memorial service, which took place a week after his death, large crowds had gathered in Tiananmen Square. They demonstrated noisily as three kneeling students tried to press a petition into the hands of Premier **Li Peng** and other government officials as they made their way into the **Great Hall of the People** to attend the service. The refusal of Li and his colleagues to accept the petition was taken as a sign of how far the government had become detached from the people. A series of sit-ins and boycotts of university classes quickly followed.

Demonstrators begin to occupy Tiananmen Square

The People's Daily raised the temperature by denouncing all this as the work of 'a small handful of plotters' who must be crushed immediately. Aroused rather than deterred by such threats, students from over 40 universities in China moved to join their fellows in Tiananmen Square. A particularly ominous portent for the government was the solidarity the transport workers showed with the students by allowing them to travel to Beijing without paying their fares.

Zhao Ziyang's unsuccessful appeal

A prominent government figure, **Zhao Ziyang** (Chao Tzu-yang), tried to appease the protesters by making a public statement in which he suggested that *The People's Daily* had gone too far. But the demonstration in Tiananmen Square had begun to develop a momentum. By the second week of May a group of 300 students had gone on hunger strike. For the first time the government made direct contact with student representatives, urging them to call off the strike. A number of China's leading writers added their voice to this appeal, but at the same time pleaded with the government to recognise the protest as a genuinely democratic and patriotic movement.

Gorbachev's visit to Beijing

The students declined to abandon their protest because they believed that events had given them two advantages that they could exploit:

- The protesters were convinced that the wide international media coverage that they were receiving, with foreign camera crews and journalists from every continent having taken up residence in the square, restricted the Chinese government's freedom of action.
- Student leaders also calculated that the government's hands were tied by the imminent arrival in Beijing of Mikhail Gorbachev, the first Soviet leader to be invited to China since

Key figures

Li Peng
(1928–) Soviet-trained, hardline Communist, who was totally opposed to any concessions being made to the democracy movement.

Zhao Ziyang
(1919–2005) Party General Secretary (1986–9), a major economic reformer under Deng, he became distrusted by his government colleagues because of his apparent sympathy towards the democracy movement.

Key terms

Great Hall of the People
A large parliament building on the west side of Tiananmen Square.

The People's Daily
The official CCP newspaper, and the government's mouthpiece.

the Sino-Soviet rift. His visit explained the presence of the world's press in Beijing. The students revered Gorbachev as the progressive leader of a socialist state who was introducing into his country the very reforms that they were demanding for China. They believed that while he was present in China the government would not dare to crush their demonstration.

Government attitudes harden

Key date

Gorbachev's visit to Beijing: 16–19 May 1989

The visit of Gorbachev may have indeed delayed the authorities from taking firm action, but their anger at having to change his schedule and itinerary made the hardliners still more resolute against the protesters. With Tiananmen Square now occupied by rebellious students, the plan to impress Gorbachev with the type of organised mass rally that the PRC customarily put on for important foreign visitors had to be curtailed. The talks between the Soviet and Chinese leaders did go ahead, but in a strangely unreal atmosphere. What should have been a historic Sino-Soviet summit had been overshadowed; the truly historic events were happening elsewhere in Beijing.

On 19 May, the sixth day of the hunger strike and the day that Gorbachev left China, Zhao Ziyang again went down to the square to address the students. He tearfully promised them that the issues over which they were protesting would eventually be resolved. Li Peng also spoke briefly to the students, but his was a perfunctory visit; it seems that he and Deng Xiaoping had already decided that the demonstrations were to be ended by force. It was this that gave particular poignancy to Zhao's parting words to the students, 'I came too late, too late. We are too old to see the day when China is strong. But you are young. You should stay alive.'

Martial law imposed

That same evening Zhao was dismissed from his post and Li Peng, in a broadcast speech in which he condemned the students as 'rioters' who were putting the future of the People's Republic of China at risk, formally declared the imposition of martial law. The news of the government's intention to apply 'firm and resolute measures to end the turmoil' rallied the students who had begun to waver. They voted to end the hunger strike, but to continue their occupation of the square. It is arguable that this is what the hardliners in the government wanted. Were the demonstrators to have peacefully dispersed at this point it would have deprived the authorities of the chance to make an example of them.

The reaction of Beijing residents

However, things did not go entirely the government's way. When news of the demonstrators' determination to stay in the square became known thousands who had earlier given up now returned, their numbers swelled by the ordinary people of Beijing. It was these Beijing residents who blocked the roads and avenues leading to Tiananmen Square and prevented the first wave of troops, sent to impose martial law, from reaching the square. The troops were bewildered by this show of popular resistance. After discussions with the leaders of the demonstration their commanders ordered their men to withdraw to the outskirts of Beijing.

The PLA move in

These events proved to be merely the lull before the storm. With Zhao removed and Li Peng and Deng now prepared to exercise full authority, the plans for ending the protest were activated. Crack troops, led by commanders specially appointed by President **Yang Shangkun** and Deng Xiaoping, advanced on Beijing. By 2 June 350,000 PLA soldiers had surrounded Tiananmen Square and had secured the routes leading to it. This time the troops were not to be deterred by the pleas of the local people.

Yang Shangkun (1907–98) President of the PRC and a leading figure in the PLA, he gave Deng his strong-arm support in crushing the student protest.

Key figure

The massacre, 3–4 June 1989

The PLA commanders described the action as a 'full military campaign' to overcome the determined resistance of the 'rebels' occupying Tiananmen Square. The troops were instructed to reclaim the square 'at all costs'. Tanks and armoured personnel carriers rumbled into position. At 10.00 pm on the night of 3 June the first shots were fired into the demonstrators. Shooting continued intermittently through the hours of darkness and into the morning. By midday on 4 June the occupation was over.

Pro-democracy demonstration crushed in Beijing: 1989

Key date

The scene was one of carnage. Twisted barricades crushed by the PLA tanks lay strewn around, mixed with the accumulated garbage of the 6-week occupation. At regular intervals, lines of exhausted, injured and broken-spirited students were marched away for interrogation and imprisonment.

The number of dead and injured will probably never be known precisely, but calculations suggest that the figure ran into thousands. Included in the figures are the people killed in the surrounding streets and the PLA soldiers beaten to death by outraged crowds. Despite the news blackout that the government immediately imposed, the information that leaked out regarding the number of victims treated in Beijing's hospitals confirmed that a massacre had occurred.

In the following weeks, demonstrators who had escaped from Tiananmen Square, but had not been able to flee the country were rounded up. Reprisals followed. Those identified as ringleaders were given stiff prison sentences. CCP officials who had shown sympathy for the protesters were dismissed for their wrong-headedness, while those who had resisted the demonstrators were promoted for their loyalty to the party.

The significance of the massacre

Looking at the Tiananmen Square protest in relation to the powers at the government's disposal, commentators have suggested that the demonstration could have been dispersed by organised police armed with no more than water cannons and tear gas. This was the normal way in which student riots were dealt with in Asian countries. The students were unarmed and far

Key question
What did the events in Tiananmen Square reveal about the character of China under Deng Xiaoping?

A lone man halts a line of tanks in Beijing on 5 June 1989. Details of who he was and his subsequent fate are still obscure, but it is thought that having been pulled away and smuggled back into the crowd he was later arrested by the authorities and imprisoned for a lengthy period. It is known that a number of the demonstrators rounded up after the massacre were still being held in prison as late as 2007. Although the incident occurred a day after the suppression of the demonstration, this photo has become one of the most immediately recognisable images relating to the Tiananmen Square massacre. Why is this?

from united over how long their protest could be sustained. Indeed, there had been a number of occasions when they were on the verge of breaking up. It would not have taken much to scatter them.

It is difficult, therefore, to avoid the conclusion that Deng and the Chinese leaders wanted a violent end to the affair. For their 2 months' defiance of the government, the protesters were to be made to atone in blood. The resort to tanks and bullets was intended to impress on the Chinese people both the seriousness of the plotters' challenge to civil order and the determination of the government not to tolerate such rebellion.

Deng's legacy

The massacre in Tiananmen Square was very much in the Chinese tradition of crushing opposition by the severest means in order to emphasise the illegitimacy of opposition itself. It was the surest confirmation that Deng Xiaoping's reforms did not include an extension of political freedoms. The CCP was willing to consider sweeping economic change in China. What it would not contemplate was giving up its authority over the Chinese people. The strange mixture of economic freedom and political rigidity was the outstanding feature of the legacy that Deng Xiaoping left China at his death in 1997.

Key date

Death of Deng Xiaoping: 1997

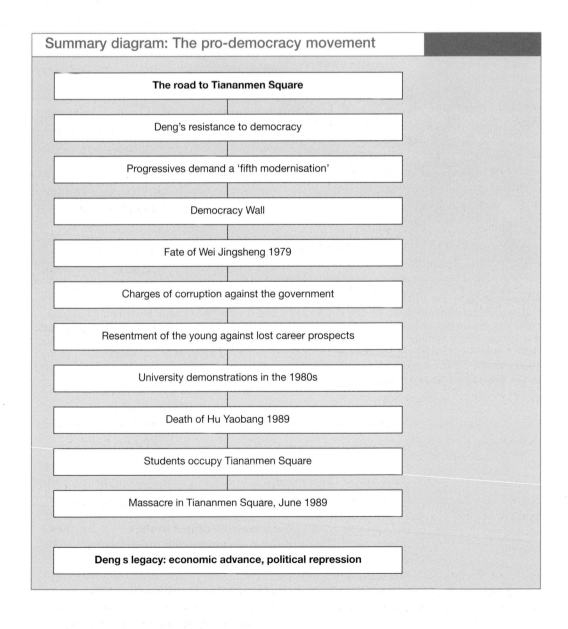

Summary diagram: The pro-democracy movement

- **The road to Tiananmen Square**
- Deng's resistance to democracy
- Progressives demand a 'fifth modernisation'
- Democracy Wall
- Fate of Wei Jingsheng 1979
- Charges of corruption against the government
- Resentment of the young against lost career prospects
- University demonstrations in the 1980s
- Death of Hu Yaobang 1989
- Students occupy Tiananmen Square
- Massacre in Tiananmen Square, June 1989

Deng s legacy: economic advance, political repression

Glossary

Agit-prop Short for 'agitation propaganda': the imposition of political ideas through entertainment.

Agronomists Experts in agricultural science.

Albania Run by an oppressive neo-Stalinist regime, it was the only Communist state in Europe to recognise China rather than the Soviet Union as the leader of the international revolutionary movement.

Ancestor worship The practice of paying respect to the deceased members of the family in a simple ceremony of remembrance. In the West this has sometimes been confused with the Christian practice of praying to the dead to ask for help.

Anti-rightist movement Rightist had no precise definition; it was applied to anyone Mao wanted to remove.

Apostate A person, group or nation that abandons its original political or religious beliefs.

Applied Communism Planning according to Marxist principles, involving state direction of the economy and the ending of private ownership.

Backyard furnaces Primitive smelting devices that every family was encouraged to build on its premises.

Bamboo curtain A figurative way of describing China's hostile and suspicious attitude towards the non-Communist world; it is similar to the notion of the iron curtain.

Barefoot doctors The teams of swiftly trained medics who were sent into China's countryside to provide a rudimentary health service.

Bolsheviks Communist revolutionaries who seized power in Russia in 1917.

Bourgeoisie The Marxist label for the middle-class capitalists who exploited the workers.

Brezhnev doctrine The demand that all Communist states toe the Soviet line. If they failed to do so, they must be disciplined by the other Marxist states acting as 'a socialist community' under the leadership of the USSR.

Bride-price The money paid to the bride's family, based on a calculation of how many children she would have.

Buddhism An ancient Chinese philosophy, which laid great stress on the individual's gaining enlightenment through meditation.

Cadres Dedicated Communist Party workers whose special task was to spy and report on fellow CCP members and the public.

Capitalist roader Those who wished to see the economy modernised on capitalist lines.

Central Cultural Revolution Group A sub-committee of the Politburo, this body was established in May 1966 to direct the Cultural Revolution. Its 17 members included the Gang of Four.

Chauvinism Exaggerated and aggressive belief in the value of one's own nation.

Chinese Communist Party Formed in 1921 and committed to a Marxist revolution in China.

Class enemies Those reactionaries who refused to accept the new China that the Communist government was creating.

Coexistence A willingness among nations with opposed ideologies to live and let live.

Cold War The period of tension (1945–91) between the Communist Eastern bloc, led by the USSR, and the Western democratic nations, led by the USA.

Collectives Areas where the peasants farmed communally rather than for themselves individually.

Collectivist principle The Marxist notion that social advance can be achieved only by the proletarian class acting together as a body and not allowing individuals to follow their own interests.

Comintern Communist International, the body set up in Moscow in 1919 to organise world-wide revolution.

Communes Organised regions where the collectives were grouped together.

Communism with a human face The idea that Marxist governments, without losing their commitment to the Communist ideal, should act in a less authoritarian manner and show understanding of the real needs of ordinary people.

Communist Cuba In 1959 Communist guerrilla forces led by Fidel Castro had taken power in Cuba.

Communist faith The intensity with which Communists held their beliefs in revolution may be legitimately compared to the conviction that inspires the followers of a dogmatic religion.

Concubinage The practice of men keeping women, not as wives but as mistresses (concubines).

Confucianism A pattern of thought based on the teachings of Confucius (551–479 BC), who emphasised the need for harmony in human relations.

Conjugal visits Time set aside for couples to have sexual relations.

Conscript army Troops who have been compulsorily called up.

Conservatoire A specialist music college.

Continuing revolution Mao's notion that revolution was not a single event but a continuous process.

Corrective labour In Communist theory, a form of imprisonment that brought the prisoner to see the error of his ways.

Counter-revolutionaries Used by hardline Maoists to describe those in the party who favoured more moderate policies.

Cult of personality A reference to the unlimited power that Stalin had taken into his own hands at the expense of the party.

Dalai Lama The leader of Tibet's Buddhist faith, who became a powerful symbol of national resistance to the Chinese occupation.

Decadent tendencies Clinging to bourgeois values, the most obvious examples being the wearing of Western-style clothes, jewellery or make-up.

Denominations Separate groups within a faith, e.g. Catholicism and Protestantism within Christianity.

De-Stalinisation A campaign begun in the USSR 3 years after Stalin's death to reveal the truth about his development of a 'cult of personality', a reference to his having put his own reputation and interests above the needs of the Communist Party during his rule between 1929 and 1953.

Détente A policy aimed at easing relations between the Eastern bloc and Western nations by encouraging mutual acceptance of coexistence.

Dialectic The Marxist notion that historical development occurs through a progressive series of conflicts between social classes.

Dogma   Rigid, unchanging beliefs.

Drip effect   Letting a reputation gradually erode rather than formally attacking it.

Dysentery   Severe diarrhoea and dehydration, often fatal.

Eastern bloc   The countries of eastern Europe which fell under Soviet domination at the end of the Second World War.

Endemic   A disease constantly present in particular communities.

Excommunication   Formal dismissal from the Catholic Church.

Expatriate Chinese   Chinese nationals living abroad.

Extended family   Not just parents and children, but all the relatives, including in-laws.

Fait accompli   Something done in such a way that it cannot be changed.

Feudal   The period of history in which the emperor allowed a group of rich lords to hold land in return for their loyalty and service to him. The landlords made the property-less peasants work for them.

Foot binding   The tight bandaging of the feet to prevent their growth. This had two purposes: to hobble the women so that they could not get about and to make them more attractive to men, who traditionally regarded small feet as highly erotic.

Forbidden City   Beijing's greatest monument, a spacious walled inner city that had been the home and court of the emperors between 1368 and 1911.

Foreign embassies   In international convention, these are specially protected areas which the host nation respects as being immune from local interference.

Four modernisations   Plans for the reform of agriculture, industry, defence and education, which Deng had been working on since the 1960s but could not introduce until Mao had gone.

Gang of Four   Made up of Jiang Qing and her three male associates, Zhang Chunquiao (1917–2001), Yao Wenyuan 1931–2005) and Wang Honwen (1932–92).

Genocide   The deliberate destruction of a people or ethnic group.

Going to the people   Used to describe Mao's practice of periodically travelling through parts of China, supposedly to listen to what the people had to say.

Great Hall of the People   A large parliament building on the west side of Tiananmen Square.

Great Helmsman   One of the terms of adulation in which Mao was described, a reference to his unmatchable skill in steering the 'ship of state'.

Group of Five   A set of moderate party officials led by Peng Zhen (1902–97), the mayor of Beijing.

Gruel   A thin, watery porridge.

Gulags   The labour and prison camps set up in the Soviet Union under Stalin.

Heavy industry   Iron- and steel-based products and constructions.

Heroes Monument   A large shrine, commemorating the great deeds of China's revolutionary past, at the southern end of Tiananmen Square in Beijing.

Hierarchical structure   A pattern of government in which each class or group owes obedience to the authority above it.

Hong Kong   The Chinese city-port that had been a British Crown colony since 1898 and was not scheduled to return to China until 1997.

Hungarian rising   An attempt in 1956 on the part of the Communist government of Hungary to break away from Soviet control.

Ideograms   Literally pictures; Mandarin symbols had begun as pictures of the ideas they described.

Imperialists   The advanced capitalist nations which had become powerful through exploiting weaker countries.

Inherently capitalistic   Selfish and grasping by nature.

Intellectuals   Mao classed intellectuals as those who did not do a proper job, e.g. writers, teachers, artists and lawyers.

Iron rice bowl   The system that provided workers with a guaranteed job and protected their wages.

Khampas   The nomadic yak herdsmen of Tibet.

Kulaks   A word borrowed from Stalin's USSR to describe the rich peasants who exploited their poorer neighbours. As in the USSR, the existence of a kulak class was a deliberately created myth.

Labour-contract scheme   An agreement between employers and workers, based on the principle of higher wages in return for greater effort and higher productivity.

Lama   A form of Buddhism which had become a defining characteristic of Tibetan culture.

Laogai   Meaning 're-education through labour', it came to be used to describe the vast prison-camp system established under Mao.

'Lift-off'   Increasing output and production at such a pace as to turn China into a modern industrial power.

'Loss' of China   Refers to the USA's dismay at mainland China's becoming Communist in 1949.

Lysenkoism   The agricultural theories of Trofim Lysenko.

Malaria   A debilitating feverish condition, caused by parasites passed on by mosquito bites.

Mandarin Chinese   Of China's many languages and dialects, Mandarin is the predominant one, used by the majority of people. It is the official language of government, administration and law.

Manufactured goods   Raw materials turned into sellable products.

Market   The system of allowing the economy to run freely according to the play of supply and demand without interference by the state.

Martial law   The placing of the civilian population under military authority and discipline.

Marxist   A believer in the theories of the German revolutionary Karl Marx (1818–83), who used the notion of the dialectic to explain history as a continuous conflict between the 'haves' and the 'have-nots', the exploiters and the exploited.

Marxist–Leninist   The official Communist ideology based on the theories of Karl Marx as interpreted by Lenin, the Russian revolutionary.

Marxist revolution   In October 1917, the Bolshevik (Communist) Party, led by Lenin, seized power in Russia.

Middle classes   Broadly made up professionally qualified people, such as lawyers, administrators and financiers.

Ming Tombs   The burial ground of the emperors of the Ming dynasty (1368–1644).

Monkeys to disrupt the palace   Mao's imagery is drawn from the practice in the imperial court of having monkeys as pets. The uncontrolled animals had been notorious for causing mayhem.

Morals of the Red Guards One of the boasts of the Red Guards was that they had risen above bourgeois thoughts of sex. This was why they dressed in plain unisex blue or khaki uniforms and made themselves look as physically unappealing as possible.

Moscow The capital of the USSR, the only foreign country Mao ever visited.

Nadir The lowest point.

National capitalists Those who had run China before 1949.

Nationalists A Chinese revolutionary party created in the early twentieth century and based on the 'Three People's Principles': socialism, democracy and national regeneration.

Neo-capitalism A return to the corrupt bourgeois system based on greed, individualism and profit-making.

Nuclear family Mother, father and their children, considered as a unit.

Packing Controlling the membership of the committees in such a way that they always contained a majority of Maoists.

Panchen Lama Second in spiritual authority to the Dalai Lama.

Panmunjong truce The 1953 agreement that brought the Korean War to an end, but decided little since the two sides simply agreed to recognise the division of Korea at the 38th parallel.

Papacy The Catholic Church's system of government, headed by the Pope.

Paper tigers One of Mao's favourite expressions; he applied it to anything or anyone whose power, he believed, was more apparent than real.

Paranoia A persecution complex, the feeling a disturbed person has that everybody is plotting against them.

Party line Official CCP policy.

Patriarchal Male dominated.

Patriotic health movements Government-sponsored schemes for providing Chinese people with basic information on health and hygiene.

People's Liberation Army The new name for the Red Army, which Mao had built into a formidable force in the 1930s and 1940s and which had carried him to power in 1949. The PLA's loyalty to Mao was his greatest single asset as leader of the PRC.

Permanent (or continuous) revolution The notion that revolution is not a single historical event, but a continuing and developing process.

Pinyin A modernised form of Mandarin.

Plenum A full, formal, authoritative gathering.

Pogrom A state-organised persecution against a particular group of people.

Politburo An inner core of some 20 leading members of the Communist Party.

Political correctness A requirement that people conform to a prescribed and restricted set of opinions and vocabulary when expressing themselves to show that they have accepted the ideology of the leaders of society.

Power struggles From the time of his helping to found the CCP in the 1920s through to his triumph in 1949, Mao had fought a series of fierce battles to assert his authority over the party.

Pragmatism A way of tackling problems that is based on the actual situation rather than on abstract theory.

Prague spring The attempt of the Czech Communist government in 1968 to liberalise some of its policies and assert its independence from Soviet control.

Productivity   The efficiency with which an article is made, measured by the time and cost involved in its production.

Progressive thinkers   Those with a forward-looking attitude who in the 1970s were beginning to demand that power and privilege in China should not be the monopoly of the leaders of the CCP.

Proletariat   The Marxist term for the revolutionary workers.

Public utilities   Gas, electricity and the transport system.

Quality control   The mechanism for monitoring industrial products so that they always meet a consistent standard.

Rectification of conduct campaigns   A series of ferocious purges by which Mao removed any member of the CCP he suspected of opposing him.

Red Army   The title given to the Communist troops that Mao led, later to be known as the People's Liberation Army (PLA).

Red Guards   The revolutionary students whose name derived from their practice of wearing red arm bands, supplied to them by Maoist officials. Red was the traditional colour of the Communist movement.

Republic   A form of government in which there is no monarch and power is exercised by elected representatives.

Reunification campaigns   The Chinese government's euphemism for forcibly bringing the invaded provinces into line in the 1950s.

Reuters   An international press agency.

Revisionism   Betraying the Communist cause by abandoning basic revolutionary principles.

San gang   The three relationships that in Confucian theory held society together.

Shanghai Forum   A group of hardline leftist radicals, who believed in the harshest measures being taken against those who opposed Mao.

Shanghai wing   Between its formation in 1921 and its taking power in 1949, the CCP had undergone a series of power struggles between various factions. One of these was the Shanghai group, renowned for its hard-line Marxism and its ferocity against opponents.

Sino-centric   Having Chinese interests at the centre of things with all other considerations secondary.

Sino-Indian War   In 1962 a long-running territorial dispute, compounded by India's granting sanctuary to the Dalai Lama, led to an outbreak of fighting between Indian and Chinese troops on the Tibetan border.

Sinologists   Experts on China.

Sino-Soviet agreement of 1950   A consequence of Mao's meeting with Stalin in Moscow; the USSR agreed to provide the PRC with vital resources that the PRC would pay back with interest over time.

Slogan-ridden society   The Soviet Union, particularly under Stalin, used mass public propaganda in order to train the people into conformity and obedience.

Social fascism   First used by Stalin to denote those Communists and socialists who were willing to compromise with their political enemies.

Socialist concepts   The structuring of the economy by the government with the aim of spreading equality.

Socialist integrity   The notion that a true work of art in Communist China must portray the triumph of the workers and peasants over their class enemies.

Soviet   A system of government organised on Communist principles.

Soviet satellites   The various countries that had fallen under Soviet control between 1945 and 1948.

Spearheads of the erroneous line Leaders who had tried to persuade the party to follow policies that ran counter to Mao's wishes.

Special Economic Zones   The areas, containing China's main export industries and companies, which were earmarked for immediate and concentrated development.

Sputnik   The first Soviet satellite to be successfully launched into orbit around the Earth in 1957.

Stalin's Five-Year Plans   Between 1929 and 1953, Stalin revolutionised the Soviet economy by a series of government-directed 5-year plans aimed at achieving a massive increase in industrial output.

Stalin's USSR   Between 1929 and 1953, the Soviet Union (USSR) was under the rule of Joseph Stalin.

Stalinist purges   During his leadership of the USSR Stalin had introduced a series of fierce purges to crush any opposition that might develop.

State subsidies   A scheme of payments, introduced in Mao's time, to supplement workers' or businesses' low income.

Superpowers   The description given to nations which possess advanced nuclear weapons.

Test Ban Treaty   Signed in 1963 between the USSR and the Western nuclear powers, in which the parties pledged to end their atmospheric testing of atomic weapons.

The People's Daily   The official CCP newspaper, and the government's mouthpiece.

Triads   Chinese secret societies, usually of a criminal kind, involved in drugs, gambling and prostitution.

Trotskyists   Followers of Stalin's great rival, Lev Trotsky, who believed in the necessity of world revolution at any price.

Tsampa   A mushy paste made from ground barley.

UN Security Council   The permanent five-member body (originally made up of the USSR, the USA, Britain, France and Nationalist China) responsible for settling international disputes.

Unequal treaties   Agreements forced on China in the nineteenth century which obliged it to surrender territory and accept trade on Western terms.

US State Department   The US body responsible for foreign policy, equivalent to the British Foreign Office.

Vatican   The spiritual and administrative centre of the Catholic Church in Rome, where the Pope has his official residence.

Veto   Each single member of the UN Security Council has the right to block the collective decisions of the other members.

Vietnam   In 1978, Chinese forces actively supported a Cambodian invasion of Vietnam. PRC government propaganda portrayed this as a great military success. In fact, the Chinese forces were heavily defeated and forced to withdraw.

Vietnam War   Between 1963 and 1975, the USA fought unsuccessfully to prevent South Vietnam being taken over by the Communists of North Vietnam.

Warlords   Powerful local generals in China who exploited the weakness of the central government to set themselves up as rulers in their own areas.

Xiang   Village or township.

Xinhua   The PRC's government-controlled news agency.

Yaks   These are hardy animals, perfectly adapted for the high altitude of the Tibetan plateau. They provide milk, meat and clothing and were thus an essential part of Tibet's rural economy.

Yellow peril   A term first used in the nineteenth century to suggest that China's vast population was preparing to spread out of Asia to swamp Europe, with Russia as the first victim.

Zhongnanhai   A building compound off Tiananmen Square that housed the government offices and ministers' residences.

Glossary of names

Chinese names in their *Pinyin* and Wade–Giles forms

Pinyin	**Wade–Giles**	*Pinyin*	**Wade–Giles**
Anhui	Anhwei	Nanjing	Nanking
Beijing	Peking	Peng Dehuai	Peng Teh-huai
Bo Yibo	Po Yipo	Peng Zhen	Peng Chen
Chen Boda	Chen Po-ta	Quemoy	Jinmen
Chen Duxui	Chen Tu-hsiu	Qin Shi Huang	Shi Huang-ti
Chiang Kaishek	Jiang Jieshi	Qinghai	Tsinghai
Chongqing	Chungking	Rao Rashi	Jao Shu-shi
Daxing	Tsa-hsing	Shaanxi	Shensi
Deng Xiaoping	Teng Hsiao-ping	Shandong	Shantung
Duan Qirui	Tuan Chi-jui	Shantou	Swatow
Fang Lizhi	Fang Li-chih	Shanxi	Shansi
Feng Xuxiang	Feng Yu-hsiang	Sun Yatsen	Sun Yat-sen
Fuzhou	Foochow	Sichuan	Szechwan
Fujian	Fukien	Taiwan	Formosa
Gao Gang	Kao Kang	Wang Dengxing	Wang Tung-hsing
Gansu	Kansu	Wang Hongwen	Wang Hung-wen
Guangzhou	Canton	Wang Jingwei	Wang Ching-wei
Guangdong	Kwangtung	Wang Jinxi	Wang Ching-hsi
Guangxu	Kuang Hsu	Wuhan	Wuchang
Guangxi	Kwangsi	Xian	Sian
Guizhou	Kweichow	Xiamen	Amoy
Guomingdang	Kuomingtang	Xie Fuzhi	Hsieh Fu-chih
Hangzhou	Hangchow	Xinhua	Hsinhua
Henan	Honan	Xinjiang	Sinkiang
Heilongjiang	Heilunkiang	Xizang	Hsi-tsang
Hebei	Hopei	Xu Shiyou	Hsu Shih-yu
Hefei	Hofei	Yanan	Yenan
Hua Guofeng	Hua Kuopfeng	Yangzi	Yangtze
Hubei	Hupei	Yan Jioqi	Yan Chao-chi
Hu Yaobang	Hu Yao-pang	Yan Xishan	Yen Hsi-shan
Jiang Jieshi	Chiang Kai-shek	Yao Wenyuan	Yao Wen-yuan
Jiang Jingguo	Chiang Ching-kuo	Ye Jianying	Yeh Chien-ying
Jiang Qing	Chiang Ching	Zhang Chunqiao	Chang Chun-chiao
Jiangxi	Kiansi	Zhao Ziyang	Chao Tzu-yang
Lin Biao	Lin Piao	Zhuhai	Chuhai
Liu Shaoqi	Liu Shao-chi	Zhou Enlai	Chou En-lai
Mao Zedong	Mao Tse-tung	Zhu De	Chuh The
Mao Yuanxin	Mao Yuan-hsin	Zunyi	Tsunyi

Index